SUDAN ARCHAEOLOGICAL RESEARCH SOCIETY
PUBLICATION NUMBER 4

Kulubnarti III

The Cemeteries

William Y. Adams, Nettie K. Adams,
Dennis P. Van Gerven,
David L. Greene

BAR International Series 814
1999

Published in 2016 by
BAR Publishing, Oxford

BAR International Series 814

Sudan Archaeological Research Society Publication Number 4
Kulubnarti III

© The Sudan Archaeological Research Society and the Publisher 1999

ISBN 9781841710273 paperback
ISBN 9781407351469 e-format
DOI https://doi.org/10.30861/9781841710273
A catalogue record for this book is available from the British Library

BAR Publishing is the trading name of British Archaeological Reports (Oxford) Ltd.
British Archaeological Reports was first incorporated in 1974 to publish the BAR
Series, International and British. In 1992 Hadrian Books Ltd became part of the BAR
group. This volume was originally published by Archaeopress in conjunction with
British Archaeological Reports (Oxford) Ltd / Hadrian Books Ltd, the Series principal
publisher, in 1999. This present volume is published by BAR Publishing, 2016.

BAR
PUBLISHING

BAR titles are available from:

BAR Publishing
122 Banbury Rd, Oxford, OX2 7BP, UK
EMAIL   info@barpublishing.com
PHONE   +44 (0)1865 310431
FAX   +44 (0)1865 316916
www.barpublishing.com

KULUBNARTI III

The Cemeteries

CONTENTS

PREFACE

This volume completes the report on the excavations at Kulubnarti in Northern Sudan. Although long delayed it makes a very welcome addition to the small numbers of definitive publications on the excavations of medieval sites in Nubia. *Kulubnarti I - The Architectural Remains* by William Y. Adams reported on the settlement archaeology on the island of Kulubnarti while *Kulubnarti II - The Artifactual Remains* by William Y. Adams and Nettie K. Adams dealt with the finds from those sites.

   Kulubnarti III - The Cemeteries is concerned with the funerary remains uncovered in two cemeteries, one on the island of Kulubnarti, the other on the adjacent left bank of the Nile. Part I by William Y. Adams includes detailed descriptions of the grave types and sets them within their Nubian medieval context. Part II by Nettie K. Adams examines the finds made in the graves, most noteably the extremely well preserved textiles, a category of material so often missing from other sites where the conditions of preservation have been less favourable. In Part III Dennis P. Van Gerven and David L. Greene look in detail at the physical anthropology of the two cemeteries and report on the physical well-being and lifestyles of the individuals as reflected in their skeletal remains. The bodies were often very well preserved and this has allowed, in many cases, certainty of sexing even of juveniles, something which the bone evidence alone can rarely do.

   The Kulubnarti volumes will be an essential reference to scholars studying medieval Nubia and highlight the importance of having reports on all categories of material recovered from excavation published in detail as a coherent project.

D. A. Welsby
Honorary Secretary
Sudan Archaeological Research Society

LIST OF TABLES

LIST OF FIGURES

LIST OF PLATES

INTRODUCTION

William Y. Adams

This is the third volume of memoirs dealing with excavations carried out on the island of Kulubnarti, in Sudanese Nubia, in 1969 and 1979. The first volume, *Kulubnarti I* (1994) dealt with architectural remains from twenty sites on the island, excavated in 1969. *Kulubnarti II,* published in 1998, described artifactual finds from ten of the sites. The present volume deals exclusively with the findings from two large cemeteries, excavated partly in 1969, but much more completely in 1979. Included are descriptions of the graves and their coverings, by William Y. Adams, descriptions of the grave goods, by Nettie K. Adams, and a detailed anthropological and epidemiological analysis of the human remains uncovered, by Dennis P. Van Gerven and David L. Greene.

The island and the sites

The Nile island of Kulubnarti ("Island of Kulb" in the Mahasi dialect of Nubian) is situated about 130 km upstream from Wadi Halfa, in the *Batn el-Hajjar* region of Sudanese Nubia (Figure 1). It is very roughly trapezoidal in shape, with maximum dimensions of about 2 km from north to south and 1 km from east to west (Figure 2). Prior to the filling of Lake Nubia it was not a true island except for a few weeks each year, at the peak of the Nile flood season. At that time it was separated from the west bank by a narrow channel, so regular in its contours that an early visitor thought it must be man-made.[1] The channel however was dry during most of the year, it sides and bottom serving as *seluka-* land for the growing of legumes and other fodder crops.[2] Kulubnarti was then simply one of many headlands projecting into the river from its western bank. Since the filling of Lake Nubia, however, Kulubnarti has been a true island most of the time.

Kulubnarti is situated in the very heart of the *Batn el-Hajjar* ("Belly of Stones") - the most rugged and inhospitable terrain along the entire course of the Nile (cf. Plate 1A). Throughout this region, bare granite ridges and pinnacles are interspersed with equally barren alluvial flats, many of them deeply drifted in sand. Natural vegetation is confined to a scattered growth of acacia, *dom* palm, and halfa grass along the riverbanks and in a few large *wadis*. There is no continuous floodplain; arable land occurs only here and there in small patches along both sides of the river.[3] These features are characteristic of the island of Kulubnarti no less than of the neighboring mainland areas to the east and west. The island's surface is dominated by a number of rocky ridges and outcrops, the highest of which, near the southern end, rises to perhaps 80 m above the level of the riverbank. Between the ridges are undulating or level plains, largely devoid of vegetation, that are either drifted over with sand or strewn with fallen boulders from the heights above (Plates 1B-C).

Of the two sites reported here, Site 21-S-46 was situated within an old and long-dry *wadi* near the west side of the island, while Site 21-R-2 was located on the west bank of the Nile just opposite the southern end of the island (see Figure 2). The latter site was not, technically speaking, within the excavation concession granted to the University of Kentucky in 1969. Permission to excavate was graciously granted by the late Negm el-Din Sherif, then the Sudan Commissioner for Archaeology, because the site was the burial place for most of the people who had lived on Kulubnarti Island in late medieval times. It therefore formed a part of the Kulubnarti story, which we aimed to tell as fully as the archaeological remains would allow.

The excavations

Preliminary excavations were carried out in both of the Kulubnarti cemeteries by the University of Kentucky Expedition to Nubia in 1969. The excavation of graves was not a major objective of that expedition, whose main focus was on the investigation of three habitation sites of late medieval age.[4] In the last weeks of the season, however, when work in the three main sites had been completed, there was time enough to investigate a number of lesser sites, including the two cemeteries. Our objective was not to study the skeletal remains, since the expedition included no physical anthropologist, but only to obtain cultural information about Christian Nubian burial practices at Kulubnarti. In all, 60 graves were partially or fully opened at 21-S-46, and 40 graves were partially or fully opened at 21-R-2. In no cases however were the bones themselves disturbed, and they were reburied at the conclusion of the excavations. The excavations at 21-S-46 were conducted by Mr. Thomas Higel, and those at 21-R-2 by Mr. Frank Fryman.

---

[1] J. L. Burckhardt, *Travels in Nubia* (London, 1819), pp. 77-78. There is no real support for Burckhardt's theory that the channel is artificial.

[2] See William Y. Adams, *Nubia, Corridor to Africa* (London, 1977), p. 51, and Hassan Dafalla, *The Nubian Exodus* (London, 1975), p. 76.

[3] For fuller topographic description see Adams, op. cit. (n. 2), pp. 26-28.

[4] See William Y. Adams, *Kulubnarti I* (Lexington, 1994).

1

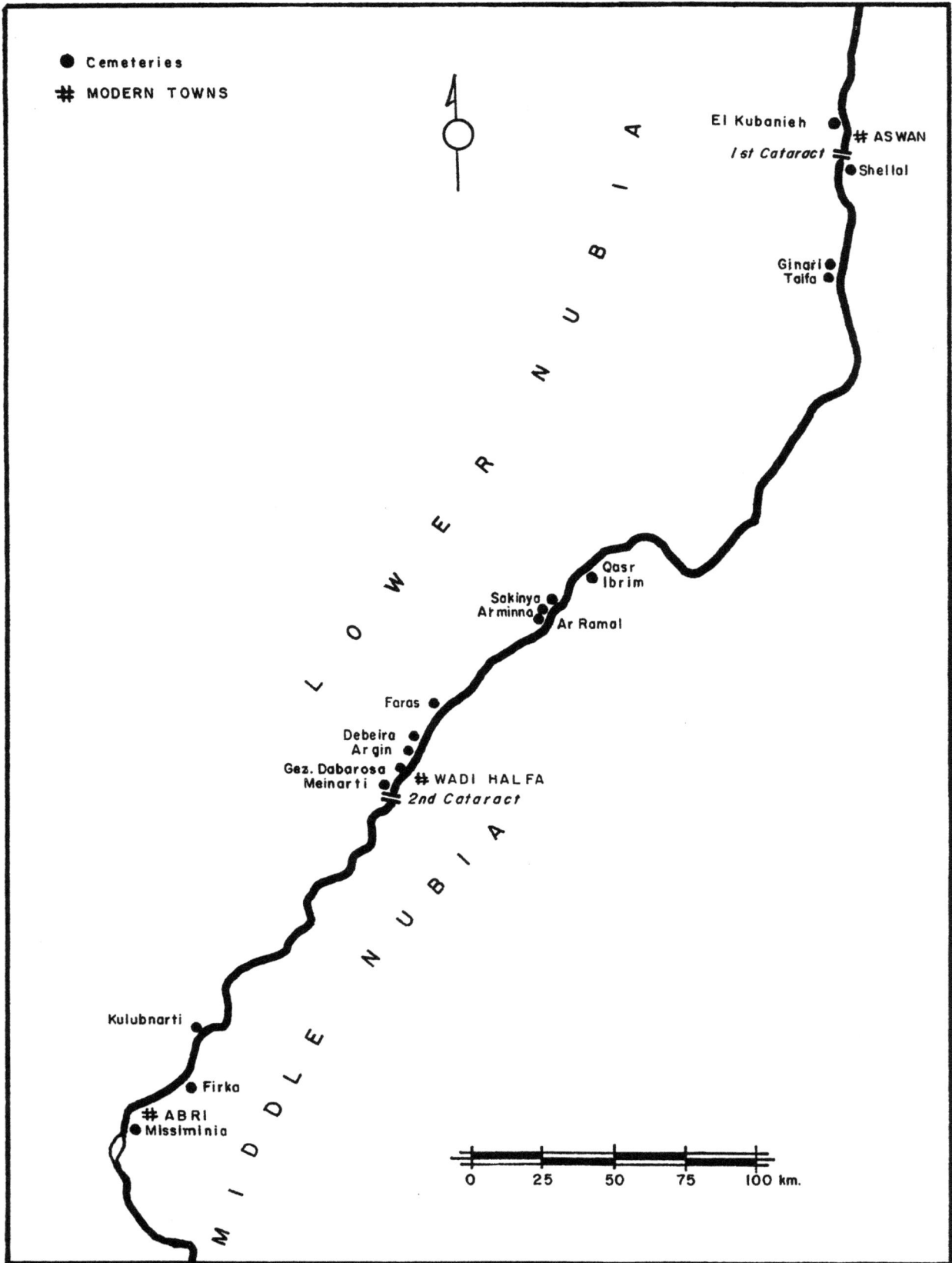

Figure 1. Map of Lower and Middle Nubia showing locations of the major cemeteries

When the 1969 excavations revealed that many of the interments at Kulubnarti were naturally mummified, preserving much of their soft tissue intact, this finding excited the interest of physical anthropologist Dennis Van Gerven, who was then at the University of Kentucky. He recognized that such preservation offered a rare opportunity for the study of many features of diet, disease, and mortality that ordinarily cannot be recovered from fully skeletonized remains. It was therefore decided to mount a further expedition, aimed specifically at the excavation of as many graves as possible, and the removal of their human remains for more detailed laboratory analysis. An application for a further research grant was made to the National Science Foundation, which had also supported the 1969 excavations.[5]

By the time a grant was actually awarded, in 1979,[6] Dr. Van Gerven had moved from Kentucky to the University of Colorado. The 1979 expedition was therefore a joint operation of the Universities of Kentucky and Colorado. Although I was nominally a co-director (because the excavation license from the Sudan Government was and is still in my name), my participation in the field work was limited to the first two weeks, during which I showed my colleagues the sites, and helped them make practical arrangements in regard to housing, labor, and other logistic matters. Actual field investigations thereafter were conducted by Dr. Van Gerven, assisted by graduate students Edward Rowan from the University of Colorado and Roger C. Allen from the University of Kentucky.

The excavations were carried out between 22 January and 17 March, 1979. Mr. Allen was wholly responsible for excavation supervision and for the purely archaeological aspects of recording and mapping, while Dr. Van Gerven and Mr. Rowan were responsible for all aspects of biological analysis. Subsequent to the excavations, a high percentage of the excavated skeletal and/or mummified remains were sent to the University of Colorado, where they were subjected to detailed analyses that will be described in Part III of this volume. Artifactual finds (chiefly shrouds) were allotted to the University of Kentucky Museum of Anthropology, where they have been studied and will be reported below by Nettie K. Adams.

Problems of documentation and sampling

Unfortunately, the original field records of the 1969 cemetery excavations have mostly been lost. In the case of Site 21-S-46 the loss is not a serious one, since the bodies themselves were not disturbed, and most were reexcavated in the course of the 1979 season. The principal loss of information is in reference to the grave superstructures, which of course were destroyed in the course of the original

excavations. Since however more than 75% of the previously undisturbed graves in this cemetery were excavated in 1979, and since the superstructures of the graves were overwhelmingly of a single type, it is a reasonable supposition that the superstructures destroyed in 1969 were mostly of the same type.

In the case of Site 21-R-2 the loss of information from the 1969 season is a good deal more serious, because in this cemetery only ten of the graves dug in 1969 were reexcavated in 1979. Moreover and more importantly, the graves dug in 1969 were located in various parts of the cemetery, and they were deliberately selected to provide a sample of the different grave types, and hopefully of the different periods of the cemetery's use. By contrast, the graves excavated in 1979 were nearly all located in one contiguous area at the site, and typological evidence suggests that those graves date from the earlier period of the cemetery's use. The 1969 graves would therefore probably have provided a more representative sample of the cemetery as a whole than do the 1979 graves, despite the much greater number of the latter. It should be added too that, although grave superstructures were numerous in this cemetery, nearly all the graves selected for excavation in 1979 were without superstructures, so that we lack a properly detailed record of the different superstructure types and their frequency. Happily, a good photographic record has survived for 28 of the 40 graves excavated in 1969, making it possible to recover information at least about superstructures, shaft types, and body positions.

From the 1979 excavations, the documentation of graves and burials is generally very satisfactory. This is not true however in regard to the recording of small finds of personal jewelry, found on a number of the bodies. There are brief mentions such as "iron cross at neck" or "bracelet on the right wrist" on the grave registration forms, but no dimensions or other details are given. Many of these objects were photographed in the field, and they were apparently given registration numbers as well, but no copy of the register was returned to the University of Kentucky. Since all the finds of small objects were taken in division by the Sudan Antiquities Service (as it was then called) at the end of the 1979 season, it appears that the only copy of the object register was surrendered at the same time. With the limited documentation in hand, it has not always been possible to determine which of the photographed objects came from which graves - a limitation that will be evident in the captions to certain of the plates.

The data base for the report

In the present volume, Part I, written by William Y. Adams, is based entirely on excavation records and maps compiled by Mr. Allen. The primary records are grave registration forms, filled out for each grave. There is, for each, a sheet describing the size and characteristics of the grave

[5] Grant no. GS-2031.
[6] Grant no. 77-270210-535.

superstructure, if any; a sheet describing the nature and dimensions of the grave shaft; a sheet describing the age and sex, and the placement and covering of the body; and a sheet describing any cultural goods found in the grave. There is also a sketch plan of the grave superstructure, and a plan of the positioning of the body in the bottom of the shaft. In addition to the registration forms, there is good photographic documentation for nearly all of the graves, including superstructures, body coverings, and the interments themselves.

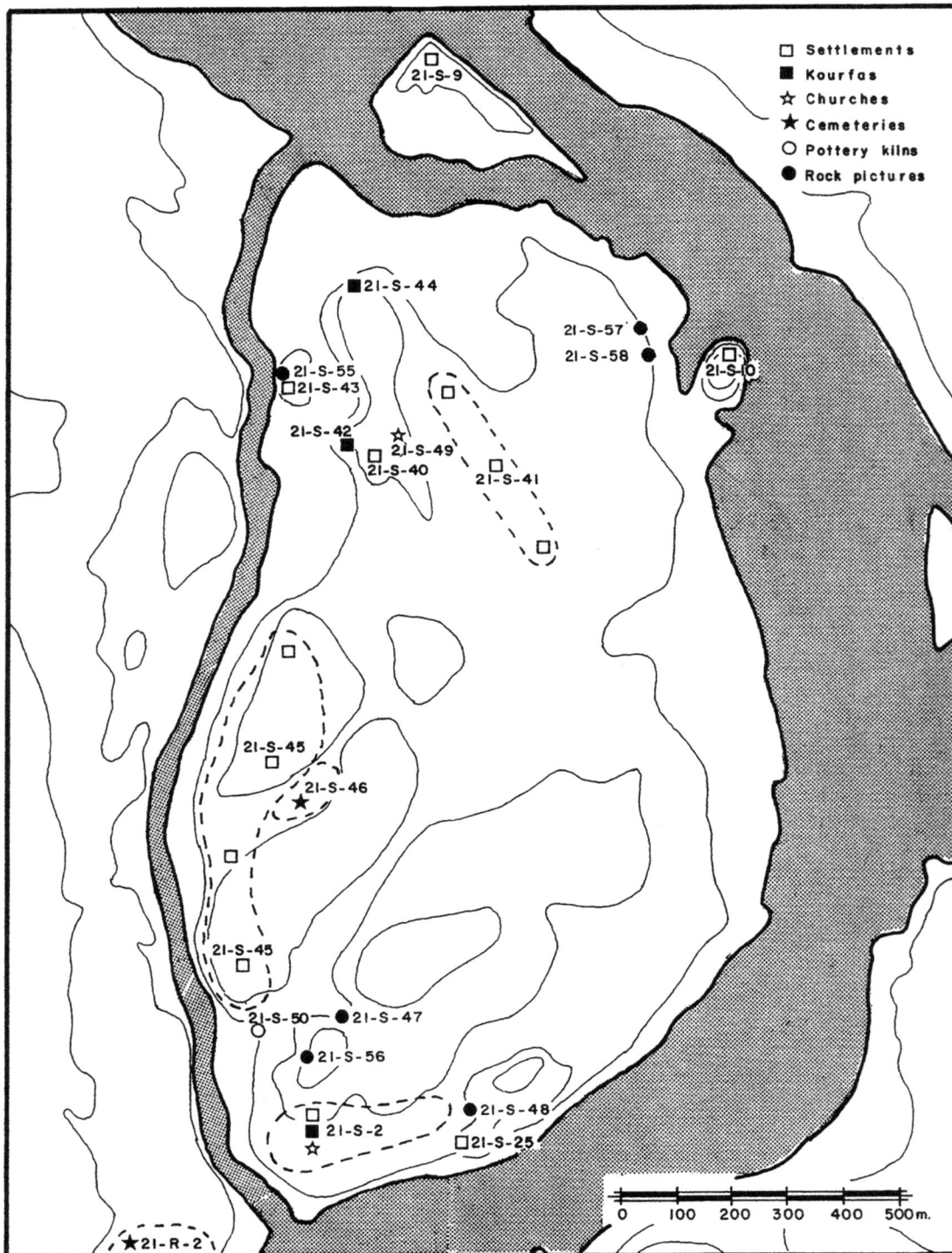

Figure 2. Map showing site locations on Kulubnarti Island.

Part II, written by Nettie K. Adams, is a description of the cultural goods found in the graves. The analysis of the body wrappings is based on the examination of the actual textiles that were allotted in division to the University of Kentucky Museum of Anthropology. They are quite well preserved in many cases, and have added substantially to our knowledge of textile materials and manufacture as well as patterns of trade in this part of Nubia during early medieval times. The descriptions of other cultural goods such as jewelry, pottery, and leather wrappings are based on the records and photographs submitted by Mr. Allen. These objects went in division to the Sudan National Museum, Khartoum.

Part III, by Dennis Van Gerven and David Greene, summarizes what has been learned from the anatomical and biological analysis of the recovered bodies, in analyses carried out at the University of Colorado. It will become obvious, from the discussion that follows, that these studies have yielded some quite unexpected results in regard to pathology and mortality at Kulubnarti. The discussion in Part III is however based wholly on the examination of skeletal and dental remains, for the analysis of soft-tissue remains has yet to be undertaken.

Some issues of terminology

Ballaña vs X-Group

For a good many years I, like many other authors, have been trying to do away with the obsolete and inappropriate term "X-Group," as a label for the post-Kushite and pre-Christian phase of Nubian history. Following the original example of Trigger,[7] I have tried where possible to substitute the term Ballaña, as a label for a period and for a culture.[8] But the older term, as a label for pottery types and for grave types, simply will not go away; it is too convenient and too embedded in the literature. It will therefore still be used in this volume as a designation for pottery and grave types, while the term Ballaña will be used to designate the civilization and the period that gave them birth.

Post-Christian vs Islamic

We were able to show, in *Kulubnarti I* and *Kulubnarti II,* that although the organized practice of Christianity in Nubia had probably ceased by A.D. 1500, there is little or no evidence for the practice of Islam until about two centuries later.[9] It therefore seems inappropriate to use the term "Islamic" as an automatic label for graves and other cultural phenomena dating after 1500, when in fact many of them preceded the actual adoption of the new faith. In this

volume, as in its two predecessors, we will use instead the term Post-Christian, except in the case of cultural manifestations that can be clearly associated with the practice of Islam.

Middle Nubia vs Upper Nubia

The arbitrary division of Nubia into two very unequal parts, called Upper and Lower Nubia, is a legacy of ancient Egyptian colonial usage. It has very little relevance, either topographically or historically, when applied to the post-pharaonic, and in particular to the post-Kushite, periods. Physiographically, the region between the Third and Fourth Cataracts is much more similar to Lower Nubia than it is to the intervening region between the Second and Third Cataracts. Historically, there was never in post-Kushite times a uniformity of culture, of language, or of polity throughout the region designated as Upper Nubia. On the contrary, the cultural features found in the *Batn el-Hajjar* and the Abri-Delgo Reach often show more affinity to those in Lower Nubia than they do to those in the Dongola Reach. It was the locality of the Third Cataract, for example, which marked the southern limit of the Ballaña culture, as it did also the boundary between Mahasi and Dongolawi speakers and, later, the frontier between Ottoman and Funj dominion.

In short and in sum, the region between the Second and Third Cataracts marks a kind of transition zone between Lower Nubia and the true Upper Nubia, and it does not fit comfortably into either. In this volume, therefore, I will introduce the term Middle Nubia as a designation for the region in question, comprising the *Batn el-Hajjar* and the Abri-Delgo Reach. It will then be possible, in later pages, to speak of a Middle Nubian mortuary complex, without suggesting that it will or should be found south of the Third Cataract as well.

Kulubnarti and Kulbincoing

Of the two cemeteries reported in this volume, only one, 21-S-46, was actually located on the island of Kulubnarti. Site 21-R-2, although certainly utilized by the residents of Kulubnarti, was situated on the west bank, just below the hamlet of Kulbincoing and across from the southern tip of the island. In a strictly technical sense therefore this site should not be referred to as a Kulubnarti cemetery. Since its excavation was undertaken as part of the Kulubnarti Project, however, it will here be considered as a Kulubnarti Cemetery, and will be labeled as such.

Chronology and periodization

Throughout this volume I will, for descriptive purposes, subdivide the culture of medieval Nubia into a series of phases, according to the same scheme which I have employed in many previous works, and as shown in the following table:[10]

---

[7] Bruce G. Trigger, *History and Settlement in Lower Nubia*, pp. 131-140. *Yale University Publications in Anthropology,* no. 69 (1965).

[8] e.g. in Adams, op. cit. (n. 2), pp. 392-424.

[9] See especially William Y. Adams and Nettie K. Adams, *Kulubnarti II* (London, 1998), p. 93.

[10] For the original formulation of the scheme see William Y. Adams in *Kush*, vol. 12 (1964), pp. 243-247.

Early Christian I (EC1)	A.D. 600 - 750
Early Christian II (EC2)	" 750 - 850
Classic Christian I (CC1)	" 850-1000
Classic Christian II (CC2)	" 1000-1100
Late Christian I (LC1)	" 1100-1300
Late Christian II (LC2)	" 1300-1400
Terminal Christian	" 1400-1500

Acknowledgments

Any list of acknowledgments must necessarily begin with thanks to the National Science Foundation, which provided the entire funding for the 1979 Kulubnarti excavations, as it did also for the excavations of 1969 and 1970.[11] As always, and for all expeditions, the support and encouragement of the Sudan Antiquities Service was also invaluable. Our thanks must go above all to the late Negm el-Din Mohammed Sherif and to the late Gamal Mohammed Hassan - the two individuals to whose memory we have dedicated the previous volumes in this series. The people of Kulbincoing village were once again gracious hosts and congenial neighbors during the time when the excavations were in progress.

We are also greatly indebted to Elisabeth Crowfoot, who introduced the study of archaeological textiles to Nettie K. Adams. Her teaching and example have been invaluable, and always an inspiration. Together, Miss Crowfoot and Mrs. Adams opened the boxes of Kulubnarti textiles when they first arrived from the field, and compiled the initial catalogue. Additionally, Laura Turner, of the University of Kentucky, helped to organize the textile collection, and Edward K. Adams performed a great service by consolidating the field notes into a more accessible form. To all we owe our deepest gratitude.

Finally, we must once again thank the Sudan Archaeological Research Society for its generous agreement to publish this long-delayed monograph.

---

[11] The 1979 excavations were supported by Grant no. 77-270210-535.

PART I
THE GRAVES

William Y. Adams

Site 21-S-46

This cemetery of some 300 graves is located at the western side of Kulubnarti Island, roughly halfway between its northern and southern ends. The graves were dug into the hard, dry bed of an ancient wadi, flanked on either side by low, rocky ridges (Plates 1A-B). The area of graves extended over about 90 m from east to west, with a maximum extent of 25 m from north to south (Figure 3). Sixty graves were excavated and then refilled in 1969, and 218 graves, including most of the original 60, were excavated in 1979.

The exact number of graves in Cemetery 21-S-46 is not known, since no effort was made to scrape the surface in order to locate grave shafts that might have been sanded over. The excavators believed that there might have been as many as 50 such graves. The number of graves actually recognized and numbered was 242, and of that number 223 were partially or fully excavated. Eight graves were not excavated because their orientation suggested that they were Muslim burials, eight others were not excavated because apparent Muslim burials had been intruded into them, and three were not excavated for reasons not given. Among the excavated graves or presumed graves, nine were found after preliminary excavation to have been unfinished (usually because they encountered *jebel* rock), or to be pits which apparently were never meant to be graves. There were in addition three shafts which had all the characteristics of grave shafts, but which proved to contain no bodies. Subtracting all of these from the total of numbered graves, then, the total of bodies actually uncovered was 215. A summary resumé of the graves and burials in Cemetery 21-S-46 is given in Table 1; detailed information about each grave is given in Table 2, and about each burial in Table 3.

The wadi bed at 21-S-46 was at a level at least 10 m above that of the Nile floodplain, and it had never within recent millennia been subjected to flooding or capillary action from the river. The only wetting that occurred would have been the result of the very infrequent and scanty rains that fall in this part of Nubia. As a result, skeletal material was well preserved in the case of nearly all the burials at 21-S-46. On the other hand, the amount of fleshy tissue that was preserved varied substantially from one burial to another, and it was absent altogether in a few cases. The reasons for this differential preservation are not entirely clear.

Chronology

At least two and perhaps as many as five of the burials at 21-S-46 were of Ballaña ("X-Group") date (cf. Plates 1C-D), and eight were presumed to be of Islamic date. All of the remainder could be identified fairly securely, on the basis of orientation and body positions, as dating from the Christian Nubian period. The question of chronology is nevertheless a difficult one, as in nearly all Christian Nubian cemeteries, because of the lack of distinctive grave goods. In those places where tomb superstructures were accompanied by votive lamps - a common practice in many Christian Nubian cemeteries - an approximate dating is often furnished by the type of vessel used as a lamp.[1] At 21-S-46, however, no lamps were found.

The problem of dating was further exacerbated by the lack of nearby settlement remains with which the burials at 21-S-46 could be clearly associated. The only settlement close by was Site 21-S-45, a scattering of very rude stone huts which extended over a large area both north and south of the cemetery. These structures yielded both Classic and Late Christian sherds,[2] but at Cemetery 21-S-46 most of the burial features suggest an Early Christian dating for the graves. Again, although most Christian Nubian cemeteries were associated with a church, there were no church remains on the island of Kulubnarti datable to the Early Christian period. The nearest church to 21-S-46 was a very primitive affair on the west bank, excavated by the German Expedition to Kulb in 1969.[3] However, there was no secure evidence on which to date that extraordinary structure.[4]

There are nevertheless a number of factors to suggest an Early Christian (7th to mid 9th century) dating for many and perhaps most of the graves at 21-S-46. The fact that at least two graves were of "X-Group" types indicates that

[1] For the chronology of lamp development see William Y. Adams, *Ceramic Industries of Medieval Nubia (Memoirs of the UNESCO Archaeological Survey of Sudanese Nubia,* vol. 1, 1986), pp. 98-99 and 103-104.

[2] See William Y. Adams, *Kulubnarti I: the Architectural Remains* (Lexington, 1994), p. 267.

[3] Erich Dinkler in E. Dinkler, ed, *Kunst und Geschichte Nubiens in Christlicher Zeit* (Recklinghausen, 1970), pp. 263-265.

[4] For discussion see William Y. Adams and Nettie K. Adams, *Kulubnarti II : the Artifactual Remains,* p. 97. SARS Publication no. 2 (1998).

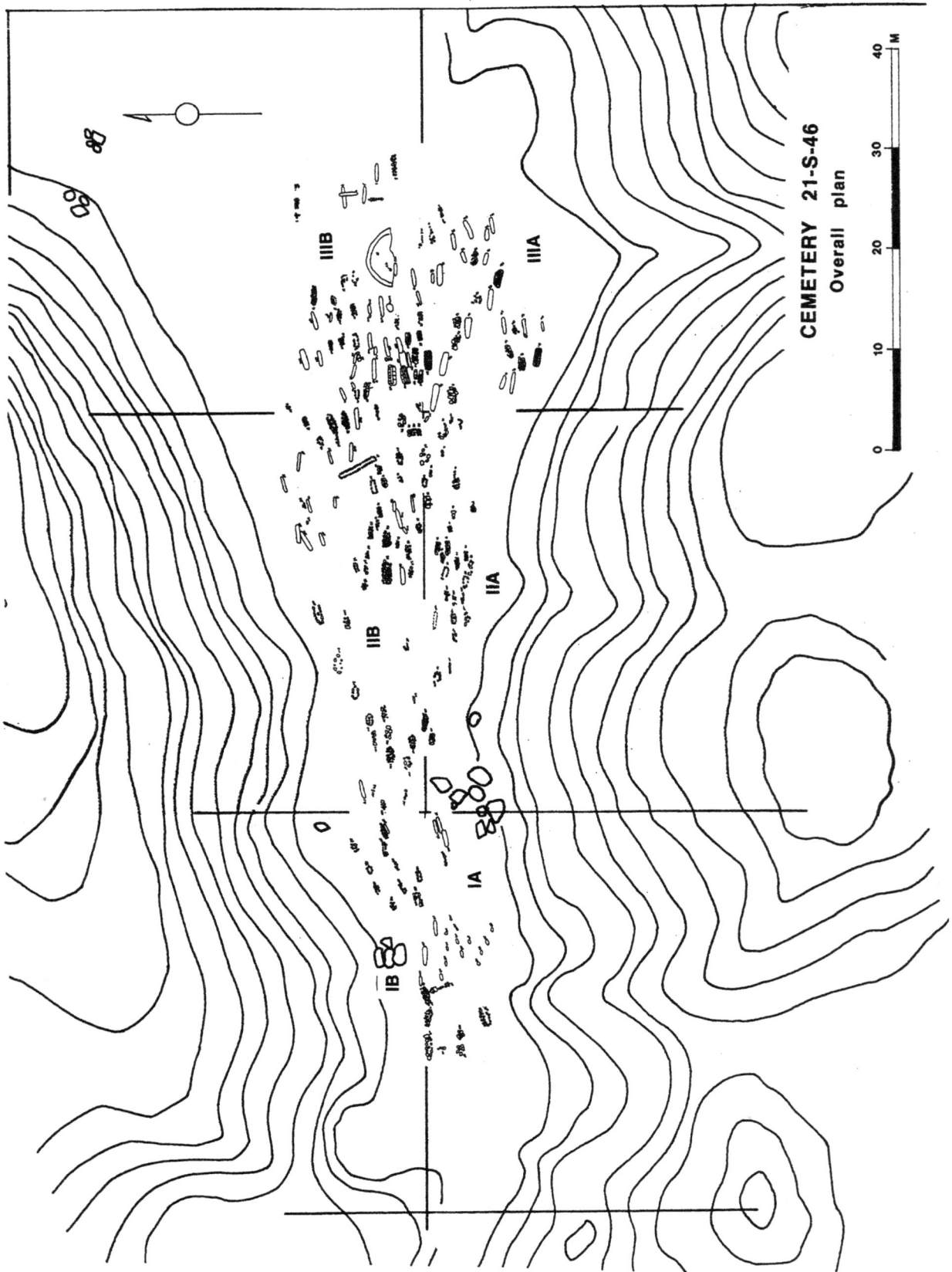

Figure 3. Site 21-S-46: overall plan.

TABLE 1

TABLE 1
CEMETERY 21-S-46 - SUMMARY OF GRAVES AND BURIALS

	No.	%.
Graves numbered	242	
Non-graves or unfinished	9	4
Disturbed - not excavated	8	3
Islamic - not excavated	8	3
Otherwise not excavated	3	1
Graves excavated	214	89
Superstructures	149	61
Stone pavement	118	49
Stone outline	16	7
Stone alignment	5	2
Stone + brick pavement	1	T
Brick pavement	9	4
Destroyed in 1969 excavations	51	21
None	42	17
Lamp boxes identified	3	
Orientation		
270-290°	40	18
220-269°	178	82
Grave shafts excavated	218	
Slot	142	65
Side niche north	44	21
Side niche south	1	T
Round or oval pit	3	1
Form uncertain	28	13
Burials uncovered	215	
Head covering		
Stones all along	48	22
3 stones, sides and top	36	17
2 stones at sides	5	2
1 stone at side	4	2
3 bricks, sides and top	22	11
2 bricks at sides	3	1
Sherds	3	1
Foetal burial in pot	8	4
Uncertain	1	T
None	85	39
Body covering		
Stones all along	48	22
Stones to waist or knees	3	1
Foetal burial in pot	8	4
Uncertain	1	T
None	155	72
Body position		
Dorsal	119	55
¼ left	10	5
Left side	57	27
¼ right	1	T
Right side	7	3
Ventral	2	1
Flexed	3	1
Foetal burial in pot	8	4
Uncertain	8	4

TABLE 1
CEMETERY 21-S-46 - SUMMARY OF GRAVES AND BURIALS (cont.)

		No.	%.
Head position			
	Facing up	55	25
	Facing left	109	51
	Facing right	20	9
	Facing down	4	2
	Foetal burial in pot	8	4
	Uncertain	19	9
Arm position			
	On pubis	110	51
	At sides	57	27
	On chest or abdomen	1	T
	Under chin	1	T
	Asymmetrical	7	4
	Foetal burial in pot	8	4
	Uncertain	31	14
Leg position			
	Straight	126	58
	Slightly flexed	57	27
	Flexed	7	4
	Asymmetrical	3	1
	Foetal burial in pot	8	4
	Uncertain	14	6

Ages at death	Male	Fem.	?	Total	%.
Under 1 year			39	39	18
1-5 years	5	2	57	64	30
6-10 years	1	1	31	33	15
11-15 years	1	1	16	18	8
16-20 years	2	2	1	5	2
21-25 years	3	3		6	3
26-30 years	1	2		3	1
31-35 years	2	4		6	3
36-40 years	7	2		9	4
41-45 years	5	3		8	4
46-50 years	7	7		14	7
51-55 years		9		9	4
Uncertain	1	0	0	1	T
Totals by sex	35	36	144	215	
Percentages by sex	16	17	67		

TABLE 2
CEMETERY 21-S-46 - REGISTER OF GRAVES

Burial no.	Sector	Superstructure	Lamp box	Orient-ation	Shaft type	Dimensions (cm)			Condition
						L	W	D	
1	IIIB	Stone pavement	-	266°	Slot	180	41	120	Poor
2	IIIB	Stone pavement	-	268°	Slot	195	51	77	Mediocre
3	IIIB	(No record*)							
4	IIIB	(No record*)							
5	IIIB	(No record*)							
6	IIIB	Stone pavement	-	(shaft and burial not found)					
7	IIIB	(No record*)							
8	IIIB	Stone pavement	-	273°	Slot	235	43	110	Poor
9	IIIB	Stone pavement	-	276°	(Disturbed - not excavated)				
10	IIIB	Stone pavement	-	281°	(Disturbed - not excavated)				
11	IIIB	Brick?	+	?	(Disturbed - not excavated)				
**12	IIIB	Round stone pave.	-	250°	Side niche N	180	77	165	Poor
13	IIIB	Stone pavement	-	277°	Slot	117	26	65	Mediocre
14	IIIB	Stone outline	-	277°	Slot	121	35	105	Mediocre
15	IIIB	Stone pavement	-	268°	Slot	90	35	80	Poor
16	IIIB	Stone pavement	-	268°	Slot	131	32	115	Good
17	IIIB	Stone pavement	-	255°	Slot	108	30	115	Good
18	IIIB	Stone pavement	-	261°	Slot	205	38	125	Good
19	IIIB	(No record*)		259°	Slot	180	37	?	Poor
20	IIIA	(No record*)		259°	Slot	185	37	90	Poor
21	IIIA	(No record*)		269°	Slot	194	55	165	Good
22	IIIA	(No record*)		254°	Slot	59	25	65	Poor
23	IIIA	Stone pavement	-	259°	Slot	102	33	70	Good
24	IIIA	(No record*)		274°	Slot	297	32	72	Good
25	IIIA	Stone pavement	-	264°	Slot	172	44	85	Good
26	IIIA	Stone pavement	-	263°	Slot	109	38	105	Good
**27	IIIB	Stone pavement	-	268°	Side niche N	83	38	85	Good
28	IIIB	Stone pavement	-	265°	Slot	122	35	85	Good
29	IIIB	Stone pavement	-	232°	Slot	83	37	90	Good
30	IIIB	Stone pavement	?	251°	Side niche ?	161	41	141	Good
31	IIIB	Stone pavement	-	274°	Slot	135	34	92	Good
32	IIIB	(No record*)		263°	Slot	177	38	135	Mediocre
33	IIIB	Stone pavement	-	269°	Slot	113	45	85	Good
34	IIIB	Stone pavement	-	253°	Side niche N	96	38	75	Good
35	IIIB	Stone pavement	?	261°	Side niche N	117	78	105	Good
36	IIIB	Stone pavement	-	262°	Slot	140	48	100	Good
37	IIIB	Stone pavement	-	264°	Slot	119	44	115	Good
38	IIIA	Stone pavement	-	258°	Slot	136	45	90	Good
39	IIIA	Stone pavement	-	242°	Slot	115	33	95	Excellent
40	IIIA	Stone pavement	-	290°	Slot	98	31	85	Good
41	IIIA	Stone pavement	-	261°	Slot	177	49	120	Good
42	IIB	Stone pavement	-	271°	Slot	113	42	95	Good
43	IIB	Stone pavement	-	265°	Slot	164	32	105	Good
44	IIIB	Stone pavement	-	274°	Slot	61	30	70	Good
45	IIIB	Stone outline	-	274°	Slot	81	36	95	Good
46	IIIB	(Not a grave)							
47	IIIB	(No record*)		246°	Slot	126	42	125	Poor
48	IIB	Stone pavement	-	256°	Slot	135	49	115	Good
49	IIB	Stone pavement	-	253°	Slot	140	37	105	Good
50	IIB	Stone pavement	-	263°	Slot	104	29	95	Good
51	IIIB	Stone pavement	-	250°	Slot	83	28	Good	
52	IIIB	Stone outline	-	256°	Slot	?	?	58	Poor

* Documentation from the 1969 excavations lost
** X-Group graves

TABLE 2
CEMETERY 21-S-46 - REGISTER OF GRAVES (cont.)

Burial no.	Sector	Superstructure	Lamp box	Orient-ation	Shaft type	Dimensions (cm)			Condition
						L	W	D	
53	IIB	(No record*)		252°	Side niche ?	128	43	105	Poor
54	IIB	(No record*)		?	Slot	?	?	130	Poor
55	IIB	(No record*)		260°	Slot	163	40	135	Good
56	IIB	(No record*)		(No data recorded – not re-excavated?)					
57	IIB	Stone outline	-	270°	Side niche N	74	40	90	Good
58	IIB	Stone pavement	-	266°	Side niche N	60	34	55	Good
59	IIA	Stone pavement?	-	260°	Slot	114	32	130	Good
60	IIA	Stone pavement	-	274°	Side niche N	82	37	85	Good
61	IIA	Stone alignment	-	254°	Slot	110	45	100	Good
62	IIA	Stone pavement	-	263°	Slot	166	41	80	Good
63	IIA	Stone pavement	-	?	Slot	?	?	?	Poor
64	IIB	Stone alignments	-	(Not a tomb superstructure)					
65	IIB	Stone pavement	-	274°	Slot	79	38	70	Good
66	IIB	(No record*)		258°	Slot	120	32	100	Fair
67	IIB	(No record*)		259°	Slot	155	44	115	Good
68	IIB	Stone pavement	-	241°	Slot	156	32	100	Good
69	IIB	Stone outline	-	262°	Slot	92	28	85	Good
70	IIB	Stone pavement	-	250°	Slot	72	40	70	Good
71	IIB	Stone pavement	-	232°	Slot	80	37	70	Good
72	IIB	Stone pavement	-	262°	Slot	138	60	100	Good
73	IIA	Stone outline	-	264°	Slot	101	47	93	Good
74	IIA	Stone pavement	-	260°	Slot	174	38	95	Good
75	IIA	Stone pavement	-	269°	Slot	110	30	110	Good
76	IIA	Stone pavement	-	285°	Slot	160	40	85	Poor
77	IIA	Stone pavement	-	266°	Side niche N	125	35	130	Good
78	IIA	Stone pavement	-	266°	Side niche N	103	48	105	Good
79	IIB	Stone pavement	-	266°	Side niche N	93	30	80	Good
80	IIB	Stone pavement	-	267°	Slot	200	40	80	Good
81	IIB	Stone pavement	-	271°	Side niche N	101	39	?	Good
82	IIB	Stone pavement	-	266°	Slot	138	42	95	Good
83	IIB	Stone outline	-	269°	Slot	86	30	80	Good
84	IIB	Stone pavement	-	266°	Slot	204	41	95	Good
85	IIB	Stone pavement	-	274°	Side niche N	103	39	95	Good
86	IIB	Stone pavement	-	272°	Slot	159	44	135	Good
87	IIB	Stone pavement	-	289°	Slot	73	33	85	Good
88	IIB	Stone pavement	-	269°	Side niche N	140	35	90	Good
89	IIB	Stone pavement	-	277°	Slot	83	30	64	Good
90	IIA	Stone pavement	-	269°	Side niche N	108	37	95	Good
91	IIA	Stone pavement	-	264°	Side niche N	105	25	90	Good
92	IIA	Stone pavement	-	266°	Side niche N	110	30	90	Good
93	IIA	Stone pavement	-	275°	Side niche N	114	33	105	Good
94	IIA	Stone outline	-	285°	Side niche N	107	33	100	Good
95	IIA	Stone pavement	-	276°	Side niche N	120	27	80	Good
96	IIA	Stone pavement	-	256°	Side niche N	115	42	95	Good
97	IIA	Stone outline	-	272°	Side niche N	122	47	105	Good
98	IIB	Stone pavement	-	276°	Side niche N	128	32	100	Good
99	IIB	(No record*)		268°	Slot	202	37	110	Good
100	IIB	Stone outline	+	255°	Slot	228	38	95	Good
101	IIB	Stone pavement	-	262°	Slot	149	26	105	Good
102	IIB	(No record)		(Islamic grave – not excavated)					
103	IIB	(No record)		(Islamic grave – not excavated)					

* Documentation from the 1969 excavations lost
** X-Group graves

TABLE 2
CEMETERY 21-S-46 - REGISTER OF GRAVES (cont.)

Burial no.	Sector	Superstructure	Lamp box	Orient- ation	Shaft type	Dimensions (cm)			Condition
						L	W	D	
104	IIA	Stone pavement	-	261°	Side niche N	99	37	75	Good
105	IIA	Stone pavement	-	280°	Side niche N	89	?	85	Good
107	IIA	Stone pavement	-	274°	Slot	163	42	105	Good
108	IIA	Stone pavement	-	267°	Slot	130	45	125	Good
109	IIA	Stone outline?	-	246°	Slot	239	61	130	Good
110	IIA	Stone alignment?	-	266°	Side niche N	123	49	95	Good
111	IIA	Stone pavement?	-	270°	Side niche N	114	38	75	Good
112	IIB	Stone pavement?		(Disturbed - not excavated)					
113	IIB	Stone outline	-	272°	Slot	189	42	100	Good
114	IIB	Stone outline	-	260°	Slot	123	35	95	Good
115	IIB	Stone pavement	-	273°	Slot	86	27	85	Good
116	IIB	Stone pavement	-	260°	Side niche N	137	36	100	Good
117	IIB	Stone pavement	-	(Islamic grave - not excavated)					
118	IIA	Stone pavement	-	258°	Side niche N	174	43	80	Good
119	IIA	Stone pavement	-	254°	Side niche N	88	37	90	Good
120	IIB	Stone pavement	-	239°	Slot	162	27	80	Good
121	IIB	Stone outline	-	260°	Slot	97	21	55	Good
122	IIB	Stone pavement	-	265°	Side niche N	134	47	90	Good
123	IIB	Stone pavement	?	265°	Slot	138	41	105	Good
124	IIB	Stone pavement	-	266°	Slot	118	30	95	Good
125	IIB	Stone pavement	-	259°	Slot	93	35	110	Good
126	IIB	Stone alignment	-	259°	Slot	163	48	105	Good
127	IIB	Stone pavement	-	262°	Slot	79	27	105	Good
128	IB	Stone pavement	-	(Uncertain due to poor preservation)					
129	IB	Stone pavement	-	251°	Slot?	190	43	140	Good
130	IB	Stone pavement	-	245°	Slot	132	32	90	Poor
131	IA	Stone pavement	-	(Burials immediately under superstructure)					
132	IA	Stone pavement	-	260°	Slot	92	31	115	Good
133	IB	Stone pavement	-	266°	Slot	104	43	90	Good
134	IB	Stone pavement	-	266°	Slot	130	33	80	Good
135	IB	Stone outline	-	266°	Slot	105	33	85	Poor
136	IB	Stone circle	-	254°	Slot	79	35	70	Poor
137	IB	Stone pavement	-	(Uncertain due to poor preservation)					
138	IB	Stone pavement	-	244°	Slot	93	29	75	Good
139	IB	Stone outline	-	268°	Slot	170	40	125	Good
140	IA	Stone pavement?	-	(Disturbed – not excavated)					
141	IA	(No record*)		(Round pit, c. 42 cm diameter)		Good			
142	IA	(No record*)		(Not excavated)					
143	IA	(No record*)		251°	Slot	48	37	45	Poor
144	IA	(No record*)		(Round pit, c. 50 cm in diameter & depth)		Good			
145	IA	(No record*)		269°	Slot	168	37	145	Poor
146	IB	(No record*)		264°	Slot	155	46	125	Poor
147	IA	(No record*)		264°	Slot	69	30	85	Good
148	IA	(No record*)		274°	Slot	55	14	50	Good
149	IA	(No record*)		220°	Slot	56	32	55	Good
150	IA	(No record*)		(Empty)					
151	IA	(No record*)		(Empty)					
152	IA	(No record*)		(Empty)					
153	IA	(No record*)		252°	Slot	53	38	?	Poor
154	IA	(No record*)		(Not excavated)					
155	IA	(No record*)		(Not excavated)					

* Documentation from the 1969 excavations lost
** X-Group graves

TABLE 2
CEMETERY 21-S-46 - REGISTER OF GRAVES (cont.)

Burial no.	Sector	Superstructure	Lamp box	Orient-ation	Shaft type	Dimensions (cm)			Condition
						L	W	D	
156	IA	(No record*)		267°	Slot	73	21	55	Good
157	IA	(No record*)		(Uncertain due to poor preservation)					
158	IA	(No record*)		268°	Slot	50	22	55	Poor
159	IA	(No record*)		256°	Slot	77	31	90	Good
160	IA	Stone pavement	-	(Presumed Islamic – not excavated)					
161	IA	Stone pavement	-	(Disturbed – not excavated)					
162	IA	Stone pavement	-	(Uncertain due to poor preservation)					
163	IA	Stone outline	-	272°	Slot	151	47	85	Good
164	IA	Stone pavement	-	(Islamic grave – not excavated)					
165	IA	Stone pavement	-	(Uncertain due to poor preservation)					
166	IA	Stone alignment	-	(Islamic grave – not excavated)					
167	IA	Stone pavement	-	(Islamic grave – not excavated)					
168	IIIA	(None preserved)		238°	Slot	194	35	85	Good
169	IIIA	(None preserved)		260°	Slot	113	30	68	Good
170	IIIA	(None preserved)		(Unfinished grave pit 30 cm deep)					
171	IIIA	(None preserved)		262°	Side niche N	186	60	145	Good
172	IIIA	Brick pavement	-	278°	Slot	180	60	102	Good
173	IIIA	(None preserved)		270°	Slot	195	45	115	Good
174	IIIA	(None preserved)		259°	Slot	169	36	71	Poor
175	IIIA	Stone pavement	-	262°	Slot	82	21	46	Good
176	IIIA	Brick pavement?	?	260°	Slot	173	36	55	Good
177	IIIA	Brick pavement	+	279°	Slot	202	32	86	Good
178	IIIA	(No record*)		260°	Slot	130	40	115	Poor
179	IIIA	(None preserved)		268°	Slot	105	25	55	Good
180	IIIA	Stone pavement?	?	276°	Slot	205	35	82	Good
181	IIIA	Stone pavement?	?	290°	Slot	140	33	50	Poor
182	IIIA	(None preserved)		241°	Slot	101	35	60	Poor
183	IIIB	Stone pavement	-	274°	Slot	66	43	50	Mediocre
184	IIIB	Brick + stone pav.		266°	Slot	74	46	90	Good
185	IIIB	Brick pavement	-	264°	Side niche N	164	34	100	Good
186	IIIB	Brick pavement	-	264°	Slot	195	38	108	Good
187	IIIB	Stone pavement	-	256°	Slot	200	50	90	Good
188	IIIA	Brick pavement	-	265°	Side niche N	190	50	135	Good
189	IIA	Stone pavement	-	(Grave shaft not found)					
190	IIIB	(None preserved)		258°	Slot	155	41	95	Good
**191	IIIB	(None preserved)		264°	Side niche N	185	64	155	Poor
192	IIIB	(None preserved)		264°	Slot	171	31	140	Good
193	IIIB	(None preserved)		272°	Side niche N	119	40	150	Good
194	IIA	Stone pavement	-	270°	Side niche N	85	32	85	Good
195	IIIB	Stone alignment	-	260°	Slot	107	28	95	Good
196	IIIB	Stone pavement	-	272°	Slot	94	32	70	Good
197	IIB	(None preserved)		264°	Slot	140	55	105	Good
198	IIB	(None preserved)		262°	Slot	102	43	70	Good
199	IIA	(None preserved)		274°	Slot	114	57	75	Good
200	IIB	(None preserved)		261°	Slot	182	47	140	Good
201	IIB	(None preserved)		260°	Slot	83	30	85	Good
202	IIA	Brick pavement	-	264°	Side niche ?	183	48	100	Good
203	IIIB	(None preserved)		(Burial immediately under superstructure)					Poor
204	IIIB	(None preserved)		261°	Side niche N	166	33	100	Good
205	IIIB	(None preserved)		270°	Side niche S	69	40	70	Poor
206	IIIB	(None preserved)		267°	Side niche N	205	60	105	Good

* Documentation from the 1969 excavations lost
** X-Group graves

TABLE 2
TABLE 2
CEMETERY 21-S-46 - REGISTER OF GRAVES (cont.)

Burial no.	Sector	Superstructure	Lamp box	Orient-ation	Shaft type	Dimensions (cm)			Condition
						L	W	D	
207	IIIB	(None preserved)		256°	Side niche N	202	40	155	Good
208	IIIB	(None preserved)		264°	Slot	89	25	90	Good
209	IIIB	(None preserved)		258°	Slot	92	48	90	Good
210	IIA	(None preserved)		272°	Slot	99	30	85	Good
211	IIIA	(None preserved)		274°	Slot	230	90	115	Good
212	IIIA	(None preserved)		276°	Slot	205	50	125	Good
213	IIIB	2 stones	-	252°	Side niche N	171	54	150	Good
214	IIB	Stone pavement	-	(Continuation of no. 84 superstructure)					
215	IIB	(Islamic grave - not excavated)							
216	IIB	Stone pavement	-	(Disturbed - not excavated)					
217	IIB	Stone pavement	-	263°	Slot	104	27	65	Good
218	IIB	Stone pavement	-	261°	Slot	69	26	65	Good
219	IIB	(None preserved)		?	Oval pit	53	45	70	Poor
220	IIB	(No record*)		(Islamic grave - not excavated)					
221	IIB	Stone pavement	-	248°	Slot	46	40	50	Good
222	IIIB	(None preserved)		264°	Slot	205	51	120	Good
223	IIIB	(None preserved)		252°	Slot	151	36	90	Good
224	IIB	(None preserved)		256°	Slot	169	34	100	Good
225	IIA	(None preserved)		278°	Slot	230	55	140	Good
226	IIIB	(None preserved)		258°	Slot	175	38	110	Good
227	IIB	Stone pavement	-	(Disturbed - not excavated)					
228	IIB	(None preserved)		267°	Side niche N	199	50	115	Good
229	IIIB	(Not a grave)							
230	IIIB	(None preserved)		(Uncertain due to poor preservation)					Poor
231	IIIB	(None preserved)		(Uncertain due to poor preservation)					Poor
232	IIIB	(None preserved)		(Uncertain due to poor preservation)					Poor
233	IIB	(Not a grave)							
234	IIB	(None preserved)		273°	Slot	179	55	140	Good
235	IB	(None preserved)		256°	Slot	112	36	105	Good
236	IIB	Brick pavement?	?	239°	Slot	212	38	85	Good
237	IIB	(None preserved)		260°	Slot	175	40	115	Good
238	IA	(None preserved)		260°	Slot	149	42	100	Mediocre
239	IA	(Unfinished grave)							
240	IA	(No record*)		265°	Slot	53	23	50	Poor
241	IA	(No record*)		(Foetal burial in Ware H1 pot, on side)					Poor
242	IA	(None preserved)		(Uncertain due to poor preservation)					Poor

* Documentation from the 1969 excavations lost

interments began here just before the beginning of the Christian period, and it is a reasonable assumption that there was a continuum of usage thereafter, extending into the Early Christian period. Secondly, the handful of foetal burials in pots were all contained in pottery vessels of Early Christian types. Thirdly, in those relatively few cases where bricks were employed in superstructures or as body coverings, the average size of the bricks was 37 or 38 x 18 x 8 cm, which was the typical size of Early and early Classic Christian bricks at Meinarti. Later bricks, both at Meinarti and at Kulubnarti, were typically 40 cm long.[5] Finally, the textile materials used in shrouding were nearly all of familiar Early Christian types, a finding that will be more fully discussed in Part II.

Negative evidence also tends to support an early dating

for the graves at 21-S-46. The Classic Christian graves at the nearby Site 21-S-49,[6] as well as the few structures at Cemetery 21-R-2 that could be clearly dated to the later Christian periods, had superstructures of rollag brick pavement,[7] while only three such pavements were identified at 21-S-46. This suggests that the cemetery ceased to be used at a time when the rollag structures were just coming into fashion, probably some time in the early Classic Christian period. If this assumption is correct, then the handful of Islamic graves at 21-S-46 do not indicate a continuity of occupation from Christian into Islamic times. Much more probably they reflect a reuse of the cemetery, on a very small scale, after a long period of abandonment.

[5] For brick sizes see W. Y. Adams in *Kush*, vol. 13 (1965), p.155, n. 13.

[6] See *Kulubnarti I*, p. 272.

[7] i.e. pavement of bricks laid on their edges.

Superstructures

In Christian Nubian times, as in all earlier periods since the C-Group, it was usual but not universal practice to place some kind of covering over the tops of grave shafts, at least to identify their location so as to avoid later intrusions, if not to memorialize the dead person. As previously noted, information is lacking in regard to the coverings of the 60 graves at 21-S-46 that were excavated in 1969. However, of the 182 graves recorded in 1979 that had not been excavated previously, 149, or 82%, had some kind of covering at the surface. The vast majority of these (118, or 79%) were simple pavements of flat but unshaped granite slabs, arranged roughly in a rectangle over the top of the grave (Plates 2A-D). In 16 cases there was only an outline of stones surrounding the grave (Plates 1E-F), and five graves had only a single line of stones along the central axis of the grave. One "X-Group" grave seems to have been surrounded by the usual wide ring of stones, although only half of it was preserved *in situ* (Plates 1C-D).

The stones employed in superstructures were natural granite spalls, gathered from the surface of the nearby ridges. There seems to have been little effort to select stones with a naturally rectangular shape, or to select stones of especially large size. A typical superstructure might incorporate anywhere from 20 to 40 individual stones. Sometimes, but not always, the interstices between the main slabs were filled in with small stone chips, to form something approaching a continuous pavement. In a good many cases however, the slabs were set fairly wide apart, with no effort to fill in the interstices (cf. Plates 2B-C). Since the stones were not set into any kind of mortar, they had suffered a good deal of disturbance and displacement in the course of time. The wadi in which these graves were located had served also as a common route of travel from the interior of the island to the west bank, and grave superstructures were consequently subject to damage from the feet of passing travelers and animals.

Only nine of the graves at 21-S-46 had had superstructures of brick. All of them were pavements rather than mastaba structures; that is, they incorporated in each case only one course of bricks. They were all incompletely preserved; in two cases so much so that the original arrangement of the bricks could not be determined. In four cases the bricks had been laid flat, mostly but not entirely at right angles to the long axis of the grave. The bricks in all cases had been laid edge to edge so as to form a continuous pavement, but the alternation of crosswise with lengthwise bricks was somewhat irregular (Plate 2E).

Three graves had rollag brick superstructures; that is, pavements formed of bricks laid on edge. All three exhibited the "spine-and-ribs" design, involving one or two lines of bricks running longitudinally down the middle of the superstructure, adjoined on either side by bricks laid at right angles to the axis of the grave (Plate 2F). In two cases there was a lamp box at the western end of the grave.

Superstructures of this type were found also at Site 21-S-49, where the graves were not excavated,[8] and also over many graves at Site 21-R-2 that will be described later. It is possible, though by no means certain, that these were among the latest graves at 21-S-46, an issue that will be further considered later. However, the size of bricks, in all cases where they could be measured, was 37 or 38 x 18 x 8 cm: the usual size for Early and Classic Christian bricks in other Nubian sites.[9]

Thirty-three graves, not previously excavated in 1969, exhibited no traces of superstructures when recorded in 1979. It is possible however, that some or all of them had originally had coverings of stones, which were subsequently displaced.

Grave orientations

Every one of the excavated grave shafts at 21-S-46, including those of presumed "X-Group" date, had approximately an east-west orientation, with the head of the body placed at the west end. There was nevertheless a substantial variation in the orientation of individual graves, from 220° (at the west end) at one extreme to 290° at the other. The general tendency was for graves to be oriented somewhat south of true west, such that 178 graves had orientations between 220° and 270°, while only 40 graves had orientations between 270° and 290°. Although it is impossible to speak of any one "typical" orientation, the mean of all the grave orientations at 21-S-46 was about 260°.

The variability of grave orientations at 21-S-46 is probably explained in part by the kind of grave superstructures that were employed. In the absence of the magnetic compass, the diggers of new graves had nothing to guide them except the sun and the orientation of earlier graves. However, the position of the sun was of course variable from season to season, while the rather amorphous shapes of the superstructures at 21-S-46 did not give a very precise indication of the orientation of the underlying graves. In more northerly cemeteries, where most superstructures were regular rectangles of brick or stone masonry, they gave a better guide to the orientation of the underlying graves, with the result that the shafts generally exhibited less variability in their orientations.

Grave shafts

Of the 218 grave shafts excavated at 21-S-46, 142, or 65%, were simple "slot" graves: elongate, straight-sided pits with either rounded or square ends (Plate 3A). Forty-five other graves had a vertical shaft of the same type as that just described, but with an offset, undercut niche at the bottom of the shaft, in which the body was placed. In all but one of the cases the niche was undercut along the north side of the shaft, while one grave had an offset niche at the south

---

[8] *Kulubnarti I*, p. 272.
[9] See n. 5.

16

side (Plate 3B). Unlike the so-called side-chamber graves of X-Group times,[10] however, the Kulubnarti graves seldom had an undercut niche more than about 20 cm wide, and it was not dug down to a level below that of the main grave shaft. It was not, in fact, wide enough to accommodate the full width of the interred body, which always lay partly within the undercut area and partly within the main shaft, as shown in Plate 3B. The purpose of this arrangement, which was common also in Lower Nubian cemeteries, was to allow the body to be bridged over and protected by stone slabs, leaning diagonally against the north wall of the shaft (Figure 4). At Kulubnarti, however, many of the bodies in side-niche graves had no such protecting slabs.

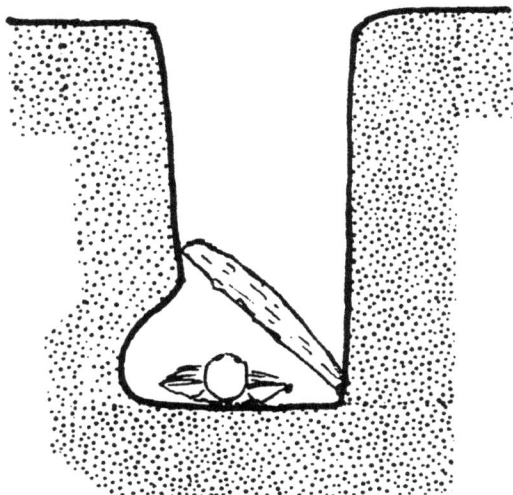

Figure 4. Diagram of side-niche grave shaft.

There were also five examples of bottom-niche graves, in which the body lay within a pit at the bottom of the shaft that was slightly narrower than the main portion of the shaft. This arrangement was made so that the body could be bridged over with horizontal stone slabs, resting on the edges of the lower pit (Figure 5).

About one quarter of the grave shafts at 21-S-46, including both slot and lateral niche graves, had carefully squared ends (most clearly visible in Plates 7E and 8C). They occurred with about equal frequency in the case of dorsal interments and of interments lying on their sides. They were considerably more common in the case of adult burials than of infants, but were not wholly lacking in the latter cases. There is, clearly, no practical explanation for this nicety, which did not in any way facilitate the process of interment, and which was not visible once the grave was filled and covered over. Like the use of an elaborate coffin in more recent times, it must have been meant simply as a gesture of respect for the dead.

[10] See George A. Reisner, *The Archaeological Survey of Nubia, Report for 1907-1908* (Cairo, 1910), pp. 307-308.

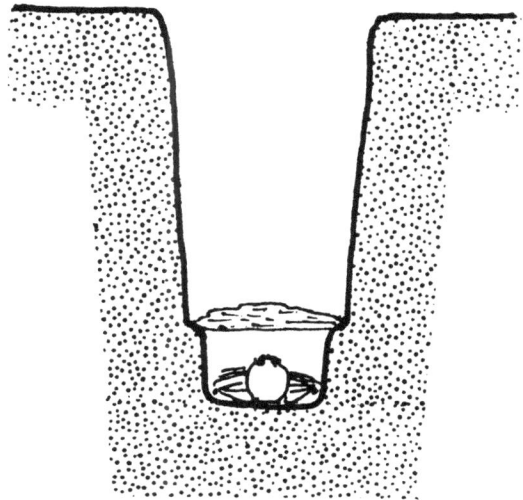

Figure 5. Diagram of bottom-niche grave shaft.

The size of grave shafts naturally varied according to the size of the individual to be buried. Nevertheless, about one-third of the graves were somewhat too small for the occupant, whose legs had to be slightly flexed at the knees to fit into the shaft. The lengths of individual shafts varied between a minimum of 51 cm and a maximum of 297 cm. Widths were obviously somewhat more uniform, averaging a little over 40 cm. Grave depths were again quite variable, and not always in proportion to the horizontal dimensions of the shaft. However, the largest graves tended also to be fairly deep. The deepest recorded grave had a depth of 165 cm, and the shallowest 50 cm. The average shaft depth for adult burials was 115 cm, while the average depth for all graves was a little under one meter.

Body coverings

In the Christian cemeteries of Lower Nubia, bodies were very commonly protected by a covering of stone slabs or bricks extending along their full length. At Kulubnarti however, the use of a covering for any part of the body below the head was uncommon. The main exception occurred in the case of side-niche graves, where stones were often laid diagonally in such a way as to seal off the niche, and the body within it, from the remainder of the shaft, as shown in Figure 4 and Plates 3C-D. The body was thus left in a very small air chamber, not filled with earth - the last survival of the immemorial pre-Christian practice of enclosing the body within some kind of unfilled chamber. It was nevertheless true that a great many of the bodies in side-niche graves had no such covering, in contrast to the situation in Lower Nubian cemeteries where bodies in side-niche graves nearly always had a covering of diagonal slabs.[11]

In addition to side-niche graves, there were also five bottom-niche graves in which an individual in dorsal

[11] See the concluding section of Part I, below.

17

TABLE 3
CEMETERY 21-S-46, REGISTER OF BURIALS

Burial no.	Head covering	Body covering	Body position	Head facing	Arms	Legs	Sex	Age
1	3 bricks	None	Left side	Left	Pubis	Sl. flexed	F	40-44
2	3 bricks	None	Dorsal	Up	Pubis	Sl. flexed	?	c. 9
3	(No record)							
4	(Islamic grave - not excavated)							
5	3 bricks	None	Dorsal	Left	Pubis	Straight	M	22-24
6	(Shaft and burial not found)							
7	3 bricks	None	Dorsal		Pubis	Straight	M	47-55
8	3 bricks	None	Dorsal	Left	Pubis	L straight; R sl. flexed	F	45-49
9	(Disturbed - not excavated)							
10	(Disturbed - not excavated)							
11	(Disturbed - not excavated)							
*12	Stones	Stones all along	Flexed	South	Chin	Flexed	M	40-44
13	3 bricks	None	Dorsal	Up	Sides	Sl. flexed	?	?
14	3 bricks	None	Dorsal	Up	R at side L on chest	Straight	?	8
15	2 stones	None	Dorsal	Up	Pubis	Straight	?	1
16	3 bricks	None	Left side	Left	Pubis	Sl. flexed	M	27-30
17	None	None	Left side	Left	Pubis	Straight	?	4-5
18	None	Stones to waist	Left side	Left	Pubis	Straight	M	20-21
19	None	None	Dorsal	Up	Pubis	Straight	M	40-44
20	1 brick	None	Dorsal	Up	Pubis	Straight	F	36-39
21	3 stones	None	Left side	Left	Pubis	Straight	F	45-49
22	2 sherds	None	Dorsal	Up	Pubis	Straight	?	3+
23	3 stones	None	Dorsal	Left	Sides	Straight	?	?
24	None	None	Dorsal	Left	Sides	Straight	?	?
25	None	None	Left side	Down	Sides	Mod. flexed	?	9 mos.
26	3 stones	None	Right side	Right	Pubis	Straight	?	4-5
*27	None	None	Left side	Down	Sides	Flexed	?	9 mos.
28	1 sherd	Stones to knees	Left side	Left	Pubis	Sl. flexed	?	6
29	3 bricks	None	Dorsal	Right	Pubis	Straight	?	10 mos.
30	None	None	Dorsal	Left	Sides	Straight	?	13
31	2 sherds	Stones all along	Left side	Left	Pubis	Sl. flexed	?	11
32	?	?	Left side	Left	Pubis	Straight	F	19
33	Stones	Stones all along	Left side	Left	Sides	Flexed	?	18 mos.
34	None	None	Left side	Left	Pubis	Straight	M	?
35	None	None	Left side	Left	Sides	Straight	?	7
36	3 stones	None	Dorsal	Up	Pubis	Straight	M	?
37	1 stone	None	Dorsal	Up	Sides	Straight	?	1
38	3 stones	None	Dorsal	Up	Pubis	Straight	?	5
39	1 stone	None	Ventral	Right	Sides	Straight	?	5-6
40	None	None	Dorsal	Right	Pubis	Straight	?	5
41	Stones	Stones all along	Dorsal	Up	Pubis	Straight	?	14
42A	Stones	Stones all along	(Infant burial in U2 amphora - head to west)					
42B	Stones	Stones all along	Left side	Left	?	Flexed	?	6
43A	Stones	Stones all along	(Infant burial in U2 amphora - head to west)					
43B	None	None	Dorsal	Up	Pubis	Straight	?	15
43C	None	None	Dorsal	Left	Sides	Straight	?	6
43D	None	None	(Disturbed by later intrusions)				?	9
44	2 stones	None	Dorsal	Up	Sides	Straight	?	9 mos.
45	None	None	Left side	Left	?	Sl. flexed	?	18 mos.
46	(Not a grave)							

* X-Group graves

18

TABLE 3
CEMETERY 21-S-46, REGISTER OF BURIALS (cont.)

Burial no.	Head covering	Body covering	Body position	Head facing	Arms	Legs	Sex	Age
47	3 bricks	None	Dorsal	Up	Pubis	Sl. flexed	?	8
48	3 stones	None	Dorsal	Left	Pubis	Straight	?	10
49	3 stones	None	Dorsal	Up	L on pubis R at side	Straight	?	9
50	3 stones	None	Left side	Left	Sides	Straight	?	4
51	2 stones + 2 bricks	None	Dorsal	?	Pubis	Straight	?	2
52	None	None	Left side	Left	Sides	Flexed	?	6
53	None	None	Dorsal	Up	Sides	Sl. flexed	F	11
54	3 stones	None	Dorsal	Left	Pubis	Straight	?	16-17
55	3 stones	None	Turned left	Left	Pubis	Straight	M	18
56	(Not re-excavated)							
57	None	None	Dorsal	Left	Sides	Straight	?	1 month
58	None	None	Dorsal	?	?	Straight	M	Neonate
59	Stones	Stones all along	Dorsal	Up	Pubis	Sl. flexed	?	5
60	None	None	Dorsal	Up	Pubis	Sl. flexed	?	9 mos.
61	Stones	Stones all along	Dorsal	Up	Pubis	Sl. flexed	?	?
62	Stones	Stones all along	Dorsal	Up	R on pubis L at side	Straight	M	13
63	None	None	(Neonate burial in U2 amphora - head to west)					
64	(Not a grave)							
65	None	None	(Infant burial in U2 amphora - head to west)					
66	None	None	Dorsal	Left	Sides	Straight	?	3 mos.
67	3 stones	None	Left side	Left	Pubis	Sl. flexed	?	13
68	Stones	Stones all along	Left side	Left	Sides	Sl. flexed	M	4
69	3 stones	None	Left side	Left	?	Sl. flexed	?	9 mos.
70	Stones	Stones all along	Dorsal	Up	Sides	Straight	?	5 mos.
71	None	None	(Neonate in amphora - head to west)					
72	Stones	Stones all along	(Foetus in H1 pot - buried with top up)					
73	Stones	Stones all along	Dorsal	Up	?	Straight	?	3
74	Stones	Stones all along	Left side	Left	Sides	Straight	F	45-49
75	Stones	Stones all along	Dorsal	Left	Pubis	Straight	?	4
76	None	None	Left side	Left	Pubis	Sl. flexed	F	45-49
77	Stones	Stones to waist	Dorsal	Up	Pubis	Straight	?	6
78	None	None	Dorsal	Left	Sides	Straight	?	4
79	None	None	Dorsal	Up	Pubis	Mod. flexed	?	3
80	Stones	Stones all along	Left side	Left	Pubis	Straight	M	27-30
81	None	None	Dorsal	Left	?	Straight	?	3
82	Stones	Stones all along	Dorsal	Left	?	Sl. flexed	?	9
83	3 stones	None	¼ left	Left	Pubis	Sl. flexed	?	1
84	1 sherd	None	Left side	Left	Sides	Straight	M	45-49
85	3 stones	None	Left side	Left	Pubis	Straight	?	5
86	Stones	Stones all along	Dorsal	Up	Pubis	Straight	?	31-35
87	Stones	Stones all along	Left side	Left	Pubis	?	?	Neonate
89	Stones	Stones all along	Dorsal	Left	?	Flexed	?	6 mos.
90	None	None	Dorsal	Left	Pubis	Straight	?	Infant
91	None	None	Dorsal	Up	Sides	Straight	F	?
92	None	None	Dorsal	Left	Pubis	Straight	?	6
93	None	None	Dorsal	Up	Sides?	Sl. flexed	?	4
94A	None	None	Dorsal	Up	Pubis	Sl. flexed	?	Infant

* X-Group graves

19

TABLE 3
CEMETERY 21-S-46, REGISTER OF BURIALS (cont.)

Burial no.	Head covering	Body covering	Body position	Head facing	Arms	Legs	Sex	Age
94B	None	None	Dorsal	Up	?	Straight	?	18 mos.
95	None	None	Dorsal	Left	Pubis	Straight	?	11
96	None	None	Left side	Left	Pubis	Sl. flexed	?	4
97	None	None	Right side	Right	Pubis	Straight	?	7
98	None	None	Left side	Left	Pubis	Straight	?	6
99	Stones	Stones all along	Dorsal	Up	Pubis	Straight	M	40-44
100	None	None	Dorsal	Up	R on pubis L at side	Straight	F	22-24
101	3 stones	None	Left side	Left	Pubis	Sl. flexed	?	9-10
102	(Islamic grave - not excavated)							
103	(Islamic grave - not excavated)							
104	Stones	Stones all along	¼ left	Up	Pubis	Sl. flexed	?	45-49
105	None	None	¼ right	Right	R on pubis L on chin	Straight	?	5
106	None	None	Dorsal	Up	Pubis	Straight	?	4
107	Stones	Stones all along	Dorsal	?	Pubis	Straight	M	45-49
108	3 stones	None	Left side	Left	Pubis	Sl. flexed	?	10
109	Stones	Stones all along	¼ left	Left	Pubis	Sl. flexed	?	40-44
110	None	None	Left side	Left	Sides	Straight	?	3-4
111	None	None	Left side	Left	Pubis	Sl. flexed	?	18 mos.
112	(Disturbed - not excavated)							
113	3 stones	None	Right side	Right	?	Sl. flexed	?	8
114	3 stones	None	Left side	Left	?	Straight	?	5
115	3 stones	None	Dorsal	Up	Sides	Straight	?	3
116	None	None	Dorsal	Left	Sides	Straight	?	11
117	(Islamic grave - not excavated)							
118	None	None	Left side	Left	Pubis	Sl. flexed	F	45-49
119	None	None	Left side	Left	?	?	?	6 mos.
120	None	None	Dorsal	Left	Pubis	Sl. flexed	?	6 mos.
121	None	None	Left side	Left	Pubis	Straight	?	?
122	Sheepskin	None	Left side	Left	Sides	Straight	?	?
123	3 stones	None	¾ right	Down	Sides	Sl. flexed	?	5
124	3 stones	None	Left side	Left	Pubis	Sl. flexed	?	5
125	3 stones	None	Dorsal	Right	Sides	Straight	?	5
126	3 bricks	None	Dorsal	Left	R on pubis L under	Straight	?	16
127	Stones	Stones all along	Dorsal	Up	?	Straight	?	6 mos.
128	3 stones	None	Dorsal	Left	Pubis	Straight	?	6
129	3 stones	None	¼ left	Left	Sides	Straight	F	50+
130	Mud	None	Dorsal	Left	Pubis	Straight	?	?
131*	None	None	Flexed R side	Front	Flexed	?	?	9 mos.
132	3 bricks	None	Right side	Right	Pubis	Mod. flexed	?	3
133	3 stones	None	Dorsal	Right	Sides	Straight	?	6 mos.
134	3 stones	None	Dorsal	Left	?	Sl. flexed	?	?
135	None	None	Left side?	Left	Sides	Straight	?	4
136	None	None	Dorsal	Left	Pubis	Straight	?	5
137	3 stones?	None	Dorsal	Right	Pubis	Straight	?	17
138	3 bricks	None	Dorsal	Up	Pubis	Straight	?	5
139	3 stones	None	Left side	Left	Pubis	Sl. flexed	F	7
140	(Disturbed - not excavated)							
141	(Foetus in Ware H1 pot, buried with top down)							

* X-Group graves

TABLE 3
CEMETERY 21-S-46, REGISTER OF BURIALS (cont.)

Burial no.	Head covering	Body covering	Body position	Head facing	Arms	Legs	Sex	Age
142	(Not excavated)							
143	None	None	Dorsal	Right	?	?	?	Neonate
144	Foetus in Ware H1 pot, buried upright)							
145	None	None	Dorsal	Up	Pubis	Straight	F	40-44
146	3 bricks	None	Left side	Left	Pubis	Straight	F	40-44
147	Stones	Stones all along	Dorsal	Up	?	Sl. flexed	?	?
148	None	None	Right side	Right	Pubis	Sl. flexed	?	Neonate
149	None	None	Dorsal?	Left	?	?	?	Neonate
150	(Empty)							
151	(Empty)							
152	(Empty)							
153	None	None	(Disturbed)				?	Foetus
154	(Not excavated)							
155	(Not excavated)							
156	2 stones	None	Left side	Left	Sides	Straight	?	Neonate
157	None	None	?	Left	?	?	?	Neonate
158	None	None	Dorsal	Left	Sides	?	?	?
159	None	None	Dorsal	Left	Sides	Straight	?	6 mos.
160	(Islamic grave – not excavated)							
161	(Disturbed – not excavated)							
162	None	None	Left side	Left	Pubis	Sl. flexed	M	45-49
163	3 bricks	None	Left side	Left	Pubis	Straight	F	45-49
164	(Islamic grave – not excavated)							
165	2 bricks	None	Dorsal	Up	Sides	Straight	M	31-35
166	(Islamic grave – not excavated)							
167	(Islamic grave – not excavated)							
168	3 bricks	None	Right side	Right	Sides	Straight	M	?
169	3 bricks	None	¼ left	Left	Sides	Sl. flexed	M	5
170	(Unfinished grave)							
171	None	None	Left side	Left	Pubis	Straight	F	36-39
172	3 bricks	None	Left side	Left	Sides	Straight	F	40-44
173	1 stone	None	Dorsal	Left	Pubis	Straight	M	40-44
174	3 bricks	None	Left side	Left	Pubis	L sl. flexed R straight	F	50+
175	None	None	Right side	Right	Sides	Sl. flexed	?	1-2
176	3 bricks	None	Left side	Left	Pubis	Sl. flexed	F	50+
177	3 bricks	None	Right side	Right	Pubis	Sl. flexed	?	?
178	2 stones	None	Dorsal	Left	Sides	Sl. flexed	?	9-10
179	3 bricks?	None	Left side	Left	Sides	Sl. flexed	?	18 mos.
180	2 bricks	None	Left side	Left	Pubis	Straight	M	9-10
181	None	None	¼ left	Up	Sides	Straight	?	4
182	3 stones	None	Left side	Left	Sides	Sl. flexed	?	5
183	None	None	Dorsal	Right	Abdomen	Flexed	?	Infant
184	Stones	Stones all along	Dorsal	Up	Sides	Straight	?	1+
185	None	None	Left side	Left	Pubis	Straight	F	31-35
186	Stones	Stones all along	Dorsal	Right	Sides	Straight	?	?
187	Stones	Stones all along	Left side	Left	Pubis	Straight	?	?
188	None	None	Left side	Left	Pubis	Straight	F	40-44
189	(Shaft not found)							
190	Stones	Stones all along	Dorsal	Right	Sides	Straight	?	9
*191	None	None	Flexed R side	?	Flexed		M	40-44

* X-Group graves

21

TABLE 3
CEMETERY 21-S-46, REGISTER OF BURIALS (cont.)

Burial no.	Head covering	Body covering	Body position	Head facing	Arms	Legs	Sex	Age
192	Stones	Stones all along	Left side	Left	Pubis	R sl. flexed L straight	M	40-49
193	None	None	Ventral	Down	?	Straight	?	Neonate
194	None	None	Dorsal	Up	Sides	Straight	?	>9 mos.
195	3 stones	None	¼ left	Left	Sides	Sl. flexed	?	8
196	1 stone	None	Dorsal	Left	Sides	Sl. flexed	?	4
197	Stones	Stones all along	Dorsal	Up	Pubis	Straight	?	6
198	Stones	Stones all along	Dorsal	Left	Sides	Straight	M	18 mos.
199	Stones	Stones all along	Dorsal	Left	Sides	Straight	?	9
200	3 stones	None	Dorsal	Up	Pubis	Straight	M	40-44
201	Stones	Stones all along	Dorsal	Up	Sides	Sl. flexed	?	4
202	None	None	Left side	Left	Sides	Straight	?	?
203	Stones?	Stones?	(Disturbed foetal burial in a Ware H1 pot)					
204	None	None	½ left	Left	Pubis	Straight	F	22-24
205	None	None	Dorsal?	?	?	Straight?	?	Neonate
206	Stones	Stones all along	Dorsal	Left	Pubis	Sl. flexed	M	45-49
207	None	None	Left side	Left	Pubis	R sl. flexed L straight	F	45-49
208	None	None	Dorsal	Left	Pubis	Straight	F	?
209	Stones	Stones all along	Dorsal	Left	Pubis	Sl. flexed	F	1
210	Stones	Stones all along	Dorsal	Left	?	Straight	?	3
211	Stones	Stones all along	Dorsal	Up	R on Pubis L on abdom	? Straight	?	
212	None	None	Left side	Left	Pubis	Sl. flexed	F	45-49
213	3 stones	None	Dorsal	Right	Pubis	Sl. flexed	F	25-26
214	(No separate burial - see no. 84)							
215	(Islamic grave - not excavated)							
216	(Disturbed - not excavated)							
217	None	None	½ left	Left	?	Sl. flexed	?	3
218	None	None	Dorsal	Up	?	Straight	?	?
219	Stones	Stones all along	(Not determinable because of poor preservation)				?	Neonate
220	(Islamic grave - not excavated)							
221	Stones	Stones all along	(Not determinable because of poor preservation)				?	6 mos.
222	3 bricks	None	Dorsal	Up	Pubis	Straight	M	31-35
223	2 stones	None	Dorsal	Left	Pubis	Straight	M	31-35
224	3 stones	None	½ left	Left	Pubis	Sl. flexed	F	31-35
225	Stones	Stones all along	Dorsal	Up	Pubis	Straight	M	?
226	3 bricks	None	Dorsal	Up	Pubis	Straight	M	?
227	(Disturbed - not excavated)							
228	None	None	Left side	Left	Pubis	Sl. flexed	?	?
229	(Not a grave)							
230	Stones	Stones all along	Dorsal	Right	Pubis	Sl. flexed	?	6
231	None	None	(Foetal burial in Ware H1 pot, covered by sherd)					
232	None	None	Left side	Left	Pubis	Straight	?	4
233	(Not a grave)							
234	3 stones	None	Dorsal	Up	Pubis	Straight	?	40-44
235	None	None	Left side	Left	?	Straight	?	2
236	Stones	Stones all along	Dorsal	Left	Pubis	Straight	?	17
237	3 stones	None	Dorsal	Up	Pubis	Straight	F	31-35
238	3 bricks	None	Dorsal	Up	Sides	Sl. flexed	?	Neonate
239	(Unfinished grave)							
240	None	None	Left side?	Left	?	?	?	?
241	None	None	(Foetal burial in Ware H1 pot)					
242	None	None	Dorsal	Up	Sides	Sl. flexed	?	6

* X-Group graves

position had been bridged over by slabs resting on the edges of the bottom niche - again creating an air chamber surrounding the body. However, there were also some ordinary slot graves in which a covering of stones rested directly on the corpse itself, as shown in Plates 3E-F. There were also three instances in which bodies had been covered by stone slabs extending only from the head to the waist or knees.[12]

The practice of burying foetuses and stillborn infants in pottery vessels seems to have been common through much of Nubian history, beginning well before the coming of Christianity and continuing to the present day. At Qasr Ibrim, some of these burials were found under house floors of the Christian period,[13] but they have also been found in cemeteries. There were eight examples of foetus or stillborn burials in pottery vessels at 21-S-46, of which two were in imported Egyptian amphorae (Plate 4E),[14] one was in a local imitation of an Egyptian amphora,[15] and five were in hand-made pots (Plate 4F),[16] all of Early Christian types.

Head coverings

In the absence of a more complete covering of the body, it was a common practice to place some kind of protective structure at least over the face of a deceased person, prior to the refilling of the grave. This practice was followed in about 60% of the burials at 21-S-46. In other Nubian cemeteries the protective structure was usually comprised of three large mud bricks: one standing upright on either side of the head, and one bridging across the top of the other two. At 21-S-46 however, these structures employed mainly rough stone slabs. Thirty-nine burials had a covering comprised of three slabs, one at each side of the head and one across the top (cf. Plate 7E), while five had slabs only at the two sides, and four had a slab only at one side. Only 22 burials had a face covering of three bricks, and an additional three burials had bricks at the sides of the head only (Plate 7F). Three burials had face coverings of large pottery sherds, and one individual had a piece of sheepskin wrapped around the head, with the fleece side inward.

Body positioning

Three of the bodies interred at 21-S-46 were in a contracted position, lying on their right sides. All of them are known or assumed to be of pre-Christian ("X-Group") date. All of the remaining burials were in the extended position usual in Christian graves, although in many cases the knees were slightly bent, to fit the grave shaft. The largest number, 119, were lying on their backs (Plates 4A and 4C), while 67 individuals were on their left sides (Plate 4B), eight were

on their right sides, and two were buried face down.

Even in the case of burials in dorsal position, the head was very commonly turned to one side or the other. Only 55 individuals were found to be facing upward (Plate 4C), while no fewer than 109 were facing to the left (Plate 4A), and 20 faced to the right. Two individuals, buried in a ventral position, faced downwards. The very marked preferences for burial on the left rather than on the right side (i.e. facing north), for heads turned to the left (north) rather than to the right, and for side-niche graves having the niche on the north side, are almost certainly not the results of chance; they seem to point toward some kind of canonical tradition. It was not however, shared by the Christian inhabitants of Lower Nubia, where burials were more often on the right than on the left side, and heads, though not usually turned, were turned more often to the right than to the left.[17]

In the majority of burials, both those on their backs and on their sides, the arms were arranged so that the hands met over the pubis. In about a quarter of cases the arms were extended straight down along the sides, and seven individuals had one arm at the side and one over the pubis. one individual the lower arms and hands lay over the abdomen, and in one case the hands were brought up under the chin. Legs were nearly always straight except in those cases where they had to be slightly flexed to fit the grave. However, three individuals had one leg somewhat flexed and one straight (Plate 4B). It is noteworthy once again that in those cases there the knees were bent, they were nearly always bent toward the north.

Shrouding

At least 85% of the individuals buried at 21-S-46 had been wrapped in some kind of shrouding, and this included persons of both sexes and all ages (cf. Plate 4D). In many cases however, the shrouds had survived only in a few small remnants. This suggests the probability that, in a good many instances where no wrapping was found, an original shroud had rotted away altogether. It is noteworthy that in nearly all cases where no shroud was found, the condition of the burial was also described by the excavator as poor or very poor. The materials used for shrouding exhibited a good deal of variability, and will be described in Part II.

Grave goods

Small items of personal jewelry were found in 11 burials. Seven individuals had a braided leather cord around the neck, and in four cases a small iron cross depended from it, at the chest. In one grave an iron cross was found without any accompanying cord, which may however, have rotted away. One individual had a braided leather cord around the wrist, and in three cases there were small collections of beads. These finds will be described further in Part II. It is noteworthy that ten of the 12 burials accompanied by jewelry were juveniles, a situation that was found to prevail in other

---

[12] This practice was fairly common in the Classic and Late Christian graves at Meinarti, although the covering was nearly always of large bricks rather than of stones (author's unpublished field notes).

[13] Author's unpublished field notes.

[14] Ware U2; see Adams, op. cit. (n. 1), p. 545.

[15] Ware U5; see ibid, pp. 522-523.

[16] Ware H1, Form U3; see ibid, p. 161 and p. 418.

[17] See discussion in the concluding paragraphs of Part I, below.

Christian cemeteries.[18] The items included with the dead were presumably not funerary offerings in the usual sense; they were simply articles of everyday wear that the preparers of the burials did not wish to remove.

Demography and mortality

The demographic characteristics of the Kulubnarti population will be much more fully discussed in Part III; it is sufficient here to indicate a few gross features of demography and mortality. As can be seen in Table 1, the infant mortality rate among the population buried at 21-S-46 was extremely high. Among individuals whose age could be calculated, 18% did not survive the first year of life, 48% did not survive the fifth year, and 63% did not survive the tenth year. Only nine individuals - all females - could be identified as having lived beyond the age of 50, and none could be identified definitely as having passed the age of 55. The average age at death, for all the individuals buried at 21-S-46, was 10.6 years.

Because such a high proportion of the individuals were pre-pubescent at the time of death, only 71 could be definitely identified as to sex.[19] These were nearly equally divided, with 35 males and 36 females. Longevity figures were essentially the same for the two sexes in all age brackets except the oldest (ages 51 and higher), where only females were identified.

Summary

The use of Cemetery 21-S-46 probably began just before the coming of Christianity to Nubia, and may have continued until some time early in the Classic Christian period. The cemetery was not close to any church, or to any known settlement of comparable age, so that the origin of the persons buried there remains problematical. The very simple and primitive grave superstructures, as well as the very high mortality figures, suggest in any case that this was not a well-to-do population.

Site 21-R-2

This large cemetery, estimated to contain between 500 and 600 graves, is located on the west bank of the Nile, just upstream from the south end of Kulubnarti Island. The graves are dug into a barren alluvial surface which slopes gently away from the foot of a steep, rocky ridge, until at the lower end, it merges with the Nile floodplain (Plates 5A-D). However, the western end of the cemetery, where nearly all of the excavated graves were located, is situated in the outwash of a small wadi (seen especially in Plate 5A, at lower left). The total extent of the cemetery was estimated

at about 250 m from east to west, and 140 m from north to south, but nearly all of the graves excavated in 1979 were located in an area measuring no more than 70 x 40 m (Figure 6).

A brief, unpublished preliminary report from the 1969 season indicates that 40 graves were numbered and documented at 21-R-2. They were selected from different parts of the cemetery, and were intended to provide a representative sample of the different kinds of graves present: those with stone superstructures, with brick superstructures, and without superstructures; and vaulted chambers as well as the more conventional slot graves. The preliminary report indicates that there were at least 15 vaulted chambers, of which three were opened.

As previously noted, the original field notes as well as the plan of Cemetery 21-R-2 have been lost. There is, fortunately, a photographic record for 28 of the 40 graves, which allows the recovery of certain kinds of information. In a number of cases the photographs show grave superstructures only, leaving some doubt as to whether the underlying shafts and burials were actually excavated. The number of graves for which full photographic documentation exists is 20, of which seven can be identified as graves that were re-excavated in 1979. In sum, then, the 1969 records add only 13 to the total sample of 188 graves opened in 1979. Despite its small size, however, this addition to the sample is important because it includes eight graves with brick superstructures, while only four such graves were excavated in 1979.

The photographs from 1969 of course provide information only about superstructure and grave shaft types, and body positioning; they provide no information about exact grave orientations or dimensions, or about the ages and sexes of the interments. It is clear from the photographs however, that all of the interments were adults. A summary resumé of the graves and burials in Cemetery 21-R-2, recorded both in 1969 and in 1979, is given in Table 4. Detailed information about each grave is given in Table 5, and information about each burial is given in Table 6.

During the 1979 excavations, numbers were assigned to 205 known or presumed graves, on the basis of surface indications. After excavation, seven of them proved to be unfinished or not to be graves, and an additional ten were not excavated for one reason or another. The total of fully excavated graves was therefore 188. Seven of them could be identified, on the basis of photographs, with graves excavated in 1969, and two others were presumed also to have been excavated in the earlier season, although they could not be matched with any particular grave shown in the photographs.

Unlike the graves excavated in 1969, all but six of those excavated in 1979 were concentrated in one contiguous area at the far western end of the cemetery, measuring about 70 m from north to south and 40 m from east to west (Figure 7). This area was probably selected because it occupied the

---

[18] See Reisner, op. cit. (n. 10), pp. 100-101; André Vila, *La Prospection de la Vallée du Nil au Sud de la Cataracte de Dal,* fasc. 14 (1984), p. 192; and author's unpublished field notes from Meinarti.

[19] Sexes could be determined occasionally in the case of pre-pubescents because of the preservation of genitalia.

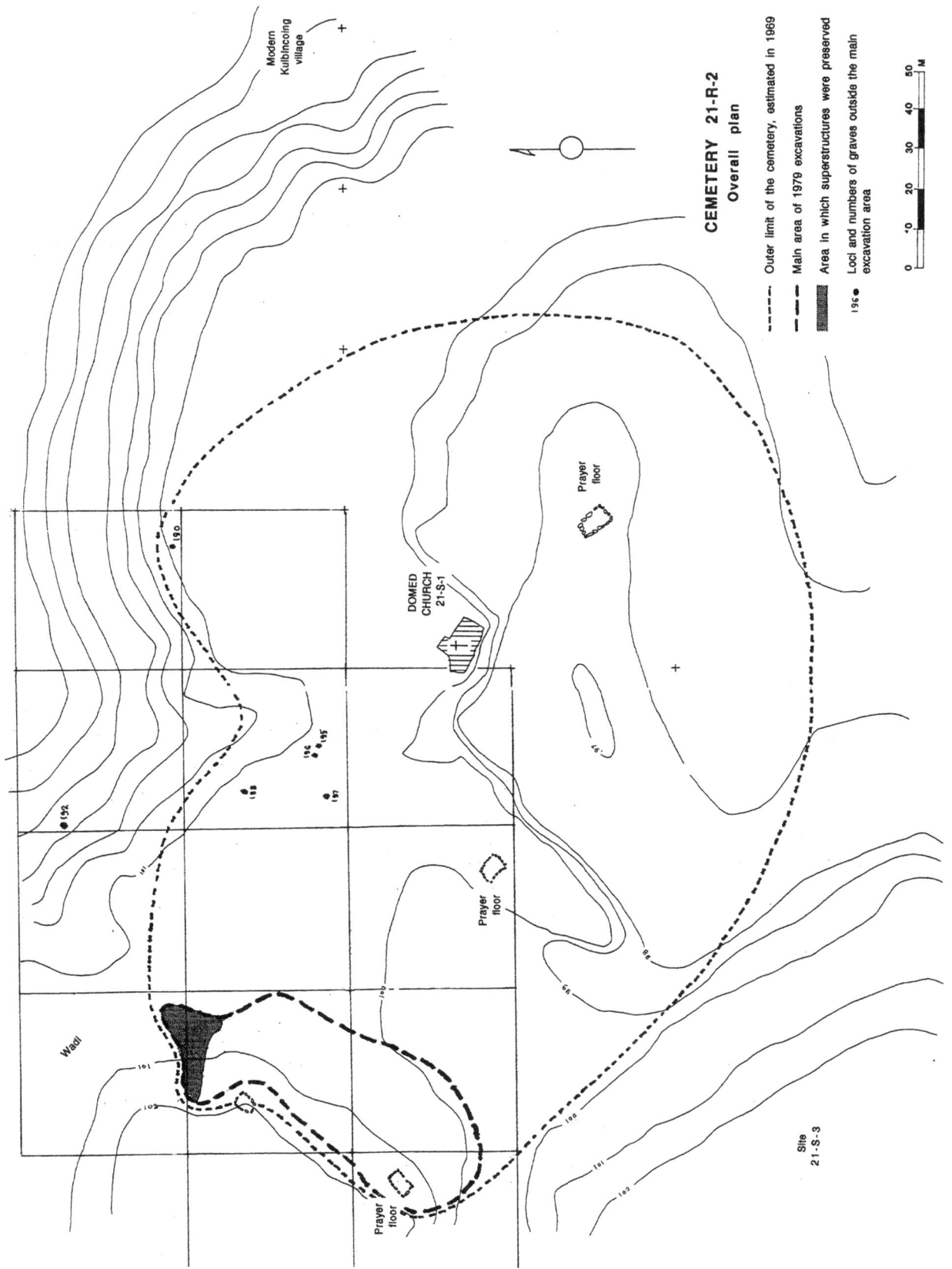

Figure 6. Site 21-R-2: overall plan.

25

highest ground in the cemetery, where the burials would be least likely to show damage from floodwater or capillary action. It means however, that the graves excavated in 1979 cannot be taken as a representative sample of the cemetery as a whole. Indeed it seems clear on typological grounds that nearly all of them are of Early Christian date, contemporary with the burials at 21-S-46.

The choice of graves to be excavated in 1979 was justified in one respect. Fleshy tissues were just about as well preserved as they were at 21-S-46, and the collection of such material was of course the single over-riding objective of the expedition. On the other hand superstructures in much of the excavated area were very poorly preserved, or absent altogether, apparently as a result of surface deflation.

Chronology

During the 1969 excavations we failed to recognize any graves of Early Christian types at 21-R-2. We hypothesized instead that the use of the cemetery had begun in Classic Christian times and continued until the recent past. It therefore, seemed a logical assumption that the use of 21-R-2 had begun when 21-S-46 ceased, the two together representing a continuum of usage from perhaps A.D. 600 until the 20th century.

This assumption was based on a number of observations and inferences. To begin with, the graves in the central part of the cemetery were closely adjacent to the Domed Church 21-R-1, a building that had previously been dated, somewhat tentatively, to the Classic Christian period.[20] Most of the graves near the church had brick pavement superstructures of the "spine and ribs" type that was rare at the Early Christian Cemetery 21-S-46, but was found in association with the Classic Christian church at 21-S-49.[21] Moreover, the single votive lamp that was recovered in 1969 was of a Classic Christian type.[22]

Continued use of the cemetery in Late Christian times was confirmed in the case of the vaulted Tomb B3, because this burial was accompanied by a pottery *qulla* of Ware U13 - a Lower Egyptian product whose importation into Nubia did not begin until around A.D. 1200.[23] On the basis of this somewhat slender thread of evidence we assumed that most or all of the other vaulted tombs at 21-R-2 were also of Late Christian date - especially since no vaulted tombs had been found at 21-S-46. However, and more importantly, the assumption of Late Christian usage was based on our conviction that Cemetery 21-R-2 was the burial place for dwellers at the nearby Late Christian site of 21-S-2, situated

on the southern tip of Kulubnarti Island.[24]

Finally, the use of 21-R-2 in post-Christian times was attested by a number of graves of recognizably Islamic type; that is, with orientations approximately from north to south. Moreover, within the cemetery there were and are three cleared rectangular areas lined with stones, which are used as prayer floors by the current residents at the neighboring village of Kulbincoing. And since the occupation at 21-S-2 had continued from Late Christian times until the recent past, we assumed that there had been a continuum of usage in the cemetery as well.

Unfortunately, our conjectural dating of Cemetery 21-R-2 in 1969 was neither confirmed nor disconfirmed by the findings of 1979. What is immediately obvious, however, is that the great majority of the graves excavated in 1979 exhibit no distinction, typologically, from those at 21-S-46 (Table 7). There is the same prevalence of rough stone superstructures, about the same frequency of lateral niche graves, nearly always on the north side of the tomb shaft, the same usage of materials to cover the head and body of the deceased, the same frequency of burials inhumed on the left side, but very rarely on the right, and the same propensity to turn the head of the dead person towards the north. Finally and very importantly, the textiles employed as shrouding were virtually the same in the two cemeteries, and were overwhelmingly of earlier medieval types. Later medieval burials would have been expected to exhibit a much higher proportion of cotton textile than was actually found.

On typological grounds, then, the conclusion seems inescapable that most of the graves excavated in 1979 were of Early and perhaps early Classic Christian date, and therefore, contemporaneous with the burials at 21-S-46. We should probably have anticipated this, because the western end of Cemetery 21-R-2 is located just below the walled settlement 21-R-3, which can be securely dated on the basis of sherd finds to the Early and the earlier part of the Classic Christian period.[25] Nearly all the graves excavated in 1979 were in that portion of the cemetery most immediately adjacent to Site 21-R-3.

The findings of 1979 therefore, enlarge upon but do not negate our earlier conclusions in regard to Cemetery 21-R-2. As previously noted, all but six of the 188 graves selected for excavation were in one limited, contiguous area, comprising less than one-eighth of the total area of the site (Figure 6). For the remainder of the graves, there is neither more nor less reason today than there was in 1969 to assume a dating in the Classic Christian, Late Christian, and Post-Christian periods. The only correction to our original hypothesis that is clearly required is the realization that the

---

[20] For documentation see Somers Clarke, *Christian Antiquities in the Nile Valley* (Oxford, 1912), pp. 45-49; Ugo Monneret de Villard, *La Nubia Medioevale*, vol. I (Cairo, 1935), pp. 234-235; and W. Y. Adams in *Journal of the American Research Center in Egypt*, vol. 4 (1965), p. 132.

[21] *Kulubnarti I*, p. 272.

[22] Ware R7; see Adams, op. cit. (n. 1), pp. 491-492.

[23] See ibid, p. 577.

[24] See *Kulubnarti I*, pp. 21-183. There was a church at 21-S-2, but it was built directly on a solid rock shelf, and there was no possibility of an adjoining cemetery.

[25] See Dinkler, op. cit. (n. 3), pp. 267-271. The dating is confirmed by my own examination of sherd material from the site.

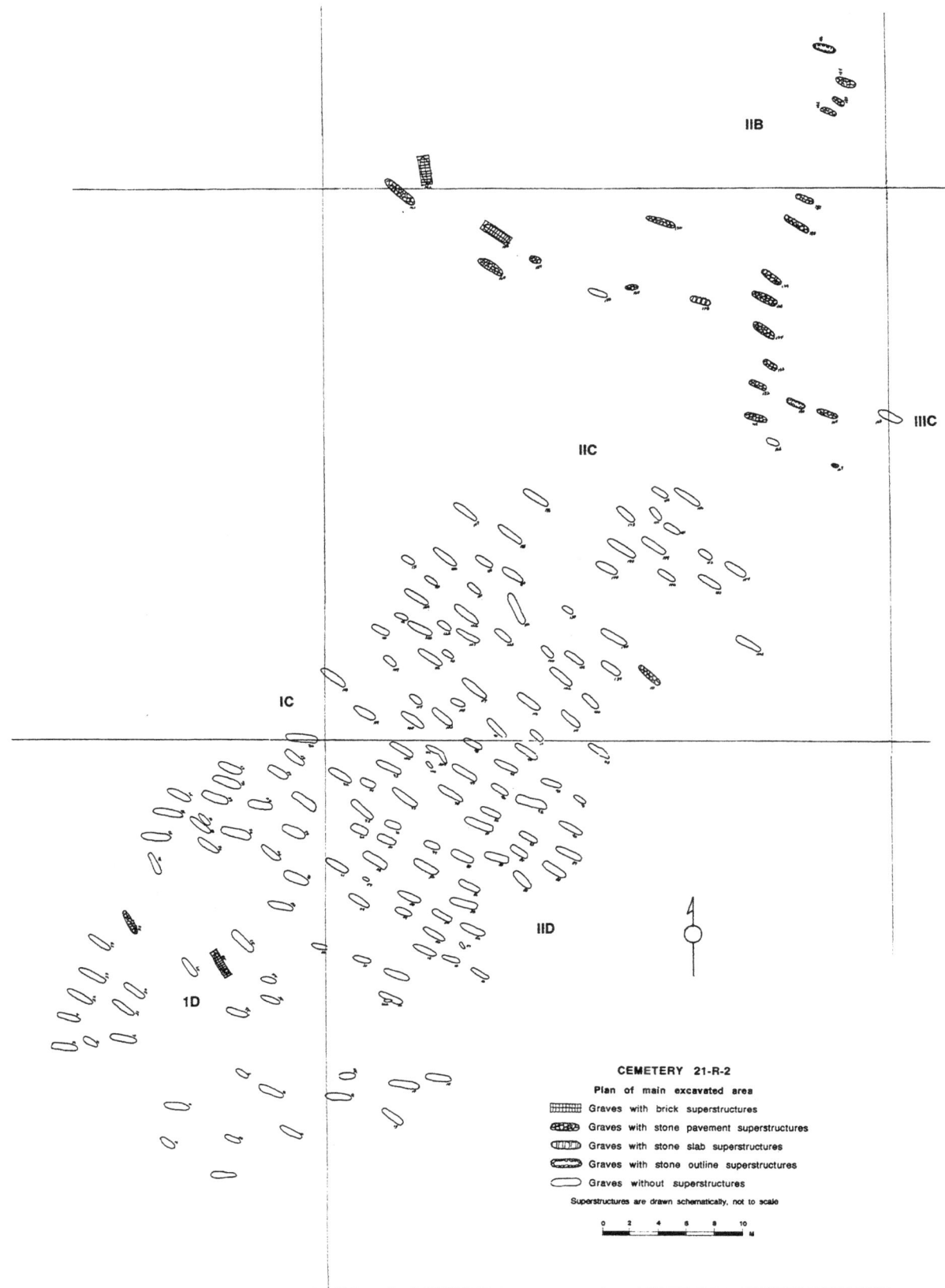

Figure 7. Site 21-R-2: plan of graves in main excavation area.

27

TABLE 4

CEMETERY 21-R-2 - SUMMARY OF GRAVES AND BURIALS, COMBINING DATA FROM 1969 AND 1979

	No.	%.
<u>Graves numbered</u>	226	
Non-graves or unfinished	7	3
Numbered but not excavated	10	4
Partially excavated	6	3
Graves excavated	203	90
<u>Superstructures</u>	43	20
Stone pavement	22	10
Stone outline	2	1
Stone alignment	1	T
Stone slabs	2	1
Stone + brick pavement	1	T
Brick pavement	12	6
Gubba	1	T
Destroyed in 1969 excavations	2	1
No recorded information	6	3
None	172	80
<u>Lamp boxes identified</u>	0	
<u>Orientation</u>		
270-316°	90	43
242-269°	92	44
No record	27	13
<u>Grave shafts excavated</u>	209	
Slot	163	78
Side niche north	33	16
Side niche south	2	1
Chamber	1	T
Vault	3	1
Form uncertain	7	3
<u>Burials uncovered</u>	203	
<u>Head covering</u>		
Stones all along	42	21
Bricks all along	2	1
Mud all along	1	T
3 stones, sides and top	48	24
2 stones at sides	1	T
1 stone at side	2	1
2 stones + 1 brick	4	2
3 bricks, sides and top	49	24
2 bricks at sides	3	2
1 brick over face	5	3
Brick fragments	4	2
Sherds	1	T
Uncertain	9	4
None	32	16
<u>Body covering</u>		
Stones all along	42	21
Bricks all along	2	1
Mud all along	1	T
Stones over pubis only	1	T
Uncertain	6	3
None	151	74

28

TABLE 4

		No.	%.
Body position			
	Dorsal	88	43
	1/4 left	7	3
	Left side	88	43
	1/4 right	3	1
	Right side	9	5
	Ventral	2	1
	Uncertain	5	4
Head position			
	Facing up	51	25
	Facing left	122	60
	Facing right	23	11
	Facing down	1	T
	Uncertain	6	3
Arm position			
	On pubis	127	63
	At sides	39	19
	Under chin	1	T
	At chest	1	T
	Asymmetrical	20	10
	Uncertain	15	7
Leg position			
	Straight	121	60
	Slightly flexed	75	37
	Flexed	2	1
	Asymmetrical	1	T
	Uncertain	4	2

Ages at death (1979 burials only)	Male	Fem.	?	Total	%.
Under 1 year	2		8	10	5
1-5 years	3	4	32	39	20
6-10 years	3		14	17	9
11-15 years	2	3	10	15	8
16-20 years	5	8		13	7
21-25 years	8	4		12	6
26-30 years	3	5		8	4
31-35 years	5	6		11	6
36-40 years	7	17	1	25	13
41-45 years	11	6		17	9
46-50 years	2	8		10	5
51-55 years	2	7	1	10	5
Uncertain	0	1	3	4	2
Totals by sex	53	69	69	191	
Percentages by sex	28	36	36		

29

first use of this cemetery, like that of 21-S-46, belongs to the Early Christian period. Also if the graves at the western end of the cemetery are most probably early, while those in the central part (close to Church 21-R-1) are more probably of the Classic period, it seems a logical inference that Cemetery 21-R-2 in the course of its long history grew in a generally eastward direction.

Two of the graves at 21-R-2 may be of pre-Christian date, although this could not be definitely confirmed in either case. Grave 185 was a wide rectangular chamber covered by stone slabs, and having a north-south orientation. It had evidently been identified by robbers as a pre-Christian grave, because it had been plundered at some time in the past. It contained the disturbed remains of four interments, but there were no surviving traces of grave offerings. This tomb was one of several located on top of a low projecting ridge, well above and away from the other graves of Cemetery 21-R-2; it was the only one of the group to be excavated. It seems possible that these are relics of an earlier occupation, and they should perhaps have been given a separate site number.

Grave H1, recorded but not opened in 1969, was a vaulted chamber surmounted by a brick *gubba*. The superstructure is certainly of Late Christian or Islamic date,[26] but the underlying chamber may be earlier, since it seems to have a north-south orientation. Local tradition identifies this tomb with Sitt Zuleiha, a female Muslim saint, and for this reason the tomb was not excavated.

The early dating assigned to most of the excavated graves at 21-R-2, contradicting as it does our previous expectations, clearly raises more problems than it solves. The most vexing of those problems involves the conspicuously different mortality rates of the populations buried at 21-R-2 and at 21-S-46; an issue that will be considered further in later pages.

Superstructures

At first glance, a conspicuous difference between Cemeteries 21-S-46 and 21-R-2 would appear to be reflected in the differential frequency of superstructures at the two sites. While more than 80% of the excavated graves at 21-S-46 had had superstructures prior to the 1969 excavations, more than 80% of those at 21-R-2 had none. It seems almost certain however, that this evidence cannot be taken at face value, given the fact that the use of surface markings was usual in Christian Nubian cemeteries. Their absence at 21-R-2 is probably explained by the fact that the western portion of this cemetery, where most of the excavated graves were situated, had been subjected to surface deflation, as a result of downwash from the wadi which opened here. Some confirmation for this may be found in the fact that the average depth of grave shafts without superstructures was 94 cm, while the average depth of shafts having

superstructures was 120 cm - about the same as at 21-S-46.[27] It is noteworthy too that nearly all of the preserved superstructures were in a kind of straggling line along the uppermost margin of the cemetery (Figure 6).

Among the recorded superstructures at 21-R-2, the great majority were stone pavements, similar in every way to those at 21-S-46 (Plate 6A), and there were also once again a few stone outlines (Plate 6B). Again however, this figure cannot be taken as representative of the cemetery as a whole, because in 1969 we observed a large concentration of brick pavements in the central part of the side, close to the Domed Church 21-R-1.

The 12 brick superstructures that were actually excavated in the two seasons of work at 21-R-2 were mostly, though not all, in poor condition. In three cases the arrangement of the bricks could not be made out because of poor preservation, and in another case it could not be made out because the structure was plastered over. It was evident however, that all of the superstructures were of rollag brick; there were no instances of bricks laid flat as at 21-S-46. Three superstructures were of the "spine-and-ribs" type, with a central line of bricks running longitudinally, and transverse bricks on either side of it, like three of the graves at 21-S-46 (Plate 6D). Another grave differed from the foregoing only in that it had a double rather than a single line of bricks running longitudinally, and one superstructure was formed of transverse bricks only, without a longitudinal course. A superstructure of the latter type was observed also at 21-S-49.[28]

Tomb B4 had an unusually large rollag brick superstructure of a very uncommon design, shown in Figure 8 and Plate 6E. The central portion involved a longitudinal

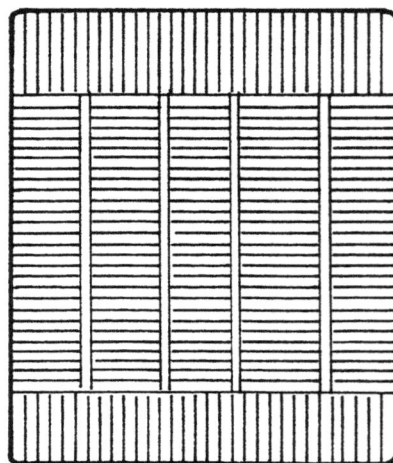

Figure 8. Site 21-R-2: superstructure of Tomb B4.

[26] See Ugo Monneret de Villard, *La Nubia Medioevale,* vol. III (Cairo, 1957), pp. 72-77; and W. Y. Adams in Tomas Hägg, ed., *Nubian Culture Past and Present* (Stockholm, 1987), p. 333.

[27] These figures were calculated for the burials of adults (age 13 and over) only, since the burials of juveniles tended to be shallower.
[28] *Kulubnarti I,* p. 272.

TABLE 5
CEMETERY 21-R-2 - REGISTER OF GRAVES

Burial no.	Sector	Superstructure	Lamp box	Orient-ation	Shaft type	Dimensions			Condition
						L	W	D	

Graves excavated in 1969 (based on photographs only)

Burial no.	Sector	Superstructure	Lamp box	Orient-ation	Shaft type	L	W	D	Condition
A1		Stone + brick pavement	-		Slot				Good
A2		None	-		Slot				Good
A3		(Re-excavated in 1979 as Grave 180, q.v.)							
A4		None	-		Slot				Good
A5		None	-		Slot				Fair
B3		Brick pavement	?		Vault				Excellent
B4		Brick pavement	?		Slot				Fair
B6		Brick pavement	-		(Shaft not excavated?)				
B7		None	-		Vault (apparently not excavated)				
SW of B7		None	-		Slot				Good
B8		None	-		Slot				Good
B10		None	-		Slot				Good
B11		None	-		Slot				Fair
N of B11		None	-		Slot				Poor
B12		None	-		(Not excavated below covering stones)				
C1		(Re-excavated in 1979 as Grave 14, q.v.)							
C2		(Re-excavated in 1979 as Grave 28, q.v.)							
C3		(Re-excavated in 1979 as Grave 149, q.v.)							
C4		Stone pavement			(Shaft not excavated?)				
C5		(Re-excavated in 1979 as Grave 53, q.v.)							
C6		(Re-excavated in 1979 as Grave 176, q.v.)							
C7		Brick pavement	?		(Shaft not excavated?)				
E1		Brick pavement	?		Slot				Good
E2		None	-		Slot				Good
E3		Brick pavement	?		(Shaft not excavated?)				
F2		None	-		Side niche N				Good
F4*		None	-		Side niche W				?
H1		*Gubba*	-		Vault			(Not excavated)	

Graves excavated in 1979

Burial no.	Sector	Superstructure	Lamp box	Orient-ation	Shaft type	L	W	D	Condition
1	ID	None	-	241°	Slot	189	37	69	Good
2	ID	None	-	281°	Slot	110	34	73	Good
3	ID	None	-	249°	Slot	185	36	81	Good
4	ID	None	-	263°	Slot	172	31	98	Good
5	ID	None	-	277°	Slot	113	27	34	Good
6	ID	None	-	256°	Slot	192	35	62	Good
7	ID	None	-	256°	Slot	178	40	104	Good
8	ID	None	-	265°	Slot	127	34	53	Good
9	ID	None	-	276°	Slot	102	39	84	Good
10	ID	None	-	268°	Slot	192	40	104	Good
11	ID	None	-	274°	Slot	178	34	95	Good
12	IID	None	-	242°	Slot	166	45	78	Poor
13	IID	None	-	275°	Slot	188	32	73	Good
14	IID	(No record*)		247°	Slot	237	68	85	Good
15	IID	None	-	242°	Slot	190	35	50	Good
16	IID	None	-	268°	Slot	143	40	82	Good
17	IID	None	-	273°	Slot	82	29	75	Poor
18	IID	None	-	262°	Slot	166	46	98	Good
19	IID	None	-	261°	Slot	168	35	82	Poor
20	IID	None	-	263°	Slot	182	40	53	Good
21	IID	None	-	(uncertain due to poor preservation)					Poor
22	ID	None	-	253°	Slot	165	40	115	Poor

* Documentation from the 1969 excavations lost   ** Possibly an X-Group grave

TABLE 5
CEMETERY 21-R-2 - REGISTER OF GRAVES (cont.)

Burial no.	Sector	Superstructure	Lamp box	Orient-ation	Shaft type	Dimensions			Condition
						L	W	D	
23	ID	None	-	(Not excavated)					
24	ID	None	-	255°	Slot	97	43	99	Good
25	ID	None	-	256°	Slot	136	32	48	Good
26	ID	None	-	263°	Slot	162	39	97	Good
27	ID	None	-	(Not excavated)					
28	ID	Brick pavement		300°	Slot	194	41	118	Good
29	ID	None	-	294°	Slot	162	33	99	Good
30	ID	None	-	272°	Slot	167	41	87	Good
31	ID	None	-	280°	Slot	180	56	99	Good
32	ID	None	-	269°	Slot	210	45	97	Good
33	ID	None	-	268°	Slot	190	45	100	Good
34	ID	None	-	278°	Slot	168	31	79	Good
35	ID	Stone pavement?	-	301°	Slot	183	37	111	Good
36	ID	None	-	308°	Slot	162	34	44	Good
37	ID	None	-	242°	Slot	190	44	93	Good
38	ID	None	-	250°	Side niche N	204	47	78	Good
39	ID	None	-	268°	Slot	169	48	80	Good
40	ID	None	-	276°	Slot	182	43	99	Good
41	ID	None	-	285°	Slot	112	25	52	Good
42	ID	None	-	277°	Slot	170	37	109	Good
43	ID	None	-	255°	Slot	223	52	125	Good
44	ID	None	-	283°	Slot	165	58	104	Good
45	ID	None	-	255°	Slot	187	36	125	Poor
46	ID	None	-	255°	Slot	182	41	115	Good
47	IID	None	-	270°	Slot	172	46	127	Good
48	IID	(Not a grave)							
49	IID	None	-	266°	Slot	113	39	74	Fair
50	IID	None	-	268°	Slot	169	33	106	Good
51	IID	None	-	262°	Slot	60	29	22	Poor
52	IID	None	-	265°	Slot	145	35	94	Poor
53	IID	None		264°	Side niche N	175	44	114	Poor
54	IID	None	-	267°	Slot	143	33	114	Good
55	IID	None	-	256°	Slot	178	51	112	Good
56	IID	(No record*)		269°	Slot	178	50	99	Good
57	IID	None	-	272°	Slot	75	36	37	Poor
58	IID	None	-	278°	Slot	202	58	112	Good
59	IID	None	-	259°	Slot	136	34	87	Good
60	IID	None	-	257°	Side niche N	123	50	97	Good
61	IID	None	-	268°	Slot	171	42	105	Good
62	ID	None	-	264°	Slot	175	40	97	Good
63	ID	None	-	270°	Slot	235	55	112	Good
64	ID	None	-	252°	Slot	171	43	109	Good
65	ID	None	-	261°	Slot	184	36	92	Good
66	ID	None	-	258°	Slot	205	38	107	Good
67	ID	None	-	260°	Slot	181	27	86	Good
68	ID	None	-	276°	Slot	158	40	112	Good
69	ID	None	-	286°	Slot	181	44	110	Good
70	IC	None	-	280°	Slot	202	41	114	Good
71	IC	None	-	(Not excavated)					
72	IID	None	-	264°	Slot	199	54	115	Good
73	IID	None	-	264°	Side niche N	186	46	93	Good
74	IID	None	-	256°	Slot	120	48	113	Good
75	IID	None	-	282°	Side niche N	187	53	128	Good
76	IID	None	-	248°	Slot	107	37	73	Good

* Documentation from the 1969 excavations lost   ** Possibly an X-Group grave

TABLE 5
CEMETERY 21-R-2 - REGISTER OF GRAVES (cont.)

Burial no.	Sector	Superstructure	Lamp box	Orient- ation	Shaft type	Dimensions			Condition
						L	W	D	
77	IID	None	-	276°	Slot	200	45	81	Good
78	IID	None	-	270°	Slot	183	45	78	Good
79	IID	None	-	257°	Slot	102	47	59	Good
80	IID	None	-	261°	Slot	162	34	78	Good
81	IID	None	-	262°	Slot	208	35	93	Good
82	IID	None	-	269°	Slot	114	30	99	Good
83	IID	None	-	271°	Slot	186	50	83	Good
84	IID	None	-	278°	Slot	112	32	87	Fair
85	IID	None	-	255°	Slot	140	40	77	Poor
86	IID	None	-	264°	Slot	132	42	77	Poor
87	IID	None	-	285°	Slot	168	47	112	Poor
88	IID	None	-	270°	Slot	192	40	104	Good
89	IID	None	-	264°	Slot	186	38	93	Good
90	IID	None	-	264°	Slot	178	36	111	Good
91	IID	None	-	261°	Slot	83	30	59	Good
92	IID	None	-	259°	Slot	205	64	105	Poor
93	IID	None	-	252°	Slot	131	38	85	Good
94	IID	None	-	276°	Slot	162	42	107	Good
95	IID	None	-	262°	Slot	174	52	90	Good
96	IID	None	-	277°	Slot	113	31	86	Good
97	IID	None	-	273°	Slot	198	41	70	Good
98	IIC	None	-	277°	Slot	105	30	49	Good
99	IIC	None	-	287°	Slot	188	33	79	Good
100	IID	None	-	302°	Slot	90	40	32	Good
101	IID	None	-	266°	Slot	110	38	92	Good
102	IIC	(No record*)		283°	Slot	165	42	80	Good
103	IIC	None	-	255°	Slot	80	32	32	Good
104	IIC	None	-	281°	Side niche N	90	30	63	Good
105	IIC	None	-	275°	Slot	186	40	96	Good
106	IID	None	-	274°	Side niche N	177	41	104	Good
107	IIC	None	-	262°	Slot	154	53	84	Good
108	IC	None	-	267°	Side niche N	222	41	106	Good
109	IIC	None	-	242°	Side niche N	82	40	76	Good
110	IIC	None	-	275°	Side niche N	120	42	65	Good
111	IIC	None	-	270°	Side niche N	80	49	67	Good
112	IIC	None	-	272°	Side niche N	206	49	92	Good
113	IIC	None	-	280°	Slot	92	34	33	Good
114	IIC	None	-	281°	Side niche N	197	48	104	Good
115	IIC	(Unfinished grave)							
116	IIC	None	-	272°	Slot	168	35	67	Good
117	IIC	None	-	276°	Slot	116	31	85	Good
118	IIC	None	-	280°	Slot	176	34	118	Good
119	IIC	None	-	286°	Slot	154	49	104	Good
120	IIC	None	-	275°	Slot	172	37	105	Good
121	IIC	(Not a grave)							
122	IIC	None	-	273°	Side niche N	182	47	106	Good
123	IIC	None	-	274°	Side niche N	136	44	94	Good
124	IIC	None	-	279°	Side niche N	106	44	58	Good
125	IIC	None	-	280°	Slot	138	43	70	Good
126	IIC	None	-	276°	Slot	210	43	92	Good
127	IIC	None	-	273°	Side niche N	176	48	128	?
128	IC	None	-	280°	Side niche N	110	30	58	Good
129	IIC	None	-	275°	Side niche N	178	36	78	Good
130	IIC	None	-	272°	Side niche N	105	30	66	Good

* Documentation from the 1969 excavations lost   ** Possibly an X-Group grave

TABLE 5
CEMETERY 21-R-2 - REGISTER OF GRAVES (cont.)

Burial no.	Sector	Superstructure	Lamp box	Orient- ation	Shaft type	Dimensions			Condition
						L	W	D	
131	IIC	None	-	269°	Side niche N	90	42	72	Good
132	IIC	None	-	278°	Side niche N	187	52	112	Good
133	IIC	None	-	265°	Side niche S	94	24	76	Good
134	IIC	None	-	271°	Side niche N	156	40	60	Poor
135	IIC	None	-	278°	Side niche N	112	36	62	Poor
136	IIC	None	-	278°	Slot	245	75	100	Fair
137	IIC	None	-	271°	Slot	75	43	30	Good
138	IIC	None	-	262°	Slot	141	44	100	Good
139	IIC	None	-	266°	Slot	158	38	107	Fair
140	IIC	None	-	270°	Slot	198	34	104	Good
141	IIC	Stone pavement	-	275°	Slot	200	47	107	Good
142	IIC	None	-	276°	Slot	158	37	90	Good
143	IIC	None	-	272°	Side niche N	219	50	98	Good
144	IIC	None	-	274°	Slot	163	38	105	Good
145	IIC	None	-	277°	Slot	195	37	86	Good
146	IIC	Stone slab	-	275°	Slot	195	45	100	Poor
147	IIC	None	-	274°	Slot	187	42	87	Good
148	IIC	None	-	280°	Slot	158	34	100	Good
149	IIC	None		269°	Slot	188	49	105	Good
150	IIC	None	-	286°	Side niche N	95	45	52	Good
151	IIC	None	-	273°	Slot	113	32	88	Good
152	IIC	None	-	273°	Slot	98	30	63	Good
153	IIC	None	-	268°	Slot	184	41	84	Good
154	IIC	None	-	275°	Slot	182	34	88	Good
155	IIC	(Not a grave)							
156	IIC	None	-	274°	Slot	185	58	108	Good
157	IIC	None	-	270°	Slot	125	40	82	Good
158	IIC	Stone slab	-	276°	Slot	137	28	80	Good
159	IIC	Stone pavement	-	?	Side niche N	?	?	?	Poor
160	IIC	Stone pavement	-	266°	Slot	200	40	111	Good
161	IIC	Stone pavement	-	316°	Side niche N	233	47	120	Good
162	IIC	Brick pavement	-	302°	Side niche N	188	50	140	Good
163	IIC	Brick pavement	-	273°	Slot	238	37	109	Good
164	IIC	Stone pavement	-	252°	Side niche N	74	28	82	Good
165	IIC	Stone pavement	-	256°	Slot	162	45	106	Good
166	IIC	Stone outline	-	259°	Slot	100	23	78	Good
167	IIC	Stone pavement	-	280°	Slot	59	22	46	Good
168	IIC	Stone pavement	-	252°	Slot	177	47	92	Good
169	IIC	Stone pavement	-	245°	Slot	100	34	46	Good
170	IIC	Stone outline	-	260°	Slot	135	34	111	Poor
171	IIC	(Not a grave)							
172	IIC	Stone pavement		262°	Slot	126	30	93	Good
173	IIC	Stone pavement	-	270°	Slot	102	40	86	Good
174	IIC	Stone pavement	-	276°	Slot	160	56	109	Good
175	IIC	Stone pavement	-	267°	Slot	190	44	115	Good
176	IIC	Stone pavement		264°	Slot	210	50	140	Poor
177	IIC	(Not a grave)							
178	IIC	2 stone slabs	-	253°	Side niche S	131	42	99	Good
179	IIC	Stone pavement	-	278°	Slot	166	36	109	Good
180	IIC	None		268°	Slot	180	58	92	Poor
181	IIB	Stone pavement	?	262°	Side niche N	106	52	74	Good
182	IIB	Stone pavement	-	266°	Side niche N	107	45	90	Poor
183	IIB	Stone pavement	-	272°	Slot	79	43	93	Fair
184	IIB	Stone pavement	-	266°	Slot	85	26	103	Poor

* Documentation from the 1969 excavations lost   ** Possibly an X-Group grave

TABLE 5
CEMETERY 21-R-2 - REGISTER OF GRAVES (cont.)

Burial no.	Sector	Superstructure	Lamp box	Orient-ation	Shaft type	Dimensions			Condition
						L	W	D	
185**	IIA	Stone slabs	-	006°	Chamber	230	90	230	Disturbed
186	IIB	Stone outline	-	243°	Slot	88	32	72	Poor
187	IIB	Stone alignment	-	(Not excavated)					
188	IVD	Brick pavement	-	284°	Slot	250	51	136	Good
189		(Not excavated - no recorded information)							
190		(Not excavated - no recorded information)							
191		(Not excavated - no recorded information)							
192	IVC	Brick pavement?	-	298°	Slot	185	41	105	Poor
193	VB	None		254°	Vault	215	63	87	Fair
194	IVC	(Unfinished grave)							
195	IVC	None	-	257°	Slot	98	25	40	Good
196	IVC	None	-	255°	Slot	116	33	80	Good
197	IVC	None	-	236°	Slot	183	40	94	Good
198		(Not excavated - no recorded information)							
199		(Not excavated - no recorded information)							
200		(Not excavated - no recorded information)							
201	IID	Brick pavement	-	250°	Slot	121	39	61	Poor
202	IID	(Superstructure and shaft disturbed)							
203	IIC	None	-	273°	Slot	183	44	88	Good
204	IID	None	-	300°	Slot	85	28	25	Poor
205	IIC	None	-	266°	Side niche N	198	40	80	Good

* Documentation from the 1969 excavations lost   ** Possibly an X-Group grave

course with transverse bricks on either side, but these in turn were bordered on the north and south by additional longitudinal courses. The whole, finally, was surrounded by a border of bricks which on the north and south sides extended in a north-south direction, while those on the east and west ends extended in an east-west direction. The surviving photo carries a suggestion that the whole structure was overlain either by thick plaster or by an additional course of bricks laid horizontally, although only small remnants of this survived. The underlying grave shaft, though larger and deeper than most, did not extend anywhere near to the full width of the superstructure, and it contained only a single interment.

Grave 188 also had a large brick superstructure of unusual design, although only a portion of it was preserved (Plate 6F). There appears to have been a central member consisting of three courses of bricks running longitudinally, bordered by bricks running at right angles. However, both the photograph and the excavator's drawing suggest that some of these latter were laid on edge, and others flat, in a pattern that cannot be fully made out. The outer margins of the structure were not preserved at any point. Here again there appeared to be a small surviving remnant of a second course of masonry. As in the case of Tomb B4, the grave shaft was unusually large and deep, but it contained only a single interment, of an adult male.

Cemetery 21-R-2 exhibited three other superstructure types not found at 21-S-46. Tomb H1 was topped by a brick-

built *gubba* of a type found in many late Nubian cemeteries both in Lower and in Upper Nubia. The lower portion is a square structure like a miniature tower, with small, arched doorways on each of its four sides; the upper portion is a slender, tapering dome. Some structures of this type may have been built in Late Christian times, but the majority, including the one at 21-R-2, are believed to be of Post-Christian date.[29] As was noted previously, the *gubba* at 21-S-2 is locally identified with the saint, Sitt Zuleiha. In the light of what we know ethnographically about saint-worship in Nubia,[30] it seems probable that someone - most probably a woman - had a dream revealing that Grave H1 was the burial place of Sitt Zuleiha, after which the *gubba* was built to commemorate her. However, there is today no very specific local tradition about who Zuleiha was, or why she is venerated here.[31]

The superstructure of Grave A1, excavated in 1969, exhibits a very irregular combination of upright bricks and stone slabs, as shown in Plate 6C. The top of the grave shaft appears to have been bordered on either side by bricks,

[29] Adams, op. cit. (n. 26), p. 333 and Fig. 7.

[30] cf. J. Spencer Trimingham, *Islam in the Sudan* (London, 1949), pp. 126-148; Nawal al-Messiri in John G. Kennedy, ed., *Nubian Ceremonial Life* (Berkeley, 1978), pp. 61-103.

[31] According to Sayyed Nuraddin Abdel Mannan, our chief authority on local lore at Kulubnarti. For other examples of the appropriation of Christian and earlier tombs as Muslim saints' tombs see Reisner, op. cit. (n. 10), pp. 308-309.

laid flat and projecting outward somewhat over the top of the shaft itself. The top of the shaft was then bridged across by a line of bricks laid on edge, forming a kind of corbel. However, this line was interrupted near the southwest end by two large stone slabs, while another slab is visible at the northeast end. It is possible therefore, that this was a crypt tomb that was not earth-filled, the slabs at the southwest end constituting a removable cover so that additional interments could be made. It appears from the photograph however, that the chamber contained only a single body, lying on its left side. The orientation of the tomb was more nearly north and south than east and west, suggesting the possibility of a pre-Christian interment.

A much less pretentious superstructure was that of Grave 158, which was covered by a single large slab of siltstone. The slab was very roughly rectangular in form, but showed no signs of deliberate shaping.

Grave orientations

The excavated graves at 21-R-2 were even more erratic in their orientations than were those at 21-S-46, varying between extremes of 28° south of west and 46° north of west (excluding possible pre-Christian tombs having a north-south orientation). The mean orientation was very nearly due west, or in other words about 10° further north than the mean orientation at 21-S-46. The reasons for variability were probably the same in both cases: the lack of clear-cut guidelines provided by previously existing graves, at the time when new ones were dug. In the case of 21-R-2 however, there was a further source of uncertainty: the lack of any topographic feature on the western horizon that could serve as an orientation point.

Grave shafts and chambers

The types of grave shafts encountered at 21-R-2 closely replicate the findings at 21-S-46. In both places simple slot graves were very much in the majority (Plates 7E-F, 8D-F), with side-niche graves comprising about one-fifth of the total at 21-R-2 (Plate 8C), as against about one-third at 21-S-46. Side-niches in both places were nearly, but not quite, all on the north side of the grave shaft. Finally, grave shafts with neatly squared ends occurred with just about the same frequency in both cemeteries, and were found in the case of both slot graves and niche graves (Plates 7E, 8C, 8D).

However, Cemetery 21-R-2 contained also a number of brick-vaulted burial chambers, which were not found at 21-S-46. Only four such tombs were recorded and numbered in 1979, and only one was fully excavated, but our preliminary notes from 1969 indicate that at least 15 vaulted tombs were recognized at that time.

The one fully excavated vault tomb, Grave 193, was a small affair, hardly larger than an ordinary slot grave. It was in fact a slot grave, 215 cm long and 63 cm wide, but instead of being filled with earth it had been roofed over, just below ground level, with a longitudinal vault in the shape of an inverted "V".[32] That is, large bricks, resting on their edges, were laid at an angle so that they leaned inward from each side of the grave, and met over the top. The space between the top ends of the bricks was chinked with mud mortar and small stones. The vault was preserved at the west end of the grave only, and there was no surviving trace of a superstructure. The tomb preserved the remains of an adult female, of undetermined age, lying on her left size. The large size of the bricks used in this construction (43 x 24 x 7 cm) suggest that it is of Late Christian date, though this is by no means a certainly.

Tomb B7, recorded and partially excavated in 1969, appears to be a fully intact brick vault, adjoined by a large square *dromos* at the west end, suggesting that it was intended for multiple interments (Plate 7B). The chamber proper was closed off at the west end, where the *dromos* adjoined, by a wall of brick masonry, which the excavator apparently did not remove. There is, as a result, no information about the contents of this tomb. A five-pointed star was incised in the mud plaster on the outer side of the closure wall. There was no surviving trace of a superstructure, but it is clear from the photographs that the ground surface surrounding the tomb was somewhat deflated.

Tomb B3, opened but not entered in 1969, was undoubtedly the most extraordinary burial chamber at Kulubnarti. It was a vaulted chamber, enclosed at both ends by straight walls of brick masonry, with the original opening at the east. There was no *dromos,* however, and it was evident that this tomb was not intended for multiple interments. The barrel-vaulted ceiling of conventional Nubian type, clearly visible in the tomb interior (Plate 7D), had been covered over and reinforced on the upper side by a kind of corbelling of additional bricks (Plate 7C). Over this there may have been a superstructure of rollag bricks, but its pattern cannot be made out from the existing photographs.

Within Tomb B3 lay the body of a tall individual extended at full length on an *angareeb* bed of traditional Nubian type, and covered over with a brightly colored, patterned blanket. The figure appeared to be lying on its right side, but this could not be determined with certainly without removing the covering blanket. At the figure's head, at the southwest corner of the chamber, was an intact *qulla* of Egyptian Ware U13, with a small vessel of some other type, most probably a lamp, resting on the top of it (Plate 7D).

The very fragile condition of these remains precluded any investigation, beyond observing and photographing whatever could be seen from the east end. The blanket when we first observed it (and as shown in Plate 7D) was so uniformly covered with dust that no trace of its design was immediately observable. We were able to view the design by blowing away a small portion of dust from the lower

---

[32] There is no surviving photograph of this tomb.

end, but when we attempted to handle the textile it immediately went to shreds in our hands. The underlying *angareeb* was found also to be in fragile condition. Lacking any facilities for conservation, we thought it best to reseal this tomb, and so it remains to the present day. Since our departure we are told that it, like the tomb of Sitt Zuleiha, has become a focus of local veneration, and now boasts a small superstructure.

Tomb H1 was the chamber underlying the *gubba* of Sitt Zuleiha. We could determine little except that there was some kind of subterranean chamber with an opening at the north end, just under the base of the *gubba*. When found it was blocked with stones set into mud mortar. We removed the stone blockage and attempted to see into the chamber, but could see little because of the accumulation of rubble in the bottom. The presence of an opening at the north end suggests a vault with a north-south orientation, which in turn suggests the possibility of a pre-Christian tomb. If such it was, it had probably been robbed in antiquity. Because of the association with the venerated Lady Zuleiha, however, we did not attempt any excavation, and we resealed the entryway tightly before out departure.

As previously noted, it is possible that Grave A1 was also a crypt, covered by a kind of corbelled vault. This can not be clearly determined from the photographs, which are the only surviving record.

One other tomb chamber at 21-R-2 requires special mention. This was Grave 185, a rectangular chamber 230 cm long and 90 cm wide, roofed over with large stone slabs (Plate 7A). It was cut into a sloping ground surface in such a way that, although most of the grave was simply dug into the earth, it had necessarily been built up with a certain amount of rough stone masonry at the north end, where it projected above ground level. The tomb was oriented almost due north and south, and had originally been entered through a door at the north end, closed by a vertical stone slab sealed in place with mud. There was presumably a *dromos* outside the doorway, although this is not clear from the photographs and notes. The door slab had been left in place by tomb robbers, who had simply lifted some of the roof slabs instead.

The contents of Grave 185 were three disturbed burials, giving clear evidence that the tomb had been ransacked. The lower parts of the bodies were however left intact, making it possible to determine that all three of the interments had been in extended position, and at least two had been lying on their right sides. The bodies were those of a male of 50 or more years, a male of about 26, and a female of about 20.

As previously mentioned, the orientation of Grave 185, as well as the fact that it had been plundered, suggests the probability that it was a pre-Christian grave, most probably of "X-Group" date, although there were no artifactual remains to confirm this. The grave was one of a small group situated on a somewhat elevated terrace, well away from the other graves of Cemetery 21-R-2, and it is possible that the whole group represents a pre-Christian cemetery.

Head and body coverings

Head and body coverings as recorded at Cemetery 21-R-2 differed in no important respect from those at 21-S-46. At least 80% of burials had some kind of covering over the head and face, and of these by far the largest number were either of three stones (Plate 7E) or of three bricks (Plate 7F): one standing upright on either side of the head, and one bridging across the top. The two types of construction were just about equally common in this cemetery, although at 21-S-46 the structures of stone were much more numerous. There were also four instances involving stones at the sides of the head, with a brick over the top. Other, partial coverings, found occasionally, were comprised of two stones or two bricks, or in a few instances a single stone or a single brick.

As at 21-S-46, only about one-fifth of the burials had any kind of body covering below the head, and the covering when present consisted in nearly all cases of stone slabs. Most of these were not laid directly on top of the body; they were laid diagonally in such a way as to seal off a side niche, containing the burial, from the main grave shaft (Plate 8A). There were however, a few slot graves in which stone slabs had been laid directly on top of the body (Plate 8B), as well as two burials covered from head to foot with mud bricks, and one with slabs of mud.

Body positioning

The prevalence of burials lying on their left sides, already noted at 21-S-46, was even more conspicuous at 21-R-2. Forty-seven percent of individuals were lying either fully or partially on the left side (Plate 8C), as against 43% on their backs (Plate 8D), and 6% fully or partially on the right side (Plate 8E). There was one case of a ventral burial. No burials in flexed position were found at 21-R-2.

The propensity to turn the heads of deceased individuals toward the left, or in other words north, was equally marked in both of the two cemeteries excavated. In both places over 50% of the heads were turned to the left, while about 25% were facing straight up, and 10% were facing to the right. Remaining cases were uncertain. Placement of arms was also very nearly the same at the two sites, with over 50% of individuals having the hands meeting over the pubis, while most of the remainder had their hands at their sides. In both places most of the legs of the deceased were extended straight, with the remainder being very slightly flexed.

Shrouding

All but 19 of the excavated burials at 21-R-2 retained some traces of shrouding (Plate 8F), and nearly all of those that did not were otherwise in poor condition, suggesting that an original shroud had rotted away. Shrouding practices were essentially the same as at Site 21-S-46, and will be further described in Part II.

TABLE 6
CEMETERY 21-R-2 - REGISTER OF BURIALS

Burial no.	Head covering	Body covering	Body position	Head facing	Arms	Legs	Sex	Age

Graves excavated in 1969 (based on photos only)

Burial no.	Head covering	Body covering	Body position	Head facing	Arms	Legs	Sex	Age
A1	?	?	Left side	Left	Pubis	Straight		
A2	?	?	Right side	Right	Pubis	Sl. flexed		
A3	(Re-excavated in 1979 as Grave 180, q.v.)							
A4	3 stones	None	Dorsal	?	Pubis	Straight		
A5	None?	None	¼ right	Right	Pubis	Straight		
B3	Robe	Robe	Right side?	Right?	?	Straight		
B4	3 bricks	None	Dorsal	?	Pubis	?		
B6	(Shaft apparently not excavated)							
B7	(Re-excavated in 1979 as Grave 193, q.v.)							
SW of B7	Bricks	None	Dorsal	Up	Chest	Straight		
B8	Stones	Stones all along	Left side	Left	Pubis	Sl. flexed		
B10	None	None	Dorsal	Right	Pubis	Straight		
B11	Stones	Stones all along	Dorsal	Right	?	?		
N of B11	None	None	?	?	?	?		
B12	Stones	Stones all along	(Not excavated below stone cover?)					
C1	(Re-excavated in 1979 as Grave 14, q.v.)							
C2	(Re-excavated in 1979 as Grave 28, q.v.)							
C3	(Re-excavated in 1979 as Grave 149, q.v.)							
C4	(Shaft apparently not excavated)							
C5	(Re-excavated in 1979 as Grave 53, q.v.)							
C6	(Re-excavated in 1979 as Grave 176, q.v.)							
C7	(Shaft apparently not excavated)							
E1	None	None	Right side	Right	Pubis?	Straight		
E2	None?	None?	Right side	Right	Pubis	Straight		
E3	(Shaft apparently not excavated)							
F2	?	?	Left side	Left	Pubis	Straight		
F4	Stones	Stones all along	(Not excavated below stone cover?)					
H1	(Not excavated)							

Graves excavated in 1979

Burial no.	Head covering	Body covering	Body position	Head facing	Arms	Legs	Sex	Age
1	3 bricks?	None	Left side	Left	Pubis	Straight	M	42
2	None	None	Dorsal	Left	R on abd. L at side	Sl. flexed	?	5
3	3 bricks	None	Left side	Left	Pubis	Sl. flexed	M	36
4	3 bricks	None	Left side	Left	Sides	Straight	F	40
5	None	None	Right side	Right	Sides	Straight	?	6
6	3 bricks	None	Left side	Left	Pubis	Straight	F	37
7	3 bricks	None	Left side	Left	Pubis	Straight	F	37
8	None	None	Dorsal	Right	Sides	Straight	?	7
9	3 bricks	None	Left side	Left	Sides	Sl. flexed	?	7
10	3 bricks	None	Dorsal	Up	Pubis	Straight	M	37
11	3 bricks	None	Dorsal	Up	Sides	Straight	M	42
12	3 bricks	None	Left side	Left	R pubis L at side	Straight	F	23
13	3 bricks	None	Right side	Right	R at side L pubis	Straight	M	35
14	Bricks + stone	None	Left side	Left	Sides	Straight	M	23
15	3 bricks?	None	Dorsal	Left	Sides	Straight	M	22
16	3 stones	None	Dorsal	Left	Pubis	Straight	?	7
17	Stones + brick	None	Dorsal	Left	Sides	Sl. flexed	?	9 mos.
18	3 bricks	None	Left side	Left	Pubis	Sl. flexed	F	15

TABLE 6
CEMETERY 21-R-2 - REGISTER OF BURIALS (cont.)

Burial no.	Head covering	Body covering	Body position	Head facing	Arms	Legs	Sex	Age
19	3 bricks	None	Dorsal	Left	Pubis	Sl. flexed	M	37
20	3 bricks	None	Dorsal	Up	Pubis	Straight	M	38
21	3 bricks	None	Left side	Left	Pubis	Sl. flexed	?	6
22	3 bricks	None	Dorsal	Left	Pubis	Straight	F	36
23	(Not excavated)							
24	3 stones	None	(Lower body disturbed)		?	?		
25	None	None	Left side	Left	Pubis	Sl. flexed	?	13
26	3 bricks	None	Dorsal	Left	R pubis L at side	Straight	F	24
27	(Not excavated)							
28	3 stones?	None	Dorsal	Up	Sides	Straight	M	34
29	3 bricks	None	Dorsal	Up	Pubis	Sl. flexed	F	27
30	3 bricks	None	Dorsal	Left	Pubis	Sl. flexed	F	34
31	3 bricks	None	Dorsal	Up	Sides	Straight	M	21
32	3 bricks	None	Left side	Left	Sides	Sl. flexed	F	40
33	3 bricks	None	Left side	Left	Pubis	Straight	F	24
34	3 bricks	None	Left side	Left	R pubis L at side	Straight	M	31
35	3 bricks	None	Left side	Left	Sides	Straight	F	31
36	1 brick	None	Dorsal	Left	Sides	Straight	F	17
37	None	None	Left side	Left	R pubis L at chin	Sl. flexed	F	51+
38	2 bricks	None	Dorsal	Left	Pubis	Straight	F	18
39	1 brick	None	Dorsal	Up	Pubis	Straight	M	47
40	3 bricks	None	¼ right	Right	Pubis	Straight	M	42
41	3 bricks	None	Left side	Left	Pubis	Straight	?	3
42	3 bricks	None	Dorsal	Left	Pubis	Straight	F	13
43	3 bricks	None	Dorsal	Up	R at side L at chin	Sl. flexed	M	42
44	Stones + brick	None	Dorsal	Up	Pubis	Sl. flexed	F	36
45	Bricks	Bricks all along	Left side	Left	Sides	Straight	M	37
46	Stones + brick	None	Left side	Left	Pubis	Straight	M	47
47	Stones + brick	None	Left side	Left	Pubis	Sl. flexed	M	47
48	(Not a grave)							
49	3 bricks	None	Dorsal	Left	Sides	Straight	?	5
50	3 stones	None	Left side	Left	Pubis	Sl. flexed	M	49
51	None	None	Left side	Left	Sides	Sl. flexed	?	6 mos.
52	1 brick	None	¼ left	Left	Pubis	Straight	F	47
53	None	None	¼ left	Left	R pubis L at side	Straight	F	36
54	3 bricks	None	Left side	Left	R pubis L at side	Sl. flexed	?	11
55	Stones	Stones all along	Left side	Left	Pubis	Straight	F	26
56	3 bricks	None	Left side	Left	Pubis	Sl. flexed	M	24
57	Stones	Stones?	(Lower body disturbed)				?	9 mos.
58	1 stone	None	Dorsal	Up	(Note 1)	Sl. flexed	F	31
59	3 stones	None	¼ left	Left	Pubis	Sl. flexed	?	9
60	None	None	Dorsal	Up	Pubis	Sl. flexed	F	4
61	3 bricks	None	Left side	Left	Pubis	Sl. flexed	F	19
62	3 stones	None	¼ left	Up	Pubis	Straight	M	42
63	3 stones	None	Left side	Left	Pubis	Straight	M	42
64	3 stones	None	Left side	Left	Pubis	Sl. flexed	F	41
65	3 bricks	None	Left side	Left	Pubis	Straight	F	45

Note. In Burial no. 58, both arms lacked radius, ulna, and hands.

TABLE 6
CEMETERY 21-R-2 - REGISTER OF BURIALS (cont.)

Burial no.	Head covering	Body covering	Body position	Head facing	Arms	Legs	Sex	Age
66	3 stones	None	Left side	Left	Pubis	Straight	F	47
67	3 stones	None	Left side	Left	Pubis	Straight	F	51+
68	3 stones	None	Left side	Left	Pubis	Sl. flexed	M	12
69	3 stones	None	Left side	Left	Pubis	Straight	F	51+
70	3 stones	None	Left side	Left	Pubis	Sl. flexed	F	51+
71	(Not excavated)							
72	3 bricks	None	Dorsal	Up	Pubis	Straight	F	38
73	None	None	Dorsal	Left	Pubis	Straight	M	21
74	3 stones	None	Left side	Left	Pubis	Straight	?	5
75	None	None	Left side	Left	Pubis	Sl. flexed	?	?
76	3 stones	None	Dorsal	Up	Pubis	Straight	?	5
77	1 sherd	None	Left side	Left	Pubis	Sl. flexed	M	36
78	None	None	Left side	Left	Pubis	Straight	M	52
79	Stones	Stones all along	Left side	Left	Pubis	Sl. flexed	?	4
80	3 stones	None	Dorsal	Up	R pubis L at side	Straight	F	40
81	2 stones	None	Left side	Left	Pubis	Sl. flexed	M	24
82	None	None	Left side	Left	Pubis	R straight L flexed	?	5
83	3 stones	None	Left side	Left	Pubis	Sl. flexed	F	40
84	3 stones	None	Left side	Left	Sides	Sl. flexed	F	2
85	3 stones	None	Dorsal	Right	Sides	Sl. flexed	F	25
86	2 stones	None	Dorsal	Up	?	Straight	M	6
87	3 bricks	None	Left side	Left	Pubis	Straight	M	47
88	3 bricks	None	Left side	Left	Pubis	Sl. flexed	M	42
89	3 bricks	None	Right side	Right	Pubis	Straight	F	49
90	3 bricks	None	Dorsal	Up	Pubis	Straight	F	40
91	1 brick	None	Dorsal	Up	?	Straight	F	2
92	3 stones	None	¾ ventral	Down	Sides	Straight	F	19
93	None	None	Dorsal	Right	Sides	Sl. flexed	?	10
94	3 stones	None	Dorsal	Up	Pubis	Sl. flexed	?	12
95	3 stones	None	Left side	Left	R chest L at side	Sl. flexed	F	14
96	Stones	Stones all along	Left side	Left	Pubis	Sl. flexed	?	3
97	3 stones	None	Dorsal	Up	Sides	Straight	M	44
98	3 stones	Stones W side	Left side	Left	Pubis	Sl. flexed	?	4
99	Stones	Stones all along	Dorsal	Left	Pubis	Straight	F	36
100	Stones	Stones all along	Left side	Left	Pubis	Sl. flexed	?	3
101	3 stones	None	Left side	Left	Pubis	Sl. flexed	?	4
102	None	None	Dorsal	Left	Pubis	Straight	M	38
103	Stones	Stones all along	Dorsal	Left	?	Straight	?	18 mos.
104	Stones	Stones all along	Dorsal	Up	Pubis	Sl. flexed	M	4
105	None	None	Left side	Left	Pubis	Straight	F	49
106	Stones	Stones all along	Left side	Left	Pubis	Straight	F	38
107	1 stone	None	Dorsal	Up	Pubis	Straight	F	51+
108	1 stone	None	Left side	Left	Pubis	Sl. flexed	M	42
109	Stones	Stones all along	Left side	Left	?	Sl. flexed	?	Neonate
110	Mud slabs	Mud all along	Dorsal	Left	Pubis	Straight	M	6
111	Stones	Stones all along	Dorsal	Up	Sides	Straight	M	6 mos.
112	Stones	Stones all along	Dorsal	Up	Pubis	Sl. flexed	F	45
113	None	None	Left side	Left	Pubis	Sl. flexed	?	4
114	Stones	Stones all along	Left side	Left	Pubis	Straight	F	42
115	(Unfinished grave)							

TABLE 6
CEMETERY 21-R-2 - REGISTER OF BURIALS (cont.)

Burial no.	Head covering	Body covering	Body position	Head facing	Arms	Legs	Sex	Age
116	None	None	Left side	Left	Sides	Straight	?	13
117	None	None	Ventral	Right	Sides	Straight	?	4
118	3 bricks	None	Right side	Right	Pubis	Sl. flexed	F	26
119	None	None	Left side	Left	Pubis	Straight	?	36
120	None	None	Dorsal	Left	Pubis	Straight	?	15
121	(Not a grave)							
122	3 stones	None	Dorsal	Up	Sides	Straight	F	27
123	Stones	Stones all along	Dorsal	Left	Pubis	Straight	M	10
124	Stones	Stones all along	Left side	Left	Pubis	Sl. flexed	?	5
125	3 stones	None	¼ left	Left	Pubis	Sl. flexed	M	2
126	Stones	Stones all along	Dorsal	Left	Pubis	Straight	F	16
127	Stones	Stones all along	Left side	Left	Pubis	Sl. flexed	M	42
128	Stones	Stones all along	Dorsal	Up	Pubis	Straight	?	8
129	Stones	Stones all along	Left side	Left	Pubis	Sl. flexed	F	45
130	Stones	Stones all along	Left side	Left	Pubis	Sl. flexed	?	4
131	Stones	Stones all along	Left side	Left	Pubis	Sl. flexed	?	Neonate
132	Stones	Stones all along	Dorsal	Left	R pubis L at side	Sl. flexed	M	28
133	Stones	Stones all along	Dorsal	Up	Sides	Sl. flexed	?	4
134	Stones	Stones all along	Left side	Left	R pubis L at neck	Straight	?	12
135	Stones	Stones all along	Dorsal	Up	R pubis L at side	Straight	?	8
136	Stones	Stones all along	Dorsal	Up	Pubis	Straight	?	51+
137	Stones	Stones at pubis	Dorsal	Up	Sides	Straight	F	18 mos.
138	None	None	Left side	Left	R pubis L flexed	Sl. flexed	?	10
139	3 bricks	None	Dorsal	Up	?	Straight	F	31
140	3 stones	None	Left side	Left	Sides	Straight	F	51+
141	3 bricks	None	Dorsal	Up	Pubis	Straight	M	22
142	3 stones	None	Dorsal	Up	Sides	Straight	?	9
143	Stones	Stones all along	Dorsal	Up	R at chin L pubis	Straight	F	45
144	3 stones	None	Dorsal	Up	Pubis	Straight	F	34
145	3 stones	None	Dorsal	Up	Sides	Straight	M	31
146	Stones	Stones all along	Dorsal	Up	Pubis	Straight	M	15
147	Stones	Stones all along	Dorsal	Up	Pubis	Straight	M	16
148	3 bricks	None	¼ right	Right	Pubis	Straight	F	47
149	None	None	Left side	Left	Sides	Sl. flexed	F	31
150	None	None	?	Left	?	Straight	?	3
151	None	None	Dorsal	Left	Sides	Straight	?	18 mos.
152	3 stones	None	Left side	Left	Sides	Straight	?	3
153	3 bricks	None	Left side	Left	Pubis	Straight	M	38
154	3 stones	None	Dorsal	Up	R at side L pubis	Straight	F	51+
155	(Not a grave)							
156	3 stones	None	¼ left	Left	Pubis	Straight	F	37
157	3 stones	None	Left side	Left	Pubis	Straight	?	4
158	Stones	Stones all along	Dorsal	Up	Pubis	Straight	M	19
159	Stones	Stones all along	Dorsal	Up	Pubis	Straight	?	2
160	Stones	Stones all along	Dorsal	Right	Pubis	Straight	?	?
161	Stones	Stones all along	Dorsal	Up	R abdom. L pubis	Sl. flexed	F	26

41

TABLE 6
CEMETERY 21-R-2 - REGISTER OF BURIALS (cont.)

Burial no.	Head covering	Body covering	Body position	Head facing	Arms	Legs	Sex	Age
162	Stones	Stones all along	Left side	Left	Pubis	Straight	F	?
163	None	None	Dorsal	Up	Pubis	Sl. flexed	M	21
164	Stones	Stones all along	Dorsal	Right	Pubis	Straight	?	9 mos.
165	3 stones	None	Left side	Left	Pubis	Sl. flexed	?	13
166	3 stones	None	Right side	Right	?	Sl. flexed	?	6
167	2 bricks	None	¼ left	Left	Pubis	Sl. flexed	M	6 mos.
168	Brick frags.	None	Left side	Left	Pubis	Straight	M?	19
169	None	None	Left side	Left	Pubis	Sl. flexed	?	18 mos.
170	3 stones	None	Left side	Left	Sides	Sl. flexed	?	12
171	(Not a grave)							
172	None	None	Dorsal	Left	Sides	Straight	?	5
173	3 stones	None	Left side	Left	Pubis	Sl. flexed	?	1
174	None	None	Left side	Left	Pubis	Flexed	?	15
175	None	None	Dorsal	Left	Pubis	Straight	M	20
176A	Stones	Stones all along	Dorsal	Left	Sides	Straight	F	18
176B	Stones	Stones all along	?	?	?	?	?	Neonate
177	(Not a grave)							
178	Stones	Stones all along	Dorsal	Up	Pubis	Straight	?	8
179	Brick frag.	None	Left side	Left	Pubis	Sl. flexed	?	14
180	None	None	Dorsal	Up	R pubis L at side	Straight	M	26
181	None	None	Left side	Left	Pubis	Sl. flexed	?	1
182	Bricks	Bricks all along	Left side	Left	Pubis	Sl. flexed	?	3
183	3 stones	None	Dorsal	Right	Pubis	Straight	?	18 mos.
184	None	None	Dorsal	Up	?	Straight	?	2
185A	None	None	(Disturbed)	Right	Sides	Straight	M	26
185B	None	None	(Disturbed)	Right	Sides	Straight	F	20
185C	None	None	(Disturbed)	?	Sides	Straight	M	50+
186	3 stones	None	Left side	Left	R at chin L pubis	Flexed	?	2
187	(Not excavated)							
188	3 bricks	None	Dorsal	Up	Pubis	Straight	M	33
189	(Not excavated)							
190	(Not excavated)							
191	(Not excavated)							
192	3 bricks	None	Left side	Left	Pubis	Sl. flexed	F	16
193	Brick frags.	None	Left side	Left	Pubis	Sl. flexed	F	37
194	(Unfinished grave)							
195	3 stones	None	Dorsal	Up	Pubis	Straight	?	18 mos.
196	None	None	Left side	Left	Pubis	Sl. flexed	M	18 mos.
197	3 bricks	None	Dorsal	Up	Pubis	Straight	M	42
198	(Not excavated)							
199	(Not excavated)							
200	(Not excavated)							
201	3 stones	None	Left side	Left	Pubis	Sl. flexed	?	7
202	1 brick	None	Left side	Left	?	Straight	?	9 mos.
203	3 stones	None	Dorsal	Left	At chin	Straight	M	17
204	None	None	Dorsal	?	Pubis	Straight	?	2
205	Stones	Stones all along	Left side	Left	Pubis	Straight	F	40

Grave goods

Grave goods other than shrouds were confined - with one notable exception - to small items of personal jewelry which had not been deliberately buried as offerings; the persons preparing the bodies had simply not chosen to remove them. As at 21-S-46 most, but not all, of the jewelry items were found on the bodies of infants or adolescents. Four individuals, including two adults and two infants, had iron crosses at the neck, which in two cases were suspended on cords. One adolescent had a cord with a *higab* around the neck, two individuals had cords with a single quartz bead, and four individuals had braided leather cords around the neck with nothing depending from them. Two individuals had bangles on the right wrist, one had beads on a cord on the right wrist, and one individual had a cowrie shell on a cord, tied just above the elbow. One adolescent had a small copper-alloy earring. Finally, a wooden stick, apparently without carving, was buried upright in one grave.

In a different class altogether were the grave goods found in the extraordinary Tomb B3. Here, as previously noted, a tall adult had been buried on an *angareeb* bed, covered with a brightly colored blanket or robe, and accompanied at the head by a pottery *qulla*, topped by another and smaller pottery vessel (Plate 7D). Here, and only here, the material goods give evidence of a specific mortuary ritual, which will be further discussed in later pages.

Demography and mortality

The sharpest, and also the most puzzling difference between Cemetery 21-S-46 and Cemetery 21-R-2 can be seen in the mortality figures from the two sites. While at 21-S-46 only 37% of individuals had lived beyond the age of ten, the figure at 21-R-2 was 66%. The average age at death for all individuals buried at 21-R-2 was 18.9 years, as against 10.6 years at 21-S-46. In both places, there was a higher survival rate for older feamles than for males.

Assuming, as we had done all along, that there was a major chronological difference between the two Kulubnarti cemeteries, we naturally attributed the improved mortality figures at 21-R-2 to a betterment in diet and in general living conditions. This seemed consistent with architectural evidence: the well-built and often elaborate houses of the Late Christian period contrasting with the rude huts of earlier times. In view of our revised dating of most of the excavated graves at 21-R-2, however, it is evident that this issue must be rethought. It will be more fully discussed in the following section, and also in Part III.

Summary

There is a good deal of evidence, partly direct and partly inferential, to suggest that the use of Cemetery 21-R-2 persisted without interruption from Early Christian until modern times. In Early and early Classic Christian times it was probably the burial place for the dwellers at the nearby walled settlement of 21-R-3, and in Classic times it was closely associated with the Domed Church 21-R-1. In Late Christian as well as post-Christian times it probably became the burial place for the inhabitants of Site 21-S-2, on the southern tip of Kulubnarti Island, and it has been used still more recently by the dwellers at the modern hamlet of Kulbincoing, directly overlooking the cemetery.

Nevethess, nearly all of the graves that were actually excavated at 21-R-2 seem datable, on typological grounds,

to the Early Christian and perhaps the early part of the Classic Christian period. They are, therefore, generally contemporaneous with the graves at 21-S-46. The excavated graves at the two cemeteries thus do not give a full picture of the development of burial practice at Kulubnarti; they exemplify only the practices of the Early Christian period. Our observations on the unexcavated graves at 21-R-2 suggest that significant changes took place in the Classic and Late Christian periods: the replacement of stone by brick superstructures, and the increasing use of brick-vaulted burial chambers.

Comparisons and conclusions

Comparisons between the findings at the two Kulubnarti cemeteries have been made repeatedly throughout the previous section, and they are summarized statistically in Table 7. In this section, an attempt will be made to place the findings from both cemeteries within a broader historical context, by comparison with what is known from other medieval Nubian sites. These comparisons are based on a survey of data from 117 published and unpublished sites in Lower and Middle Nubia, between Aswan in the north and Abri in the south.[33]

Superstructures

Stone pavements. The rude stone pavements at Kulubnarti are characteristic of Early Christian superstructures throughout Middle Nubia. They are the single most common type of grave marking found from the Second Cataract through the *Batn el Hajjar*, but have almost never been found anywhere further north. The northernmost recorded examples were found at Debeira, about 20 km north of the Second Cataract. The great majority of stone pavements date unmistakably from the Early Christian period, but there may have been some carryover at least into the early part of the Classic Christian period.

Stone outlines, although much less common than pavements, exhibited essentially the same distribution in time and space. They were often found alongside stone pavements in the same cemeteries, but in a few cemeteries they were the only kind of superstructure observed.

Stone alignments, observed in a few cases at Kulubnarti, have not been recorded at any other cemetery, but this may be due simply to lack of precision in recording.

Flat brick pavements, represented by four examples at 21-S-46, have been recorded only in two other cemeteries, both in the area slightly upriver from Kulubnarti. Far to the south, a few graves with brick pavements were found at Soba,

---

[33] The discussion that follows is excerpted from a more detailed survey, "Toward a Comparative Study of Christian Nubian Burial Practice," to be published in *Archéologie du Nil Moyen*.

although here the pavings seem to have surrounded the graves without actually covering them.[34]

Rollag brick pavements have essentially the same distribution in space as have stone pavements. That is, they have been found almost entirely in the area from Debeira southward. Brick and stone pavements have often been found together in the same cemeteries, as at Kulubnarti, but in an equal number of cases the superstructures were of brick only. There seems to be little doubt that brick pavements are generally later in time than are stone pavements, dating chiefly from the Classic Christian period, with some possible carryover into the Late period.[35] There was nevertheless probably some period of time, at the end of the Early Christian and/or the beginning of the Classic Christian period, when both types of pavements were built.

Mastabas. To anyone familiar with the medieval cemeteries of Lower Nubia, the most conspicuous features of the Kulubnarti cemeteries is a negative one: the total absence of mastaba superstructures of stone or brick masonry. However, this again appears to be characteristic of all Christian cemeteries to the south of the Second Cataract, although mastabas have been noted at Old Dongola and at Soba.[36]

Gubba. The single gubba superstructure at Kulubnarti (attributed to the tomb of Sitt Zuleiha) is identical to other structures found at many places in Lower Nubia.[37] Most of them were certainly built in Post-Christian times, through some may date from the Christian period. Those of Post-Christian date often stand atop earlier tombs, as does the specimen at Kulubnarti.

Grave orientations

Although it is clear that Christian graves were always supposed to be oriented toward the west, it was usual practice to orient them toward "Nile west;" that is, taking the direction of the river's flow as a datum for north. This referent could not, however, be followed at Kulubnarti, where the Nile flows very nearly east and west along the southern side of the island - that is, within sight of the Cemeteries 21-R-2 and 21-S-46. As already noted, the Kulubnarti grave-diggers must instead have used either the sun or some fixed point on the western horizon as reference points. In the upshot, their graves tended more often than not to be oriented somewhat to the south of true west, in contrast to the situation in nearly all Christian graves further north. At the same time, individual graves both in Cemetery 21-S-46 and in Cemetery 21-R-2 varied enormously in their orientations; again in contrast to the situation in most other cemeteries. This was probably because previously dug graves could not be followed as models, due to the rather amorphous shape of their superstructures.

Grave shafts

The relative antiquity of slot graves and of side-niche graves was once a matter of dispute.[38] However, it seems clear now that both types of grave shafts were in use throughout the whole of the Christian Nubian period, and beyond.[39] The choice of one type or the other seems to have been almost entirely a matter of personal preference, though affected to some extent by regional traditions.

Slot graves were more numerous than side-niche graves in nearly all cemeteries, as they were at Kulubnarti. In some cemeteries in the far north of Nubia, they were the only kind of grave shaft found.

Side-niche graves, although found almost everywhere except in the far north, were far more numerous from Debeira southward than they were further north. In a few sites, at Debeira and Argin, they were the predominant form. At Missiminia, the one Middle Nubian site besides Kulubnarti that has been thoroughly excavated, they constituted about one-third of all the grave shafts,[40] as against a figure of about one-fifth at Kulubnarti.

Where side-niches were employed, they were almost universally at the north side of the grave shaft, both in Lower and in Middle Nubia. Apart from their rare occurrence at Kulubnarti, niches on the south side of the shaft were reported in only three other cemeteries. Surprisingly, however, they constituted almost 10% of the cases at Missiminia.[41]

It seems clear that the practical reason for digging a side-niche grave was to allow the interred body to be protected by stone slabs or bricks leaning diagonally over it. This practice was followed fairly consistently in Lower Nubia, but much less so at Kulubnarti and Missiminia, where many bodies in side-niche graves did not have a slab covering.

Bottom-niche graves represent a distinctive type whose use seems to have been confined to the Early Christian period.

[34] See D. A. Welsby and C. M. Daniels. *Soba: Archaeological Research at a Medieval Capital on the Blue Nile*. pp. 120-121. British Institute in Eastern Africa, memoir no. 12 (1991).

[35] See Vila, op. cit. (n. 18), p. 187.

[36] See D. A. Welsby. *Soba II: Renewed Excavations within the Metropolis of the Kingdom of Alwa*. p. 278. British Institute in Eastern Africa, memoir no. 15 (1998).

[37] See Adams, loc. cit. (n. 26).

[38] See Reisner, op. cit. (n. 10), p. 308; and Hermann Junker, *Ermenne (Akademie der Wissenschaften in Wien, Philosophisch-historische Klasse Denkschriften* 67, Band 1 Abhandlungen, 1925), p 161.

[39] See Hermann Junker, *Bericht über die Grabungen der Akademie der Wissenschaften in Wien auf den Friedhöfen von El-Kubanieh-Süd (Akademie der Wissenschaften in Wien, Philosphisch-historische Klasse Denkschriften* 62, Band 3 Abhandlungen, 1919), pls. LIII-LIV; Junker, loc cit. (n. 36); and W. Y. Adams and H.-Å. Nordström in *Kush* 11 (1963), p. 45, n. 99.

[40] Vila, op. cit. (n. 18), pp. 188-190.

[41] Ibid, p. 190

They were the preferred form of interment in the middle portion of Lower Nubia, extending about from Taifa to Arminna, but occurred only sporadically in sites further to the north and to the south. As previously noted, there were five examples at 21-S-46, but none at 21-R-2.

Carefully squared ends were present in a number of graves at both Kulubnarti cemeteries, but have been specifically noted in only one other Nubian cemetery, at Argin.[42] It seems probable however, that in many other cases they were simply not recorded, because they did not strike the excavator as a significant feature.

Vaults. Brick vaulted tomb chambers, usually but not always containing multiple interments, were employed in small numbers throughout the whole of the Christian period. They were however, far more common in Lower Nubia than further south. Apart from their occurrence at 21-R-2, they were found at only two other sites in Middle Nubia.

Body coverings

Diagonally laid slabs or, very occasionally, bricks, were the usual covering for bodies in side-niche graves. They were inserted so that their lower ends rested on the floor of the tomb, at the base of the south wall, while the upper end rested against the north wall at a point above the niche. In Lower Nubia the use of such covering in side-niche graves was nearly universal, but it was much less so in Middle Nubia, where many bodies in niche graves had no covering. This was conspicuously the case at Kulubnarti.

Horizontally laid slabs or bricks were the nearly universal covering for bodies in bottom-niche graves, both in Lower and in Middle Nubia. However, in Middle Nubia they were also employed fairly commonly in ordinary slot graves, as they were at Kulubnarti. In these cases the stones rested either directly on top of the corpse, or on a shallow filling of earth overlying the corpse.

Bricks. The use of a body covering of bricks was found in only two cases at 21-R-2, and none at 21-S-46. Elsewhere in Nubia, the use of brick coverings, in place of stone, seems to have become common at about the same time when brick paved superstructures replaced those of stone, at or near the end of the Early Christian period. They were however, much more common from Debeira southward than they were anywhere further north.

Pot burials. The burial of foetuses and stillborns in pottery vessels was practiced throughout the whole of the Christian period, although it seems to have been more common in

Early Christian times than later. Most of the known examples have been found in the area from Debeira southward. As at Kulubnarti, nearly all the burials are either in Egyptian-made amphorae or in hand-made pots of local manufacture.

Head coverings

The use of a head covering of three stones or three bricks was of course a substitute for a more complete protection of the body. Curiously enough, the only recorded instance of this practice, north of the Second Cataract, was at El-Kubanieh, at the far northern extremity of Nubia.[43] At Meinarti, however, about 80% of bodies had this kind of covering, comprised in each case of three bricks. The percentage was only slightly lower at Kulubnarti, where however, the covering in most cases was of stones rather than bricks. Head coverings have also been noted at a few other Middle Nubian sites, but they seem to have been very rare at Missiminia.[44] The evidence from Meinarti, combined with that from Kulubnarti, shows conclusively that the use of a three-stone or three-brick covering for the head persisted through the whole of the Christian period, even though it was found only at a minority of sites.

Body positioning

Burial in dorsal position, with the head to the west, was always the preferred posture for Christian Nubian interments, and in the northern part of Lower Nubia it was universal. From Arminna southward to the Second Cataract however, burials both on the right and on the left side were encountered, with those on the right being considerably more common. From the Second Cataract southward the situation was reversed, with burials on the left side being far more common than those on the right, as they were at Kulubnarti. The percentage of laterally interred individuals at Kulubnarti (36% at 21-S-46 and 53% at 21-R-2) is however, far higher than in any other known cemetery.

The choice of a lateral or a dorsal burial position does not correlate closely with any particular kind of grave shaft or any one kind of superstructure. As in the case of grave shaft forms, it seems to have been very much a matter of individual preference. It seems probable however, that burial in a ventral position represents some form of execration. It was recorded in only two cases at each of the Kulubnarti cemeteries, in one case at Meinarti, and in one case at each of two other cemeteries in northern Nubia. Ventral burials were also encountered at Soba.[45]

Head positioning

When individuals were buried on their sides, their heads were naturally turned in the same direction as was the body. However, the practice of turning the heads of dorsal burials

[42] See Manuel Pellicer and Miguel Llongueras, *Las Necropolis Meroiticas del Grupo "X" y Cristianas de Nag-el-Arab (Comité Español de la U.N.E.S.C.O. para Nubia, Memorias de la Misión Arqueológica, V, 1965)*, p. 40, fig. 11.

[43] Junker, *El-Kubanieh-Süd* (op. cit., n. 39), pl. LI, upper left.
[44] But see Vila, op. cit. (n. 18), p. 191, fig. 228, lower right.
[45] Welsby, op. cit. (n. 36), pp. 54, 55, 278.

TABLE 7

TABLE 7
CEMETERIES 21-S-46 AND 21-R-2 - COMPARATIVE SUMMARIES*

	21-S-46	21-R-2
<u>Graves numbered</u>	**242**	**226**
Non-graves or unfinished	4	3
Numbered but not excavated	7	4
Partially excavated		3
% of numbered graves excavated	89	90
<u>Superstructures</u>	62	20
Stone pavement	49	10
Stone outline	7	1
Stone alignment	2	T
Stone slabs		1
Stone + brick pavement	T	T
Brick pavement	4	6
Gubba		T
Destroyed in 1969 excavations	21	1
No recorded information		3
None	38	80
<u>Lamp boxes identified</u>	**3**	**0**
<u>Orientation</u>		
270-316°	18	43
242-269°	82	44
No record		13
<u>Grave shafts excavated</u>	**218**	**209**
Slot	65	78
Side niche north	21	16
Side niche south	T	1
Chamber		T
Vault		1
Round or oval pit	1	
Form uncertain	13	3
<u>Burials uncovered</u>	**215**	**203**
<u>Head covering</u>		
Stones all along	22	21
Bricks all along		1
Mud all along		T
3 stones, sides and top	17	24
2 stones at sides	2	T
1 stone at side	2	1
2 stones + 1 brick		2
3 bricks, sides and top	11	24
2 bricks at sides	1	2
1 brick over face		3
Brick fragments		2
Sherds	1	T
Foetal burial in pot	4	
Uncertain	T	4
None	37	16

* Figures in bold face are raw numbers; all others are percentages

TABLE 7

		21-S-46	21-R-2
Body covering			
	Stones all along	22	21
	Bricks all along		1
	Mud all along		T
	Stones to waist or knees	1	
	Stones over pubis only		T
	Foetal burial in pot	4	
	Uncertain	1	3
	None	69	74
Body position			
	Dorsal	57	43
	¼ left	5	4
	Left side	27	43
	¼ right	T	1
	Right side	4	5
	Ventral	1	1
	Uncertain	T	4
Head position			
	Facing up	26	25
	Facing left	52	60
	Facing right	10	11
	Facing down	1	T
	Foetal burial in pot	4	
	Uncertain	6	3
Arm position			
	On pubis	53	63
	At sides	27	19
	On chest or abdomen	T	T
	Under chin	T	T
	Asymmetrical	4	10
	Foetal burial in pot	4	
	Uncertain	11	7
Leg position			
	Straight	61	60
	Slightly flexed	27	37
	Flexed	4	1
	Asymmetrical	1	T
	Foetal burial in pot	4	
	Uncertain	4	2
Ages at death			
	Under 1 year	1	5
	1-5 years	30	20
	6-10 years	15	9
	11-15 years	8	8
	16-20 years	2	7
	21-25 years	3	6
	26-30 years	1	4
	31-35 years	3	6
	36-40 years	4	13
	41-45 years	4	9
	46-50 years	7	5
	51-55 years	4	5
	Uncertain	T	2
	Average age at death	**10.6**	**18.9**

to one side or the other seems to be a distinctive feature of Middle Nubian burial practice. As with so many other features, its northernmost occurrence was at Debeira. The practice was recorded at a score of cemeteries from Debeira southward, but only at Kulubnarti was it actually predominant. At Argin and at Meinarti, heads were turned more often to the right than to the left, while throughout the *Batn el-Hajjar*, as at Kulubnarti, they were turned much more often to the left. This preference seems to correlate with the preference for interment of the bodies on the left side at Kulubnarti, and on the right side at Meinarti and Argin.

Hand positioning

The positioning of hands has not been consistently reported from Christian Nubian cemeteries. Where reported, however, the practice of placing both hands on the pubis is everywhere described as usual, as was the case at Kulubnarti.

Shrouding

In the practice of shrouding, the burials at both Kulubnarti cemeteries followed the all-but-universal custom of Christian Nubia. Bodies were wrapped from head to foot in one or more pieces of textile, and then were usually tightly bound around with cords or tapes. The various garments and materials used in shrouding will be much more fully discussed in Part II; it is enough to indicate here that the materials used were in every case those characteristic of Early and Classic rather than of Late Christian Nubia.

Grave goods

Small items of personal jewelry, like those found at Kulubnarti, have been found in a good many other Christian cemeteries, both in Lower and in Middle Nubia. They are found primarily though not exclusively in Early Christian graves, and primarily though not exclusively on the bodies of infants or adolescents. By far the most common items everywhere are small iron crosses, often suspended from a cord around the neck. Other items noted at several sites are earrings, simple metal bracelets, and beads.

In a very different category are the pottery vessels found in Tomb B3 at Site 21-R-2 (Plate 7D). There is only one other known instance in which *qullas*, accompanied by lamps, were buried alongside the heads of the dead - in the tomb of Bishop Ioannes at Faras.[46] Here no fewer than five individuals were interred, each with his own accompanying *qulla*, and with lamps in four of the five cases. Ioannes himself died in the year 1005, but it is clear from the accompanying pottery that all of the other interments were made at later dates, extending probably into the 12th century.[47]

The bed burial in Tomb B3 is even more an anomaly than is the pottery, for it has no counterpart in any other tomb of the Classic or Late Christian period.[48] It recalls the common Nubian burial practice of Kushite and even earlier times.[49] It seems clear that the individual in Tomb B3 must have been someone of importance, most probably in the ecclesiastical sphere. Why he should have found his final resting place in this remote and provincial cemetery, where there was no major church or monastery nearby, is however, an enduring mystery.

Demography and mortality

We have already noted a substantial difference in the mortality figures from the two Kulubnarti cemeteries, although mortality rates in both cases were high. They are substantially similar to the figures from Argin, where almost 70% of the burials were of pre-adults,[50] and from Meinarti,[51] where about 50% of burials were pre-adults, but are markedly different from the figures from Missiminia, where only 14% of burials were of pre-adults.[52] These discrepancies will be much more fully considered in Part III.

Summary of comparisons

In nearly all respects the two Kulubnarti cemeteries exhibit the typical Middle Nubian mortuary complex of Early Christian times: stone pavement superstructures covering either slot or side-niche graves, with either dorsally or laterally extended burials, most commonly on their left sides. The only respects in which the Kulubnarti burials stand out are in the high percentage of individuals buried on their left sides, and the even higher percentage with the heads turned toward the north. Both these features were found in other Middle Nubian graves, but not with the same frequency as at Kulubnarti.

Concluding observations

The combination of cultural and biological evidence from the two Kulubnarti cemeteries suggests a wholly unexpected possibility: that this region in Early Christian times was home to two racially and culturally identical, but socially distinct, communities, one of which was considerably better off than the other. The grave types, the grave goods, and the skeletal types are virtually identical as between the two Kulubnarti cemeteries, while the figures for pathology and mortality are significantly different.

For the moment there is no obvious explanation for this anomaly. The possibility that the folk buried on the island

[46] Kazimierz Michalowski, *Faras - Fouilles Polonaises 1961-1962* (Warsaw, 1965), pp. 49-55.

[47] See Stefan Jakobielski, *Faras III* (Warsaw, 1972), p. 143.

[48] Bed burials were found in a couple of very early Christian (or late X-Group) tombs at Firka and at Sesebi, but these clearly represent a carry-over of X-Group practice. See especially David N. Edwards in *Journal of Egyptian Archaeology*, vol. 80 (1994), pp. 172 and 176.

[49] See William Y. Adams, *Nubia, Corridor to Africa* (London, 1977), pp. 203-206, 285-288, 376, 409.

[50] Pellicer and Llongueras, op. cit. (n. 42), p. 200.

[51] Author's unpublished field data.

[52] Vila, op. cit. (n. 18), p. 233.

48

were a slave population seems ruled out by their physical identity with their neighbors on the mainland. At least in more recent times, slave populations in Nubia have been drawn from the tribal peoples of the southern and western Sudan, who are markedly distinct from the Nubians in a number of their physical characteristics. The possibility that the island burials are those of a group of ethnic immigrants seems precluded by the identity of their cultural practices and grave goods with those in the mainland graves. The possibility that the poorer folk were refugees from the north seems also unlikely, given the absence of any record of military disturbances in Nubia after the Arab invasion of A.D. 652.[53] In the absence of those possibilities, we are left to imagine a single culturally homogeneous but socially stratified Nubian population; yet there is neither textual evidence nor archaeological evidence from other sites to support such an interpretation.

Ethnographic evidence does however, suggest one possible explanation. Our colleague Ali Osman Mohammed Saleh has informed us that in the Dar el-Mahas region there was, in the recent past, a kind of "floating population" of landless Nubians, who provided casual labor at the time of the date harvest or whenever there were extra labor needs.[54] At other times they were forced to lead a kind of nomadic existence, grazing their small flocks of sheep and goats up and down the riverbanks. These people, although ethnic Nubians, were looked down on as inferiors by their more prosperous fellows, and were not allowed to live among them. They made their abodes, usually temporary, on barren, uninhabited land, and especially on rocky islands. The evidence from Kulubnarti at least raises the possibility that a similar social division prevailed a millennium earlier.

Clearly, this is a matter calling for further investigation: first, to ascertain whether our conclusion is correct with regard to Kulubnarti itself, and second, to see if comparable social divisions can be recognized at any other Early Christian site. The first of these possibilities would be very much enhanced if we could identify the dwelling places of the folk buried respectively at 21-S-46 and at 21-R-2. Fortunately, two lines of investigation are still open at Kulubnarti, since the island and its hinterland have not been affected by the impounded waters of Lake Nubia. There should, on the one hand, be a much fuller investigation of the numerous rude stone huts that are scattered all over the island, and that we excavated only on a limited scale in 1969.[55] Our previous investigations suggested that these structures were mainly datable to Classic and Late Christian times, but if we could establish that some were occupied in Early Christian times, it would be logical to identify them as the dwellings of the poor folk buried at 21-S-46.

A second important line of investigation would be a much fuller excavation of the mainland Site 21-R-3, which was excavated and published only in incomplete fashion by the original German mission in 1969.[56] This walled settlement, yielding both Early and Classic Christian pottery, was most probably the home of at least some of the folk buried at 21-R-2, and its plan suggests a somewhat higher standard of housing than is represented by the rude and scattered huts. However, only further and careful excavation could establish the true level of prosperity enjoyed by the dwellers at 21-R-3.

To the south of Kulubnarti there are, presumably, many additional Early Christian sites still to be investigated. Nevertheless, it may be unrealistic to hope that much further evidence on the subject of social stratification will be adduced. Morbidity and mortality figures comparable to those from Kulubnarti could only be attained by the additional wholesale excavation of other Christian cemeteries - something that is not likely to happen when the yield of material goods is so small. As for residential remains indicative of social differences, the best chance of finding these may be at Old Dongola, but tons of sand must be removed before the Early Christian levels are uncovered at that site. In the meantime the findings from Kulubnarti remain an intriguing and an unexplained anomaly in Nubian social history.

[53] See Adams, op. cit. (n. 49), p. 451
[54] Personal communication.
[55] See *Kulubnarti I*, pp. 263-267.

[56] See Erich Dinkler in Dinkler, op. cit. (n. 3), pp. 267-270. The published plan of this site (ibid., p. 268) shows a complete layout of rooms, but I was able to establish by personal examination that many of these were not actually dug.

PART II
THE GRAVE GOODS

Nettie K. Adams

Introduction

Among the many changes brought to Nubia by the arrival of Christianity were ideas about life after death. Previously, the dead were thought to require for their afterlife the same things that make for a good life on earth. Food, water, weapons, containers, and luxury items such as jewelry, oils and perfumes were often interred with the deceased. Christian notions of immortality were strictly spiritual; in this view there was no need for the presence of any physical accouterments of life because the dead were freed from their corporeal existence, and life after death was for the soul.

The Kulubnarti cemeteries show that the Kulubnarti Christians adhered to these ideas faithfully. The only pots were those which were used for foetal burials.[1] There were no weapons or tools, no food or luxury items, although a few, mostly women and children, were buried with a piece of jewelry which they had worn in life. However, each person was wrapped in cloth before being laid into the grave, and many of the wrappings were secured with bindings. A very few were encased in leather (Plate 18E) or placed on a piece of sheepskin (Plate 18F) or on a woven mat in addition to the body wrapping.

The textile remains

Conditions of the Textiles

Although it seems certain that every body was originally wrapped in cloth, not every grave excavated contained textile remains. Some had gotten wet and disappeared; others were in such a bad state of preservation they could not be saved. Of the 214 graves excavated in cemetery 21-S-46, 122 graves contained 239 textile specimens which were removed and numbered. From cemetery 21-R-2, containing 203 excavated graves, 121 graves yielded 231 textiles. The wrapping from Grave 60 went in division to the Sudan Antiquities Service, and the skirt from Grave 136 was reported by the excavator but not recovered, leaving our collection from 21-R-2 with 229 specimens from 119 graves.

When the bodies were disinterred many of the grave wrappings were complete, or nearly so. However, the process of removing the textiles necessitated cutting with scissors in many cases, because oozing body fluids, acting as a kind of glue, had stuck the layers of cloth together when they dried. What had been recognizable as a loin cloth, tunic or other garment was thus often reduced to a few fragments of featureless cloth. After removal, all the textile specimens from each burial were numbered and placed together in boxes or bags.

The placement of the different wrappings on each burial was not generally recorded by the excavator, although there are occasional notations of "skirt" or "loincloth". Thus, information which would aid in our interpretation of this material, such as the way garments were placed on the body, whether there was more than one layer of fabric, and the configurations of the bindings, is unavailable to us now. Despite these drawbacks, the Kulubnarti cemeteries have yielded a splendid collection of very rare Early Christian Nubian textiles.

Some Earlier Studies

Although textiles from Early Christian Nubian cemeteries are rare, excavations of the cemeteries are not. Beginning with George Reisner in 1907 there are 18 reports of Christian cemeteries containing burials wrapped in cloth. Most of them have merely a mention : "wrapped only in a few coarse linen or woollen cloths";[2] "Están cubiertos con sudarios y a veces con mantos" (tr. They are covered with shrouds and at times with mantles);[3] "completely wrapped in cloth".[4]

Reisner, however, was much more complete and detailed in his descriptions. In his report on Cemetery 2 at Shellal he wrote that tape or cord was wound diagonally or spirally around the bodies, presenting a criss-cross appearance. "The cords consisted usually of three twisted strands, each made of three twisted threads of twisted fibre".[5] From the same

---

[1] With the sole exception of a *qulla* covered by a saucer lamp buried in Tomb B3 at 21-R-2.

[2] C. M.. Firth, *Archaeological Survey of Nubia, Report for 1908-1909* (Cairo, 1912), p. 40.

[3] Manuel Pellicer and Miguel Llongueras, *Las Necropolis Meroíticas Del Grupo "X" Y Cristianas de Nag -el -Arab*, p. 38. *Comité Español de la U.N.E.S.C.O. para Nubia, Memorias de la Misión Arqueológica*, V (Madrid, 1965).

[4] Unpublished field notes of William Y. Adams, V, pp. 50-52.

[5] George A. Reisner, *Archaeological Survey of Nubia, Report for 1907-1908* (Cairo, 1910), p. 100.

cemetery he mentioned that two bodies had well-preserved leather sandals.

From Cemetery 5 at Shellal he wrote of bodies clothed in shirts reaching to the knees, 115 x 65 cm approximately, with sleeves to the elbows, 60 cm long and open at the armpits. They were further wrapped in coarse white cloth, their heads wrapped separately in the same cloth.[6] A young adult woman was clothed in a shirt with a species of crochet work at the neck, and traces of embroidery.[7] From a vault containing 19 bodies he reported an old man wearing a coat (kuftan), the cloth of which inside was similar to Turkish bath toweling; the coat was fastened with a cloth button and a tape loop. An outer shroud was tied with plaited tapes. An adult woman was dressed in two shirts: one sleeved to the wrist and one to the elbow. An old man was clothed in a toweling shirt with two more undershirts. The outer shirt was sleeved to the wrist, the inner one to the elbow.[8] And finally, Reisner mentioned three children, one wearing boots.[9]

Two monographs written specifically on burial cloths by textile analysts, *Late Nubian Textiles*[10] and *Ancient Textiles from Nubia*,[11] contain detailed analyses of each textile specimen along with excellent photographs. However, most of the graves in these reports date to pre-Christian times; only four graves in *Late Nubian Textiles* and ten in *Ancient Textiles from Nubia* are attributed to the Christian period. Similarly, cemeteries from Gebel Adda[12] yielded a large textile collection, but only eight burials are from the Early Christian period.

Another work, *The Monastery of Epiphanius at Thebes*,[13] reports five well-preserved burials. It contains a very detailed description of the way the bodies were prepared for burial, listing all the steps in the process and all of the different types of textiles used. There are photographs showing the bodies as found, and in five stages of being unwrapped. The technical analysis of the binding tapes, and the discussion about the weaving of the shrouds as well as the tapes is most valuable. Although the monastery is not located in Nubia, the practices used in preparing the body for burial there were very similar to those carried out in Nubia. Finally, there is a short account of an early Christian burial found at Qasr Ibrim in the *Journal of Egyptian Archaeology*.[14] A tunic, one of three shrouds, and two types of binding tapes are briefly described.

General Characteristics of the Textiles

I have deliberately avoided using the term "shroud" when referring to the burial cloths because the word suggests a cloth made specifically for burial. Because of comparative material from other sites, shrouds from the Early Christian period are easily recognizable, and there are few true shrouds from the two Kulubnarti cemeteries. Most of the fabric which enclosed the bodies was of the type of cloth which was in every day use: light blankets, mantles and other items of untailored clothing. These were probably locally-made fabrics from sheep's wool, in the natural colors of brown or creamy white. A good many of the wrappings cannot be recognized as a specific garment or blanket, but merely as a piece of cloth.

Some people, mostly children, were buried in fragments of garments. Others were wrapped in several different kinds of cloth which had been roughly tacked together (Plate 14 E). One person, a 16- year-old woman, was laid to rest in a beautifully made cotton tunic, completely lined, which appears to have been new. This clothing style, as well as the cotton cloth made of z-spun yarns, suggests that this burial comes from a later time than the other excavated graves in 21-R-2. A few bodies were wrapped in what was probably a long-held and cherished piece of imported cloth, often patched and mended, but brightly colored in blue or red (Plates 13A, B). Professionally made funeral shrouds were found in only 28 of the 119 graves at Site 21-R-2, and in only 8 of the 122 graves at Site 21-S-46.

There is some variety in the types of bindings that were tied around the burial cloths (Plates 10A-F). Multiple threads, string, and cord occur in the greatest numbers. Braids, made by interlacing three elements together, are also found. A woven tape, which seems to have been made only for funeral purposes, was used in seven burials. In some cases, the burial cloths were tightly wrapped around the body and then secured by pinning with wooden splinters about 10 cm long (Plate 9 F).

Because of the variable preservation of the wrappings, I have divided them into two groups: recognizable objects, and fabrics. The first group to be discussed will be the textiles which can be recognized as actual objects, that is, garments, mats, or bindings. Among these there are five recognizable types of garments, one type of very unusual woven mat, and five types of bindings from the two cemeteries. The type descriptions are presented below, and the frequencies of these types for each cemetery will then follow. A few words are necessary here to explain some of the terms used in the following paragraphs.

[6] Ibid., p. 104.

[7] Ibid., p. 106.

[8] Ibid.

[9] Ibid, p. 108.

[10] Ingrid Bergman, *Late Nubian Textiles*, pp. 23-25 and pls. 5.1 and 20. *Scandinavian Joint Expedition to Sudanese Nubia Publications*, Vol. 8 (1975).

[11] Christa M. Thurman and Bruce Williams, *Ancient Textiles from Nubia* (Chicago, 1979).

[12] Unpublished field records of the Gebel Adda Expedition. Egyptian Department, Royal Ontario Museum, Toronto.

[13] H. E. Winlock and W. E. Crum, *The Monastery of Epiphanius at Thebes*. The Metropolitan Museum of Art Egyptian Expedition (New York, 1926).

[14] John Alexander and Boyce Driskell in *Journal of Egyptian Archaeology*, vol. 71 (1985), p. 14.

Fiber The material from which the object is made, i.e. wool, cotton, flax, human hair.

Spinning direction The direction of the spun yarn is designated as s or z, depending upon whether the spiral of the thread when held vertically follows the slant of the central portion of one or the other letter. An s spun yarn has the spiral slanting so: \; in z spun yarns the direction of the spiral is thus: /.

Plied Two or more yarns are twisted together, usually in a direction opposite to that of the spin of the original yarns.

Overspun Occurs when the act of spinning continues to the extent that the yarn begins to twist on itself, forming kinks.

Warp The longitudinal, passive yarns of loom-woven fabrics. They are usually under tension.

Weft The transverse, active yarns of loom-woven fabrics. The weft yarns are passed over and under the warp yarns, thus creating the weave.

Weave The structure that is produced by the pattern followed by the weft.

Plain weave The simplest weaving pattern in which the weft goes alternately over one warp, under one warp.

Balanced weave A weave in which the number of warps and wefts per centimeter are the same or nearly so. Both the warp and weft are visible.

Half basket weave A plain weave in which wefts are paired and used as one (Plate 14C).

Basket weave A plain weave in which both warps and wefts are paired and used as one.

Close weave A fabric in which the systems of warp and weft are closely spaced. (Plates 11A,B; Plate 13F).

Open weave A fabric in which the systems of warp and weft are widely spaced. (Plates 13B, C).

Tapestry weave A weave in which the weft does not progress over the full width of the fabric but turns back before reaching the edge. This weave is used to create designs with wefts of different colors. The warp is usually completely covered by the weft.

Weft faced Describes the weave where the wefts greatly outnumber the warps, and the warps are not visible (Plates 9B, 11C, 12E,13A).

Weft predominant A weave in which the wefts outnumber the warps, but do not completely cover the warps. (Plates 11D, 12F,14B).

Warp faced A weave in which the warps greatly outnumber the wefts, and the wefts are not visible (Plate 10F).

Warp predominant A weave in which the warps outnumber the wefts, but do not completely cover the wefts.

Selvedge The two side edges of the woven cloth created by the returning wefts. Most selvedges have between two and five paired warps at each edge. In a reinforced selvedge the weft passes over the warp pairs a second time before traveling to the other side (Plates 9B, 11C, 14B); in a simple selvedge the weft travels directly from one side to the other.

Selvedge pattern Selvedge patterns are small decorative marks embroidered or woven in the technique of tapestry weave. The earliest selvedge patterns in this collection have portions of the pattern within the actual selvedge, or are placed immediately next to it (Figure 9, a and b). Later ones are placed from 1 to 3 cm away from the selvedge and are much more elaborate (Figures 9, c-h; 10, c-e). Two specimens have selvedge patterns alongside both selvedges of the cloth (Figure 10, a and b). The significance of these marks is not known. They are also found at Qasr Ibrim among textiles from X-Group and Christian periods.

Borders The top and bottom edges of woven cloth which have been worked in some way to present a finished edge. Borders are often a cord along the top and bottom edge of the cloth made by twisting the loose warps together (Plates 11C, 12C). Fringe can also be found along one or both edges (Plates 9A, B; 15F). Some borders are extremely simple, consisting merely of closed loops formed when the warp was turned around the end beam (Plate 11D).

Twining A weaving technique in which pairs of twisted yarns run in the weft direction. The threads are often heavier than the surrounding wefts, and sometimes of a different color. In examples where there are two or more rows of twining next to each other, the twined rows are twisted alternately in s and z directions, which creates a chain-like pattern. This is termed countered twining (Plates 9B and 12F).

Typology of garments and textile objects from the

Kulubnarti cemeteries

Garments

Type A   Loincloth. (Plate 9A,B) This garment has the form of a trapezoid with very long sides, which was woven to that shape on the loom, not cut or hemmed. The longer end of the piece was knotted around the waist of the deceased; the shorter end opposite was then brought forward between the thighs, up behind the knot, and folded over in front of it. The area near the shorter end is sometimes decorated with rows of twining and fringe which hang down in front. Loincloths occur in undyed cotton fabric, or wool, either brown, or ivory/ cream - the natural color of "white" sheep's wool.[15]

[15] For an example of a loin cloth see Thurman and Williams, op. cit. (n. 11), p. 142, no. 178. For a technical description of the method used to create the shape see Bergman, op. cit. (n. 5), pp. 23-25, and Figs. 12, 13, and 14. Although Bergman's loin cloths are pre-Christian in date, they were constructed in the same way as the Kulubnarti specimens.

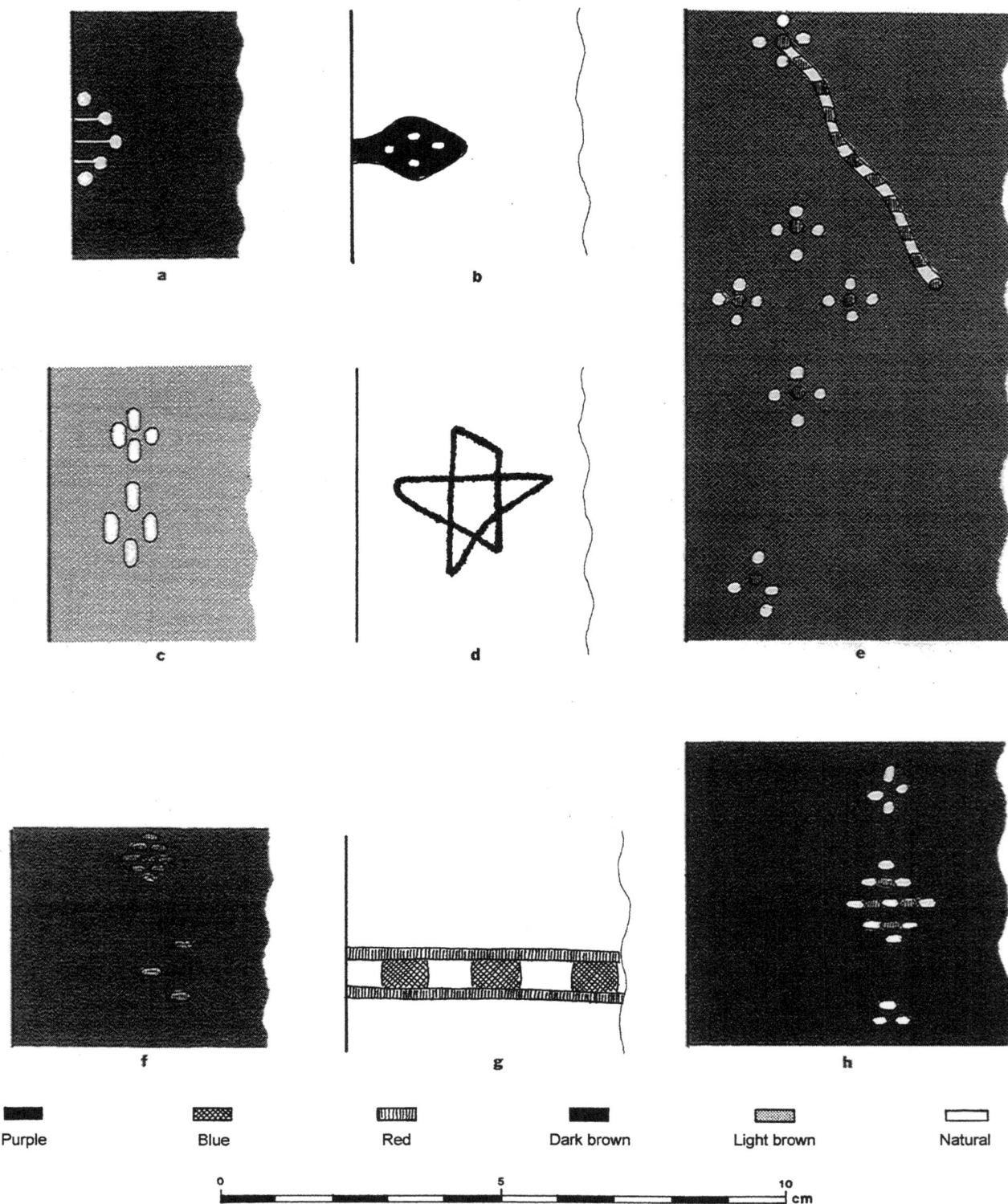

Figure 9. Textile selvedge patterns: single. a. 21-S-46, Grave 191, Cloth 12; tapestry weave in "natural" on dark brown. b. 21-S-46, Grave 188, Cloth 119B; tapestry weave in dark brown and "natural" on "natural". c. 21-R-2, Grave 34, Cloth 237A; tapestry weave in "natural" on light brown. d. 21-R-2, Grave 197, Cloth 211A; embroidered in purple on "natural". e. 21-S-46, Grave 223, Cloth 91; tapestry weave in red and "natural" with tassel on dark brown. f. 21-R-2, Grave 32, Cloth 235A; tapestry weave in red and blue on dark brown. g. 21-S-46, Grave 222, Cloth 163; tapestry weave in red, blue, and "natural" on light brown. h. 21-R-2, Grave 38, Cloth 114A: tapestry weave in red and "natural" on light brown.

54

Type B   Tunic. (Plate 9C-F) This garment evolved from the Roman tunic, and is the ancestor of the present-day *jellabiyah*. It is a flowing gown with long sleeves, a shaped neckline, and side gores. It can be made of wool, cotton, or linen. Often the neck opening was closed with a cloth button and string loop (Plate 9E). Square gussets reinforced the underarm area of the sleeves (Plate 9C).

Type C   Skirt. No specimen is now recognizable as such, but several were designated as skirts by the excavator. All are of wool, fabric types C and D. (See Fabric Type descriptions, below).

Type D   Seamed garment. The garment form cannot be described, but the placement of seams indicates that it was originally a garment of some kind, and not just several pieces of cloth sewn together. All are of wool, fabric types A, B, D, E, F, and G.

Type E   Mantle with selvedge pattern. (Plate 14A, B; Figures 9 and 10) This is usually a rectangular cloth, originally measuring more than one meter in both dimensions. It can be all one color - natural or brown - or it can have bands of alternating colors in the weft, or have stripes in both the warp and weft. The selvedge pattern is embroidered or woven in or near one or both selvedges in one or more colors of wool yarn. The garment is always of wool, and occurs in fabric types A-G.[16]

Mat
Type F   Mat (Plates 15A-F). Made of dark brown, human hair.[17] All three specimens are woven in open plain weave; one of the three has paired wefts throughout. Their dimensions range from 69 cm to 126 cm in width and 106 cm. to 135 cm in length, although the widest specimen has an incomplete length, and was probably somewhat longer than either of the complete mats. There is a certain amount of technical variation to be found among the three specimens. A more complete technical analysis will appear in the descriptions of the untyped fabrics.

Bindings
Type G   Multiple threads. (Plate 10A) They are made of wool, generally dark brown in color, or of cotton, which are always undyed. Each thread is s-spun. The threads are grouped, not twisted or plied together.

Type H   String. (Plate 10B) This is made of two or three s-spun yarns of wool, or rarely cotton, which have been plied in the z direction. Some examples are also made of goat hair and comprise two s-spun, z-plied yarns twisted together in the s direction. Seven specimens have been identified as human hair (Plate 10E, center).[18] String is usually doubled or tripled when used as binding.[19]

Type I   Cord. (Plate 10D) It can be made of multiple threads, twisted together in the z direction, or can be multiple strings, twisted together in the s direction. One specimen has been identified as human hair (Plate 10E, left).[20] Cords are between 3 and 7 mm thick.[21]

Type J   Braid. (Plate 10C). It is made of three interlaced elements. Elements can be goat hair, wool, cotton or flax, or a combination of fibers. Two elements of one specimen have been identified as human hair (Plate 10E, right).[22] Each element may consist of multiple threads, or one or more strings. If more than one kind of fiber is used, the braid has a decorative appearance, with dark and light colors intertwined. One of the three elements comprising the braid in Plate 10E is missing; it was probably a vegetable fiber - either cotton or flax.

Type K   Tape. (Plate 10 F). A woven tape, typically about 1 cm wide, made specifically for burials. The warp is comprised of dark brown wool or goat hair yarns alternating with undyed cotton or flax yarns which provide a pattern of dark and light bands. The weft is single or paired cotton or flax yarns. The weave is completely warp-faced, with no weft showing.[23]

The distribution of the 11 types above named, in each of the two Kulubnarti cemeteries, is shown in Tables 8 and 9.

---

[16] For two possible examples of selvedge patterns see Thurman and Williams, op. cit.. (n. 11), p. 125, no. 143, C; and p. 145, no. 184. For the latter the authors mention "traces of inlaid decoration in purple visible in two spots". This could be a description of two very deteriorated selvedge patterns. Bergman op. cit.. (n. 10) has an excellent color photograph of a selvedge pattern, no. 25/68:1 in Pl. 71:l, right. A discussion of selvedge patterns is found on p. 48 under Bergman's Tapestry Figure B1A, p. 51. Other photographs showing this pattern, but not as clearly as the color photo are Pls 49:1; 64:1, 2, and 3; and 65:2.

[17] A fiber sample from one of our three specimens has been identified as human hair by the McCrone Research Institute, Chicago, Illinois.

[18] Two samples were identified as human hair by H. M. Appleyard, F.T.I., of the Wool Industries Research Association, Leeds, Yorkshire, and five additional samples of string were identified as human hair by the McCrone Institute (op. cit., n. 17).

[19] For examples of string see Bergman, op. cit. (n. 10), p. 74, no. 25/290:6, last entry; p. 78, no. 141/12:1; and Pl. 19:2.

[20] Identified by the McCrone Institute (op. cit., n. 17).

[21] For examples of cord see Bergman, op. cit. (no. 10), p. 53, no. 19/l:22, last entry; p. 63, no. 25/104:2, last entry; p. 69-70, no. 25/196:1, last entry; p. 71, no. 25/213:2; p. 76-77, no. 63/2:16 and 63/3:1; and p. 78, no. 141/12:2; Pl. 19:1. Bergman terms them string, but they are like cords. For a mention only see Gebel Adda op cit. (n. 12), Cemetery II - 353, no. 29B.

[22] Identified by the McCrone Institute (op. cit., n. 17).

[23] For examples of tape see Thurman and Williams, op. cit. (n. 11) p. 144, 1b; see also Bergman, op. cit. (n. 10), p. 23; p. 76, no. 63/1G:1; and Pl. 18:2. What Bergman calls bands are similar to our tapes. Winlock and Crum op. cit. (n. 8), p. 49, describe how tapes were used to bind the body; see also their figure 10 and Pl. XI, C. For a description of the weaving technique and a very clear diagram see their p. 71. For a close-up photograph of a tape see also Pl. XXII, C. For a mention only see Gebel Adda, op. cit. (n. 12), Cemetery II - 370, no. 30B.

Fabric Types

As has been discussed earlier, many of the textile specimens cannot be identified as garments or specific objects. Since these specimens can only be described in terms of their fabric, I have devised a typology of the fabrics found in the two Kulubnarti cemeteries. The typology includes both fabrics from identifiable objects, and fragments whose original form is uncertain.

The graves which were excavated in the two cemeteries seem to be almost entirely of Early Christian date, and the fabric types found in them bear out this supposition. The corpus of textiles from the Early Christian period in Nubia is known from previous excavations at Qasr Ibrim, and exhibits the following distinctive characteristics:

1. A high percentage of woollen fabrics.
2. A much lower percentage of cotton .
3. Even lower percentage of flax.
4. Absence of silk.
5. All spinning in the s direction.
6. Nearly all weave is plain weave.
7. Selvedge marks - small areas of woven or embroidered decoration near the selvedge
8. Rare occurrence of dyed color.

Since we are dealing with comparable material from both Kulubnarti cemeteries, I shall describe the various textile types first, and then indicate their frequencies for each cemetery in tabular form. Unless otherwise specified, all spinning is in the s direction, and all weave is plain.

Typology of fabric types from the Kulubnarti

Cemeteries

Wool

Type A   (Plates 11A,B) One color dark brown, yarn thickness varies from fine to coarse and is often overspun in places. Weave is usually balanced, and may vary from close to somewhat open; however, it can also be weft-predominant or weft-faced.[24] This fabric type is found in Nubia over a very long time. It appears during the X-Group period ca. 350 A.D., and it continues throughout the entire Christian period, and into Islamic times, only disappearing in the early 19th century.

Type B   (Plate 11C) One color "natural," varying from ivory to light tan; the term "natural" is used to indicate the natural color of "white" sheep's wool which has not been dyed. Yarn thickness varies from medium to coarse and is never overspun; weave varies between balanced to weft-predominant to weft-faced, and is usually close. Two examples have paired wefts occurring in small areas of the fabric.[25]

Type C   (Plates 11D-F) Varying shades of brown, used either in random or in organized arrangements. Yarn thickness varies from fine to medium and is rarely overspun; weave is usually balanced, but can be weft-predominant or weft-faced, and varies from open to medium to close. Eight specimens have occasional paired wefts occurring in small areas of the fabric. A few specimens have a small number of dyed wefts, mostly red, occurring in the fabric.[26]

Type D   (Plate 12A) Warp: may be any one of a number of brown shades; weft may be one or more shades of brown together with natural color arranged in alternating bands of varying widths. Warp yarn thickness varies from coarse to medium; weft yarn thickness varies from fine to medium and is never overspun. The number of weft yarns per centimeter outnumbers the number of warp yarns per centimeter; the weave is usually weft-faced, but can be weft-predominant. Occasionally, up to six weft yarns, usually dyed red or blue, may be found woven in near the top or bottom edges. Six specimens have occasional paired wefts occurring in small areas of the fabric.[27]

Type E   (Plates 12B, C) Same as Type D except that the warp is entirely of natural color, and warp yarn thickness, as well as the weft, varies from fine to medium.[28] One specimen has a small band of vertical bar patterning, sometimes called "picket fence", which is produced by alternating single light and dark wefts within the area of the patterned band.[29]

Type F   (Plates 12D-F) Warp: any one of several colors - mostly natural, tan, or light brown; rarely dark brown, blue, or turquoise. Weft is the same as the warp color, plus natural, plus one or more dyed colors: blue, green, red, and/or purple, in alternating bands of varying widths. Yarn thickness varies from fine to medium and is never overspun; the number of weft yarns is greater than the number of warp yarns per centimeter. The weave is usually weft-faced, but can be weft-predominant. Two examples

---

[24] There are many examples of fabric Type A. From Thurman and Williams op. cit. (n. 11) see p. 76, no. 44; p. 79, no. 50; p. 100, no. 87; p. 107, nos 103 and 104; p. 112, no. 113; p. 119, no. 128; p. 121, nos. 133 and 134; p. 124, no. 141. See also William Y. Adams and Nettie K. Adams, *Kulubnarti II: The Artifactual Remains* , Plate 9.2C. Sudan Archaeological Research Society, Publication Number 2 (London: 1998).

[25] For examples of fabric Type B see Thurman and Williams, op. cit. (n. 11), p. 94, no. 76; and p. 142, no. 178.

[26] For examples of fabric Type C see Thurman and Williams, op cit. (n. 11) p. 58, no. 4; p. 82, no. 55; p. 94, no. 77; p. 103, no. 95; p. 124, no. 140; p. 140, no. 174; p.147, no. 186.

[27] For an example of fabric Type D see Thurman and Williams, op. cit. (n. 11), p. 81, no. 53. Also Gebel Adda, op. cit. (n. 12), Cemetery II - 497, no. 31.

[28] For an example of fabric Type E see unpublished notes from Gebel Adda Cemetery II - 547, no. 32.

[29] For an example of "picket fence" patterning see Adams and Adams, op. cit. (n. 24), Pl. 9.3c.

TABLE 8
TEXTILES OBJECTS FROM CEMETERY 21-S-46

Grave no.	Garments					Mat		Bindings			
	A	B	C	D	E	F	G	H	I	J	K
1	x							x	x		
2								**x**			
14								x			
16	**x**							**x**			
21									x		
22								**x**			
23	x							x			
25	**x**										
26								x			
28										**x**	
29								x			
33									**x**		
37							x				
40								**x**			
44								x			
45								**x**	**x**		
47								x			
48		**x**						**x**			
49							x				x
52								**x**			
53							x		x		
55											**x**
58								x			
66									**x**		
67								x			
73								**x**			
76								x			
78		**x**						**x**			
80	x										
83								**x**			
86								x			
88								**x**			
90							x				
91				**x**							
93				x							
98								**x**			
99	x										
113				**x**				**x**	**x**		
124								x			
130								**x**			
131a							x				
132				**x**							
145				x				x			
149								**x**			
168								x			
169	**x**										
172						x	x				
188					**x**						
191					x						
193							**x**				
195							x				
198								**x**			
200	x										x
207	**x**										

TABLE 8
TEXTILES OBJECTS FROM CEMETERY 21-S-46 (cont.)

Grave no.	Garments					Mat	Bindings				
	A	B	C	D	E	F	G	H	I	J	K
208								x			
212								**x**			
217							x				
222				x							
223				x							
224			x						**x**		
225	x										x
235							**x**				

have occasional paired wefts occurring in small areas of the fabric.[30] One blue specimen has a row of countered twining bordering a narrow red band (Plate 12F). Like Fabric Type A, this type persists in Nubia for a very long time, and is found throughout the Christian period.

Type G   (Plate 13A) One dyed color only, usually red or blue. Yarn thickness varies from fine to medium and is never overspun; the number of weft yarns per centimeter greatly outnumbers the number of warp yarns per centimeter. The weave is usually weft-faced, but can be weft-predominant.[31]

Type H   (Plate 13B) One dyed color only, usually dyed red or blue. Yarn is very fine in both warp and weft; weave is balanced and very open.

Cotton
Type I   (Plate 13C) Shroud. It is made of undyed yarns which vary in thickness from fine to medium. The weave is balanced and is very open, having a net-like appearance; spaces between the yarns vary between 4-7 mm. The purpose of these shrouds appears to have been primarily symbolic, as the open weave would not have protected the body from the earth. Consequently they are usually found in combination with more tightly woven fabrics, on the same body. In the single occurrence of a shroud of this type at Qasr Ibrim, it was the outermost of three shrouds, the other two being closely-woven linen shrouds.

Type J   (Plate 13D) Undyed cloth. Yarn thickness is medium, never overspun; weave varies between balanced, weft-predominant, and weft-faced.[32]

---

[30] For examples of fabric Type F see Thurman and Williams, op. cit. (n. 11) p. 80, no. 52; p. 85, nos. 62 and 63; p. 105, no. 100 A and C; p. 106, no. 101; p. 119, no. 127; p. 125, no 143; p. 129, no. 151; p. 130, nos. 153 and 154; p. 133, no. 159; p. 134, no. 161; p. 141, no. 176; p. 145, no. 183; p. 147, no. 187. Also Adams and Adams, op. cit. (n. 24) Plate 9.3B.

[31] For an example of fabric Type G see Thurman and Williams, op. cit. (n. 11), p. 92, no. 73.

[32] For an example of fabric Type J see Thurman and Williams, op cit. (n. 11), p. 140, no. 175. Also Gebel Adda, op cit. (n. 12), Cemetery II - 97, no. 27; II - 353, no. 29; II - 370, no. 30.

Flax
Type K   (Plate 13E) Shroud. It is made of undyed yarns of medium thickness generally; weave is balanced and close. The fabric has sometimes had a waxy substance applied and then has been pressed, which gives it a very characteristic and distinctive appearance.[33]

Type L   (Plate 13F) Undyed cloth. Yarn thickness varies from fine to medium, and is often uneven; weave is balanced and varies from close to somewhat open.

Untyped
Type M   Fabrics of goat hair, sheep's wool, or human hair, cotton, or flax which do not fall into any of the above categories. Each will be described individually. Grave numbers with untyped fabrics are marked with an asterisk.*

Descriptions of untyped fabrics from Cemetery 21-S-46

Grave 45   Cloth no. 154B (see Tables 10 and 11) Cotton and wool. All yarns are s-spun; weave is weft-faced plain and half-basket. Warp: s-spun undyed cotton; weft: s-spun undyed cotton used in pairs; also medium brown wool used singly and dark brown wool used in pairs; weft colors arranged in bold bands ranging from 1.5-6 cm wide extending the width of the fabric. This style, with a cotton warp and cotton and wool weft, is usually found in the later medieval period around A.D. 1200.

Grave 81   Cloth no. 73D. Wool. All yarns are s-spun; weave is weft-faced plain weave. Warp: s-spun brown and natural wool yarns; weft: s-spun dark brown wool yarns. Warp yarns alternate two brown, two natural, used singly the extant width of the specimen. Weft completely covers the warp.

Grave 122   Cloth no. 219B. Wool. This specimen is basically fabric type D, weft faced. It is fragmentary, so the

[33] For a possible example of fabric Type K see Thurman and Williams, op. cit. (n. 11), p. 144, no. 182, 1A. The description of the weave and thread count is like that for Type K, but does not include the waxy surface and pressed appearance. However, since the body was tied with a woven binding tape, which was only used for burials, it seems probable that this fabric was in fact a linen shroud.

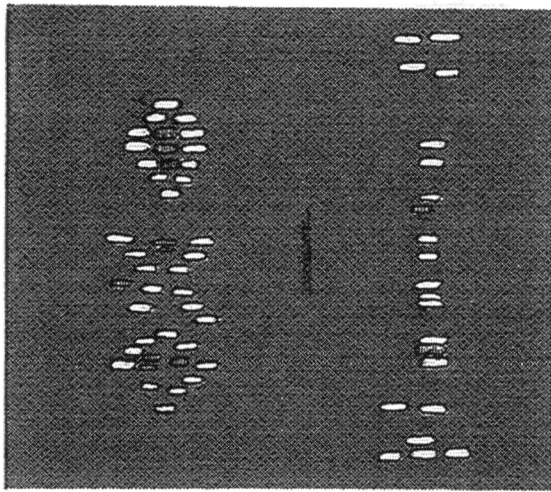

a

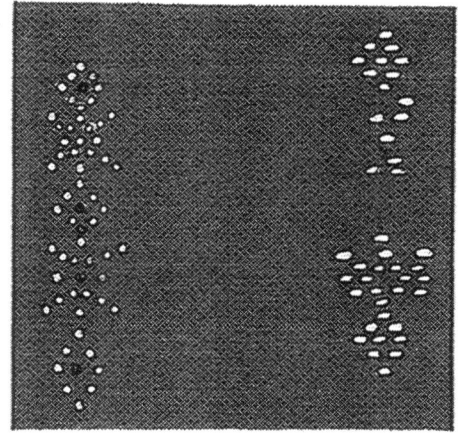

b

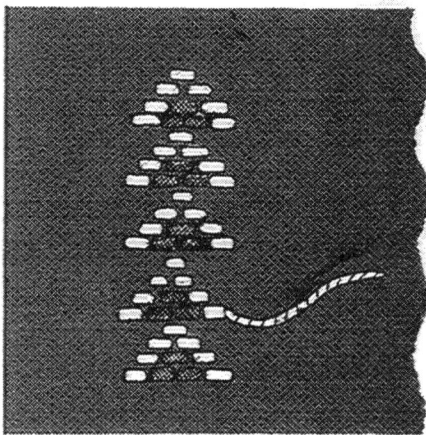

c

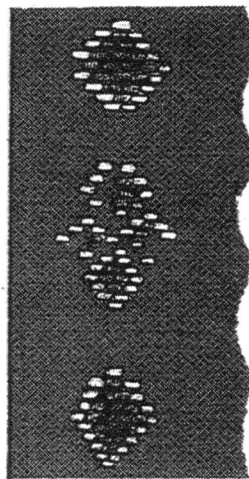

d

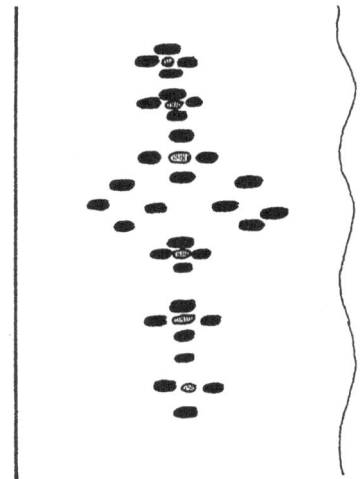

e

| Purple | Blue | Red | Dark brown | Natural |

0   5   10
cm

Figure 10. Textile selvedge patterns: double. a. 21-R-2, Grave 141, Cloth 162A; Left: tapestry weave in red and natural on dark brown; Right: embroidery in "natural" red, and blue on dark brown. b. 21-R-2, Grave 90, Cloth 199; Left: embroidery in "natural" on dark brown; Right: tapestry weave in "natural" on dark brown. Textile selvedge patterns: single. c. 21-R-2, Grave 20, Cloth 238B; embroidery in "natural" and blue with tassel on dark brown. d. 21-R-2, Grave 139, Cloth 143A; tapestry weave in red, blue and "natural" on dark brown. e. 21-R-2, Grave 118, Cloth 221B; tapestry weave in purple and red on "natural" ground.

59

TABLE 9
TEXTILE OBJECTS FROM CEMETERY 21-R-2

Grave No.	Clothing					Mat	Bindings				
	A	B	C	D	E	F	G	H	I	J	K
2								x			
5								x			
6					x						x	
13											x	
14	x										x	
16								x			
18								x			
20	x				x						
25										x		
30		x									x	
31	x							x			
32					x			x			
34					x			x			
36								x			
37								x			
38					x						
40								x		x	
41								x			
42								x			
43								x			
45	x										
55										x	
59	x										
64								x			
66									x		
68								x			
69								x			
70						x					
75											x
76		x									
80								x			
85	x										
86								x			
88	x										
89								x			
90					x						
91								x			
92									x		
102	x										
108	x						x				
112			x								
114								x			
118					x						x	
129			x								
132							x				
136			x								
139					x			x			
141					x					x	
143								x			
145	x										
151							x				
153								x			
160				x							
161			x								

60

TABLE 9
TEXTILE OBJECTS FROM CEMETERY 21-R-2 (cont.)

Grave No.	Clothing					Mat	Bindings				
	A	B	C	D	E	F	G	H	I	J	K
162		x					x				
164							x				
165								x			
168						x					
169	x						x				
174							x				
183	x										
188	x										
192		x					x				
196									x		
197					x						x
205							x				

overall pattern of the brown and natural bands is not apparent. It has a single occurrence of a tapestry join, one of only two examples of tapestry weave in the collection. A narrow brown band (5 mm) is bordered on both sides by natural bands. The brown band narrows to a point, the brown wefts turning back, and a natural band meets the brown in tapestry joins.

Grave 128   Cloth no. 72. Wool. Warp: dark brown and natural; weft: dark brown and natural; weft faced. Some wefts in both colors are paired. The natural yarns are very deteriorated, as if they had been treated with a form of bleach.

Grave 172   Cloth no. 1 (Plates 15E,F). Complete mat made of human hair. Length: 106 cm; Width: 69 cm. Hair twisted in the s direction, six yarns per cm in warp; seven per cm in weft. Weave is balanced, open and plain. There are fringes at both borders. At the starting border pairs of closed loops, 3 cm long, are z-plied and tied in knots at the edge of the weave; at the ending border groups of eight warps are z-plied and knotted at the end forming a fringe 5 cm long. Both selvedges are the reinforced type.

Descriptions of Untyped Fabrics from Cemetery 21-R-2

Grave 5   Cloth no. 240A. Wool. This fabric is basically type D. Several features set it apart from others of this type. The first is that there is a band of three pairs of blue wefts 5 mm wide in addition to the brown and natural bands. More unusual is the spinning of some of the wefts. Some of the dark brown and some natural bands have yarn which is s-spun, and then s-plied. This is rarely found in spinning, the more common combination being s-spun and z-plied. One of the natural bands has unplied, but paired wefts. All warps are unplied. The selvedge is reinforced; the ending border is a cord.

Grave 22   Cloth no. 244D. Wool. This fabric is basket weave, the only example in this collection. The light brown warp pairs are very fine, and widely spaced: four pairs per cm. The coarser natural weft pairs are more closely spaced:

seven per cm. All spinning is s; no other features are present on this tiny specimen.

Grave 26   Cloth no. 106B. Very coarse bast fiber, s-spun in both systems, balanced, fairly close plain weave, 5-6 warps per cm; 5-6 wefts per cm. Has been dyed or painted red. The fiber has not been identified but may be a coarse flax.

Grave 30   Cloth no. 239A. Wool. Warp: natural. Weft: natural with red bands. Weft-faced. This may have been part of a tunic. One narrow (5 mm) red band is bordered on both sides by a row of countered twining in natural yarns. There are two other wider red bands 5.4 cm wide. A hemmed corner is sewn with s-spun z-ply natural wool thread. Very fragmentary.

Grave 53   Cloth no. 185. Wool. This specimen is basically fabric type C, with a dark brown warp and irregular bands in dark brown, gray-brown and light red-brown. The light brown bands have paired wefts. There is a reinforced selvedge. Very fragmentary.

Grave 60   Cloth no. 217. This specimen was taken in division and is now in the Khartoum National Museum. From the black and white photograph it appears to be wool, with isolated motifs woven in tapestry weave. The ground is a color of medium intensity. The tapestry-woven motifs are of two types: one is a light color outlined in a dark color, and the reverse, a darker hue outlined in a light color. The pattern possibly represents a flowering lotus bud.[34]

Grave 69   Cloth no. 145B. A piece of tentcloth or bag, 42 x 29 cm incomplete, made from z-ply goat hair. It is warp-predominant, with a dark brown, almost black ground. One stripe, 3.5 cm. wide, is made of mixed brown and natural hairs. It is bordered on each side by four warps of the ground color, then by two warps of natural, making a very narrow

---

[34] For a complete example see Bergman, op. cit. (n. 10) front cover; Fig. 52, tapestry figure Type A1C; and Pl. 73.

TABLE 10
DISTRIBUTION OF FABRIC TYPES FROM CEMETERY 21-S-46

Grave no.	Wool								Cotton		Flax		Untyped
	A	B	C	D	E	F	G	H	I	J	K	L	M
1										x			
2				x									
13				x									
14				x				x					
15	x		x										
16	x	xx											
17									x				
18												x	
20	x												
21	fabric impression in soil only												
22		x		x									
23	x	xx				x							
24		x											
25	x												
26		x											
27										x			
28	x	x											
29		x	x									x	
33		xx	x	x									
34	xx			x									
35		x	x	x									
36	x					x							
37				x	x								
40	only the binding preserved												
42a										x			
42b				x									
43c	x												
44	x												
*45		x											x
47												x	
48										x			
49										x			
51			x										
52					x								
53												x	
55									x	x	x	x	
57				x									
58	x												
63	x		x										
65	x												
66				x									
67	only the binding preserved												
68b	x	x											
69		x											
70	x												
71				x									
73	x					x							
76	only the binding preserved												
78		x											
80	x												
*81		xx		x		x							x
82			x										
83	xxx	x		x									
85						x							

TABLE 10
DISTRIBUTION OF FABRIC TYPES FROM CEMETERY 21-S-46 (cont.)

Grave no.	Wool								Cotton		Flax		Untyped
	A	B	C	D	E	F	G	H	I	J	K	L	M
86	xx												
88						x							
89						x							
90		x											
91		x											
93		x											
94a		x											
95	x		xx										
96						x							
98										x			
99	xx												
101		xx	x										
104				x	x								
105	x												
107			x										
113	x					x	x				x		
114			x										
115		x				x							
116	x	xx		x									
119		x											
120	only the binding preserved												
*122	x		x										x
124				x									
*128													x
130				x									
131a	only the binding preserved												
132		x				x							
134	x												
135				x									
136												x	
137			x										
138						x							
144			x										
145		x											
149	x												
159						x							
163				x									
168									x				
169		xx											
*172													x
177										x			
178		x		x									
188					x				x				
191	x												
192		x											
193	x												
194	x												
195			x	x		x							
196				x		x							
198				x									
200		xx											
202			x						x				
204				x									
205	x												

TABLE 10
DISTRIBUTION OF FABRIC TYPES FROM CEMETERY 21-S-46 (cont.)

Grave no.	Wool								Cotton		Flax		Untyped
	A	B	C	D	E	F	G	H	I	J	K	L	M
207			x										
208										x			
211						x							
212	only the binding preserved												
217		xx				x							
221			x										
222						x							
223			x										
224	x	x				x							
225		x							x				
226		x				x							
228			x										
234			x			x							
235			x										
241	x												

white line. The selvedge is simple, with no paired warps. This was sewn to a piece of fabric type C.

Grave 70   Cloth no. 225C (Plates 15C,D). Mat made of dark brown human hair. Complete dimensions: L 135 cm x W 77 cm. Warp is s-spun, four per cm. Weft is s-spun, used in pairs throughout, five pairs per cm. Weave is half-basket, fairly open. One selvedge is reinforced, with two paired warps. The other selvedge is plain with two paired warps. Both edges are finished with warp cords, s-twisted. There is a coarse darn located near the center of the piece. It measures *c*. 13 x 10 cm and is made of mixed light and dark fibers. Their identification is uncertain - they may be human or goat.

Grave 80   Cloth no. 188A (Plate 14D). Coarse linen cloth with unusual spinning. The yarns are s-spun, s-plied. This spinning style is common in linen fabric dating to the Egyptian dynastic periods, and is also found in Ptolemaic and Roman times on Nubian sites. This specimen was probably produced the same way the earlier yarns were: by rolling the flax fibers along the thigh to produce a twist, and splicing in additional fibers, thus producing the plied areas.

Grave 102   Cloth no. 169B. Wool. This is basically fabric type B, with some additions. The specimen is much patched and very fragmentary. In one area there are three rows of countered weft twining in z-spun yarn, each row separated by 2.3 cm of ground weave. Row one employs purple and natural yarns, which results in a chevron pattern, alternately purple and white. The next twined row is in natural yarns only. The third row appears to have some purple yarns present, but it is difficult to be sure. In another area there are two z-spun natural yarns run in parallel, over three, under three. A hem is sewn with z-spun blue wool thread; a z-

spun peach-colored wool thread has been crudely stitched along the very edge of the hem as a decoration.

Grave 118   Cloth no. 221C. Wool. This is very like fabric type B except that one incomplete band, 5.5 cm wide, has a half-basket weave with two wefts used as one. It is very nearly weft face. Adjoining the band of half-basket weave is an incomplete band, *c*. 5 cm wide, of single wefts. This small fragment may be part of fabric type F from the same grave (Cloth no. 221B). Cloth 221B has a natural warp, with a weft of natural and purple in weft-faced bands. On the part of this specimen that remains, there is no half-basket weave present, but it is technically possible that 221B and 221C could be from the same cloth.

Grave 167   Cloth no. 133A (Plate 14C). Cotton. This is essentially fabric type J, except that the weave is half-basket with two wefts used as one, and in some places three wefts are used as one. The warp is tightly spun and in places is overspun. The weft is coarser and more loosely spun. This small fragment is composed of two pieces sewn together with a simple basting stitch of s-spun, z-ply "natural" wool thread.

Grave 168   Cloth no. 190 (Plates 15A,B). Mat made of brown human hair. Incomplete length: 86 cm. Complete width: 126 cm. Warp is s-spun, four per cm. Weft is s-spun, 10 per cm. Weave is plain weave, weft predominant. Both simple selvedges have two paired warps each. One edge has knotted fringe made of warp ends 4 cm long. Very faint bands of somewhat lighter and slightly redder wefts occur irregularly.

Grave 192   Cloth nos. 201A , B. Both cotton. This is a very finely-made tunic, completely lined. The outer layer of the garment (201A) is made from very fine undyed z-spun

64

TABLE 11

DISTRIBUTION OF FABRIC TYPES FROM CEMETERY 21-R-2

Grave No.	Wool								Cotton		Linen		Untyped
	A	B	C	D	E	F	G	H	I	J	K	L	M
2	only the binding preserved												
4				x									
*5													x
6				x			x						
7		x		x									
12	x												
13		x						x					
14	xx												
15		x	x										
16	only the binding preserved												
17							x						
18			x										
19	x			x					x				
20		x				x							
*22		x	x										x
25	x												
*26				x									x
29						x							
*30													x
31		xx				x							
32				x									
33		x						x					
34		xx	x				x						
35			x										
36											x		
37				x									
38						x							
40			x										
41		x		x									
42									x				
43										x	x		
45										x	x		
49		x		x			x						
*53													x
55						x	x						
56								x					
57a	x			x									
59	x								x				
*60	textile specimen taken in division												x
63		x											
64					x				x				
65					x	x							
66			x										
67						xx							
68											x		
*69			x										x
*70		x		x									x
73									x	x			
75	x								x				
76		x											
*80									x				x
83				x									
84		x											
85				x	x				x				

TABLE 11
DISTRIBUTION OF FABRIC TYPES FROM CEMETERY 21-R-2 (cont.)

Grave No.	Wool								Cotton		Linen		Untyped
---	A	B	C	D	E	F	G	H	I	J	K	L	M
86					xx								
87		x											
88		x							x	x			
89				x		x							
90				x	x								
91		x											
92			xx										
94											x		
95									x	x			
98				x									
99		xx		x	x								
100				x									
101				x									
***102**													x
103				x									
104				x									
106					x								
107			x										
108		x											
109	x												
110						x							
111									x				
112			x										
114	x								x	x			
117			x										
***118**			x			x							x
119			x						x				
122				x					x				
124		x				x							
127												x	
128	x												
129				x									
131	x		x										
132									x				
135					x								
137	x												
138									x				
139				x									
141						x							
142				x								x	
143				x									
144		x											
145		x											
146												x	
147									x				
150			x	x				x					
151									x				
152									x				
153		x											
158		x											
160				x	xx				x				
161				x									
162												x	

TABLE 11
DISTRIBUTION OF FABRIC TYPES FROM CEMETERY 21-R-2 (cont.)

Grave No.	Wool								Cotton		Linen		Untyped
	A	B	C	D	E	F	G	H	I	J	K	L	M
164				x									
165	only the binding preserved												
166		x		x									
*167					x								x
*168													x
169		x											
170									x				
174				x									
183		x											
188		x											
*192													xx
195												x	
196	x										x		
197		x											
205		x							x	x			

yarns: warp: 21 per cm; weft 24 per cm. The spinning and weaving are very even and professional looking. The garment is completely lined with 201B, a coarser fabric: warp and weft both 11 per cm. The sewing is very fine and was clearly done by a professional. In its very fragmentary condition the style is impossible to reconstruct. Fabric of this type was not available in Nubia until about A.D. 1200, so this grave is quite a lot later than the others which were excavated in this cemetery.

Conclusions from the Textiles

Apart from the objects of human hair, the collection fits well into the corpus of Nubian textiles from the Early Christian Period. To review these characteristics, they are:

1. A high percentage of woollen fabrics.
2. A much lower percentage of cotton.
3. An even lower percentage of flax.
4. Absence of silk.
5. All spinning in the s direction.
6. Nearly all weave in plain weave.
7. The presence of selvedge marks - small areas of woven or embroidered decoration near the selvedge.
8. Rare occurrence of dyed color.

Fiber frequencies. Leaving out the bindings, there were 184 woven specimens from Cemetery 21-S-46 and 183 from Cemetery 21-R-2. To address the first four characteristics of the above list, the frequencies of the various fibers of the woven textiles from the two cemeteries have been put in tabular form in Table 12. [35]

[35] Percentages have been rounded.

TABLE 12
FIBER FREQUENCIES AT CEMETERIES 21-S-46 AND 21-R-2

	21-S-46	21-R-2
Wool	86%	74%
Cotton	8%	17%
Flax	4%	6%
Silk		
Human hair	Trace	1%
Goat hair		Trace
Unidentified		Trace

From these figures it is evident that the frequency relationships among the woven cloths from the two cemeteries follow the general pattern of textiles of the Early Christian period. However, the presence of human hair which was used for bindings and for the three mats is unique in my experience. In analyzing hundreds of textile fragments of the Early Christian period from the town site of Qasr Ibrim I have never seen human hair made into any sort of object. At this writing I have not found any comparative material. The obvious conclusion is that human hair was used only in a mortuary context. However, the darn in Cloth number 225C calls that conclusion into question.

It is not hard to imagine that human hair bindings could be readily and quickly made, given the expertise in spinning that nearly all people had. Perhaps family members made the bindings of their own hair as an act of mourning. But the three mats, which contain nothing but human hair, could not have been quickly made. The hair had to be twisted into yarn, some of that yarn used for the warp which was set up on a loom, then the weaving of the mat, and the knotting of the fringe. One of the specimens has faint bands of very slightly lighter and redder hair alternating with slightly darker bands. This type of decorative weaving takes time and planning. Until more can be learned about the use of human hair in a mortuary setting the examples from the Kulubnarti cemeteries will stand as a unique funerary practice.

The next characteristic is the spinning direction of yarns. All yarns used in the woven fabrics from the two cemeteries are spun in the s direction with the exception of Cloth numbers 201a and b from Grave 192 in Cemetery 21-R-2. This grave was some distance from the other excavated graves of that cemetery, and the style of the cotton fabric shows clearly that it is from a much later period, and does not belong in the corpus of Early Christian textiles.

Turning to the weave types, only one fabric was not plain weave. This was Cloth number 217 from Grave 60 in Cemetery 21-R-2. The woven patterns of this cloth were done with tapestry weave, a technique which is found in the Early Christian period, but was much more common during earlier (Meroitic and X-Group) and later (Classic Christian) periods. It was clearly a valued piece of imported material. Cloth 219B of Grave 122 from cemetery 21-S-46 has a narrow band 1 cm wide in which natural yarns meet dark brown yarns in tapestry joins. The specimen is otherwise all of plain weave. Tapestry weave was used to produce 11 of the selvedge patterns, but they are basically just tiny dots of color laid into the plain weave of the mantle.

Selvedge marks occur on four fabrics from 21-S-46, and on nine from 21-R-2. The significance of these small marks is not known. They are seen on textiles from the Late X-Group period, and they continue in more elaborated forms into Classic Christian times.

The use of dyed color is very sparing in this collection. Of the fabrics made entirely of dyed yarns, types G and H, there are only two from 21-S-46. From 21-R-2 there are nine. Fabric type F contains some dyed yarns, usually in bands alternating with one or more shades of brown, tan or "natural". Cemetery 21-S-46 had 21 of type F; there were 13 from 21-R-2. Fabric type C has shades of brown used in organized or in random arrangements; some examples, but not all, have a few dyed wefts, often near the end or the beginning of the weaving. There are usually no more than six, so the effect is that of a very narrow colored line. From 21-S-46 there are 20 specimens of type C; there are 18 from 21-R-2. Not all of these specimens of type C contained the colored wefts.

Family Grave Plots? One piece of information which the textiles might provide is a clue to the presence of family plots in the cemeteries. None of the graves was marked with the name of the deceased, so family plots, if there were such, would have to be identified by some other means. In looking at the distribution tables of the fabric types and checking the cemetery maps, patterns emerge from both cemeteries which might point to the existence of family grave plots.

From 21-S-46 there are four groups of contiguous graves in which the deceased was buried in the same fabric type. They are: graves 22, 23, 24; graves 68b and 69; graves 90 and 91; and graves 115 and 116. All of these contained fabric type B, the cloth made of wool from "white" sheep. From 21-R-2 there are four groups of contiguous graves. In the first, the bodies were wrapped in fabric type C: they are graves 33, 34, 35. The next two groups contain fabric type E: graves 64 and 65, and graves 85 and 86. The final group contains fabric type B: the graves are 87 and 88.

The graves in each group were contiguous and appeared on the map to be no more than two meters apart. Whether these patterns reflect the presence of actual family grave plots can never be proved by the textiles. But they do provide a clue which might be followed up by physical anthropologists making skeletal and dental comparisons or even perhaps DNA analyses.

Comparisons Between the Two Cemeteries. Numerical comparisons between the collections of the two cemeteries are perhaps not totally valid because of differential preservation of the organic remains, and the fragmentary and disarticulated condition of the collected textiles. However, some observations can be made and should be taken for what they are worth. Table 12 sets forth the percentage frequencies for the *fibers* of the two cemeteries. A comparison of the *fabric* type frequencies is presented in Table 13, below.

TABLE 13
FABRIC TYPE FREQUENCIES AT CEMETERIES 21-S-46 AND 21-R-2

Categories	Fabric types	21-S-46		21-R-2	
		No.	%	No.	%
Undyed wools	A,B,C,D,E	131	71.1	108	59.0
Dyed wools	F,G,H	25	13.5	21	11.4
Cottons	I,J	15	8.1	29	15.8
Linens	K,L	8	4.3	11	6.0
Shrouds	I,K	8	4.3	28	15.3
Untyped	M	5	2.7	14	7.6

Some Assumptions. Before numerical comparisons can be meaningfully interpreted, certain assumptions should be stated. The first is that wool fabrics, because of their much greater frequency, were much less costly than cotton and linen cloth. We know that flax was not grown in Nubia until much later in the Christian period, if at all, and although cotton was the dominant fiber in earlier times, it had become very scarce by the Early Christian period. Importation to such an isolated area as the *Batn el Hajjar*, far from main trade routes, would have made cotton and linen fabrics more expensive than wool.

The next assumption is that the undyed woollens, fabric types A, B, C, D, and E were the basic textiles of Nubia. They were made from the wool of brown sheep, so numerous in the Nile Valley, and from "white" sheep, a less common breed. All of these fabric types were probably made at Kulubnarti, and were the bulk of the textiles to be found in the village.

A final assumption is that dyed fabrics were more precious than undyed. As cloth is easily transported, it is probable that dyed yarns or complete dyed cloths were imported, with the same added value that attached to cotton and linen fabrics. It is unlikely that dyeing was done at Kulubnarti, for this is a very specialized craft, requiring knowledge, materials, and equipment not readily available in this small farming community.

The textile remains from the two cemeteries are very similar; for the most part, the bodies were interred in cloths which were part of their lives. In some cases, new fabrics were used for the dead. In other burials, fragments of several cloths were put together to make one wrapping by stitching or by pinning the pieces together with wooden splinters. In rare instances, a brightly colored or patterned fabric, cherished and strongly associated with its owner, went with that person to the grave.

The frequency tables however, do reveal subtle differences between the two cemeteries. Table 12 shows that cemetery 21-S-46 has 12% more fabrics of wool than cemetery 21-R-2; the latter cemetery almost makes up for that difference with higher percentages of both flax and cotton. That factor seems to suggest that 21-R-2 had a higher percentage of somewhat more prosperous people than did 21-S-46.

Turning to Table 13, we see a greater frequency of undyed wools in Cemetery 21-S-46. This suggests a stronger reliance on the basic, homemade fabric by the people of that cemetery compared to those of 21-R-2. However, the frequencies of dyed wool fabrics is almost the same for both cemeteries. Again, the difference is made up by frequencies of the linens and especially the cottons, both more costly, imported textiles.

The shrouds, both cotton and linen types, were imported for burial use only. A shroud represents a luxury obtained only with discretionary income. Cemetery 21-R-2 had more than three times the number of shrouds than did 21-S-46. Again, this difference suggests that more people of 21-R-2 had the resources to procure trade goods than did those of 21-S-46.

A final comparison is that between the untyped fabrics. Most of them were probably made at Kulubnarti, and are untyped because of small technical differences in the weaving from the typed fabrics. They reflect more on the imagination on the weaver's part, than on the prosperity of the owner. The three mats woven of human hair, Cloth numbers 1, 190C and 225C present more of a problem of interpretation, since nothing is known about any others, and at this writing, they are unique. They occur in both cemeteries, and we do not know if they were locally made or brought from elsewhere.

Leaving out the three specimens from a later period: Cloth number 154B from 21-S-46 and 201A and 201B from 21-R-2, there are only two among the untyped examples which were probably imported. They are Cloth number 133A from Grave 167 and Cloth number 217 from Grave 60. Both were from cemetery 21-R-2. So again, we see evidence that the people of 21-R-2 were slightly more thriving than those of 21-S-46.

Putting all the evidence together from the two cemeteries, it appears that, with three exceptions of later periods from 21-R-2, the two populations were chronologically and culturally identical. Most of their fabrics were homemade from the wool of their sheep. Both groups were able to afford some imported goods, especially textiles dyed in bright colors. They both also imported shrouds and other fabrics of cotton and linen, but the people of 21-R-2 had the resources to acquire a few more of these luxuries than those of 21-S-46.

The non-textile finds

There are forty-seven objects from the two cemeteries which are not textiles. They were registered and taken in division by the Sudan Antiquities Service to the Sudan National Museum in Khartoum. It should be reiterated that the present authors were not the excavators of these graves; the descriptions that follow are based on the somewhat limited photographic and documentary records that are available to us.

Body wrappings

Three corpses were interred wrapped in a sheepskin with the wool still adhering to it. None was older than eight years. The only example for which we have further information was a four year old, completely encased in sheepskin with both dark and light wool (Plate 18F). It is not clear if this represents more than one skin or just one multicolored skin. The burial bundle was tied with cord, probably made from several yarns of wool twisted together. The field description reads, "Sheepskin finished with strip of leather alongside edge which runs down center of body". This feature cannot be seen in the photograph.

Seven bodies were partially or completely wrapped in leather. Two are reported to have had their legs wrapped in leather; a 27 year old male had leather around the pelvis. It is not now known if this was a leather kilt, or simply a wrapping. A fourth person had the head covered with cloth and a leather sheet covered the body from the neck to the knees. Three small children were completely encased in leather wrapping (Plate 18E). There is no sign that the body bundles were tied with cord.

Pottery

Pottery forms the largest group of the non-textile remains. Thirteen pieces were recovered from the two cemeteries. Two specimens, a bottle with a cup inverted over it, are both of X-Group Ware R1 (Plates 16A,B).[36] They were found in an X-Group grave.

The fragment of a Late Christian saucer (Plate 16E) is Ware R17, a red ware which has a floral design in cream. It was collected from the surface of cemetery 21-R-2 during the 1969 field season, and is curated in the Webb Museum of Anthropology at the University of Kentucky. There is no documentation in regard to the bowl shown in Plate 16F, which was probably picked up on the surface of the cemetery. The vessel has clearly been used as a lamp, and therefore, was most probably a votive lamp left at the head of one of the grave superstructures. The pottery ware cannot be identified from the photograph, but the owner's graffito visible close to the rim suggests a Late Christian date.

The rest of the pottery remains are pots and amphorae which contained the bodies of foetuses and newborns. All are from cemetery 21-S-46. The amphorae which are described are all of Ware U2. One pot is listed as being handmade. Unfortunately, the roll of film containing all the photos of pots and amphorae was spoiled. The two shown in Plates 16C and D were collected from 21-S-46 during the 1969 field season and are curated in the Webb Museum of Anthropology at the University of Kentucky.

Crosses

The 417 graves excavated from the two cemeteries yielded eleven crosses . The arms are all the same length, some with a knob at the end of each arm. They vary in size from 1.3 cm in each direction, to 4.5 cm. They are described as being made of iron (Plate 17A), silver or bronze. Most of them were found suspended from a fine, twisted leather thong around the neck of the deceased (Plate 17E). One was found loose in the fill of the grave shaft. A tiny cross, more elaborate than the rest, is surrounded by a decorative frame, with a four-pointed figure positioned between the frame and the suspension loop (Plate 17C). It also was hung by a thin twisted thong. All of the crosses were found in the graves of women and children.

Beads

A number of beads were recovered. They are described in the field notes as being made of carnelian, quartz, yellow glass, glass, and silver or lead. The photographs also show beads that appear to be of agate and other small stones, and very small faience beads. With the single exception of five small beads found loose in the fill of the grave of a 42 year-old male, the beads were all from the graves of women and

[36] See William Y. Adams, *Ceramic Industries of Medieval Nubia*, pp. 461, 469-470. *Memoirs of the UNESCO Archaeological Survey of Sudanese Nubia*, vol. 1 (1986).

children.

Although some of the beads were found loose in the fill, others were found *in situ* on the bodies. Three examples were single globular beads strung on a string or leather cord around the neck. A single cowrie shell was reported as being "around the right elbow". One photo is entitled "beads"; the eighteen beads appear to be strung, but it is not certain if they were found together or if they were a miscellaneous lot strung together by the excavator (Plate 17B). The largest one of the group is dark colored and diamond-shaped. The next eight on the string are of various shapes and colors, and appear to be mostly small stones. There is one small globular bead, and the remainder are small tubular beads which may be faience.

Two of the bead specimens described as bracelets are strung with several beads and were found around the wrists. One example consists of 16 mostly globular beads alternately light and dark, with the exceptions of one place where there are two light beads together, and one where there are three dark beads in a row (Plate 17D). The diameter of the circle is less than 4 cm. The second example consists of five small beads, one of which is tubular in shape, and appears to be made either of gold or of glass filled with gold (Plate 17F).

Other jewelry

Four pendants, two bangles and one earring were also found. Three of the pendants appear to be single, elongated beads which were suspended from twisted leather (Plate 18C). All three were found around the necks of children. A fourth pendant seems to be made of metal, finely engraved stone, or perhaps even decorative knots. There appears to be a vertical row of two or possibly three cube shapes, *c.* 7 mm along each side. They are suspended from plied string or fine twisted leather thong (Plate 18D).

Two bangles, both probably of iron, were recovered. One is from the wrist of a 51+ year old woman and is 6 cm. in diameter. The other is 4.5 cm. in diameter, and was found on an 18 month-old child (Plate 18B).

There is a mention of a bronze loop earring from a 12-year old, but no other documentation. A photograph of a tear-drop shaped object entitled "earring", is 1.5 cm. long and 1 cm. wide. It is not clear what the material is, whether metal, stone, or glass.

A number of bodies are said to have been found with a simple leather cord around the neck. Most are from the graves of children, although one was worn by a 31-year old woman and one by a woman 51+ years old. No photographs or other information is available.

Miscellaneous

The partial remains of a leather shoe were found in the grave of a 33-year old man. The rounded end of the sole of either the toe or the heel is 7 cm. wide. A leather scrap also shows in the photograph, but it is not possible to recognize the shoe style from it.

Two bodies were buried lying on mats. One, from the

grave of a 5-year old, is a palm leaf mat, ubiquitous in Nubian households from early times until today. The other person is described as being laid on small *gerid* mats, made from the centrum of the palm branch. This is most commonly found used in roofing and in beds. It was from the grave of a l6-year old female.

The same 16-year old female was found with a leather-encased amulet around her neck. It is *c*. 2 cm square, tied to a short string or fine leather thong. The contents of the amulet were not disclosed (Plate 18A).

Both of the burials which contained mats also contained staffs. The five-year old's grave contained a long rod lying along the north side of the body. In the grave of the 16-year old the field notes say, "wood stick stands upright at north end of grave". A 42-year old woman had a "staff... under the body". The most complete description concerning wooden sticks found in the graves is that of a 47-year old man. "A long pole extending the length of the grave was found resting on top of the body. It is *c*. 3 cm in diameter". There are no data to suggest that any of these people were crippled, or that the staffs were personal belongings.

General Conclusions

The goal of this study has been to try to learn something about the lives of Nubians of the Early Christian period. Physical anthropologists can tell us, in many cases, how they died, but they can also give us much information about how they lived. The grave goods, on the other hand, do not tell us very much at all about the deceased, but about how his or her living relatives and friends regarded that person. In that way, clues from the textiles, crosses, and small bits of finery lead us back to the villages and the lives of their inhabitants. It is hoped that in the future the habitation sites will be excavated. Then perhaps, we shall have a broader picture of the lives as well as the deaths of the Early Christian Nubians.

PART III
THE HUMAN REMAINS

Dennis P. Van Gerven and David L. Greene

Introduction

Excavation and Field Analysis

A joint expedition sponsored by the Universities of Colorado and Kentucky was undertaken in 1979 in order to excavate the human remains from the two cemeteries at Kulubnarti. Between January and April, 1979, 218 individuals were disinterred from cemetery 21-S-46 located on the island and 188 were disinterred from cemetery 21-R-2 located on the mainland adjacent to the modern village of Kulb. Analysis of pottery and architectural associations indicates that the island cemetery represents an early Christian population (*c.* 550-750). Textile remains as well as grave features including vaulted brick tombs and a clear transition from Christian (east-west oriented) to Moslem (north-south) grave orientations, indicates that the mainland cemetery spans the Christian period (550-1450+).

The island cemetery was located in a small, narrow wadi bounded to the east, north and south by jebel (Figure 3). The western end was marked by an abrupt slope to the river channel separating the island from the west bank of the Nile. The presence of an X-group (Ballaña) grave at the far eastern end suggests that the cemetery grew from east to west. The entire wadi bottom was surveyed and mapped and all identified graves were excavated. In all, 218 individuals were exhumed. While preservation varied, the majority of remains were in excellent condition including many mummified individuals. Indeed, several newborns had preserved twine still attached to the umbilicus. Additionally, last trimester foetuses were preserved within pottery urns placed within small graves.

The mainland cemetery 21-R-2 was more complex. Larger and less clearly bounded by natural features, time and resources forbade complete excavation. It was, therefore, decided to focus excavation on that portion of the cemetery with the highest concentration of identifiable grave features (Figures 6-7). Recent analysis of textile body wrapping suggests that these graves, like their island counterparts, may be early Christian. The two cemeteries may not, however, represent a single community. Architectural features associated with each suggests that the island community may have been impoverished while the mainland

folk enjoyed substantially better economic circumstances. Preservation however, was comparable. The mainland individuals were often mummified and skeletal preservation was excellent. Here again, both sexes and all ages from last trimester foetuses to the elderly were represented.

Following excavation, all remains were removed to a field laboratory where a preliminary assessment of age at death and sex was recorded. The remains were also examined for obvious signs of pathology. The remains were then prepared and packaged for shipment by lorry from the site to Wadi Halfa where they were subsequently shipped by train to the Sudan Antiquities Service at Khartoum. The remains were then inspected by Antiquities Service personnel and shipped to laboratories at the University of Colorado where they continue to be curated.

Laboratory Analysis

Following their arrival at the University of Colorado, a systematic assessment of age and sex was conducted. Given the virtual completeness of all remains, multiple criteria could be utilized. Whereas the diagnosis of sex is typically limited to skeletal features present only in the adult skeleton, the presence of soft tissues at Kulubnarti broadened and strengthened the assessment. In many cases the assignment of sex was made certain for both adults and sub-adults by the presence of preserved genitalia. When appropriate soft tissues were absent, sex was determined for adults using standard skeletal features including dimorphic features of the pelvis, cranium and long bones.

Estimations of age at death were based on seriation using all available dental and skeletal criteria. The technique involved arranging all individuals simultaneously in a graded developmental sequence using known standards of dental eruption, epiphyseal union, and age changes in the pubic bones. In addition, population-specific patterns of dental attrition and skeletal degenerative changes were utilized. Individuals were then categorized into developmental age categories based on patterns of shared similarities. Given the greater number and sensitivity of sub-adult criteria, infants (birth through 2 years) were categorized into quarter year categories, children (older than 2) and adults were grouped into whole years. The ages were then grouped into broader age groups as illustrated in Table

73

TABLE 14

AGE CATEGORIES AND SAMPLE SIZES FOR
THE KULUBNARTI CEMETERIES

Age	21-S-46 Frequency	21-R-2 Frequency
Birth to 1 year	48	12
2 to 3	24	20
4 to 6	45	22
7 to 9	12	9
10 to 12	18	8
13 to 15	8	11
16 to 20	5	12
21 to 25	6	12
26 to 30	3	7
31 to 35	6	11
36 to 40	9	25
41 to 45	7	17
46 to 50	14	11
51+	9	8
Total	**214**	**185**

14. The frequencies and total sample sizes for the two cemeteries represent all individuals for which age could be assessed.

The following report of the Kulubnarti remains is based on multiple lines of investigation conducted over an 18 year period by a number of scholars in addition to the authors. The authors particularly wish to acknowledge the work of Dianne Mittler[1] who investigated the skeletal evidence for nutritional anemia, James R. Hummert[2] and Katherine Moore,[3] who examined patterns of growth and development, Nicole Yeagley[4] and Midori Albert[5] who investigated patterns of dental and skeletal asymmetry, Rosemary Beck and Susan G. Sheridan who investigated dental enamel defects,[6] and lastly, Katherine Moore's analysis of age-related bone loss.[7]

[1] Diane Mittler and Dennis P. Van Gerven in *American Journal of Physical Anthropology* (hereafter cited as *AJPA*), vol. 93 (1994), pp. 287-297.

[2] James R. Hummert, *Childhood Growth and Morbidity in a Medieval Population from Kulubnarti in the Batn el Hajar of Sudanese Nubia*. Ph.D. Thesis, University of Colorado, Boulder, 1983.

[3] Katherine P. Moore, S. Thorp and Dennis P. Van Gerven in *Human Evolution*, vol. 1 (1986), pp. 325-330.

[4] Nicole Yeagley, *The Effects of Environmental Stress on Juvenile Development: a Study of Fluctuating Dental Asymmetry in Two Nubian Populations*. Honors Thesis, University of Colorado, Boulder, 1995.

[5] A. M. Albert, *Assessment of Variability in the Timing and Pattern of Epiphesial Union Associated with Stress in Teenage and Young Adult Skeletons from Medieval Kulubnarti, Sudanese Nubia*. Ph.D. Thesis, University of Colorado, Boulder, 1995.

[6] Reported in Dennis P. Van Gerven, R. Beck and J. R. Hummert in *AJPA*, vol. 92 (1990), pp. 413-420.

[7] Katherine P. Moore, *Osteopenia in a Medieval Population from Sudanese Nubia*. Ph.D. Thesis, Univesity of Colorado, Boulder, 1987.

Population relationships

Craniology

Using an approach borrowed largely from Egyptology, the earliest archaeological surveys of Nubia[8] focused intensively on cemetery remains and funerary architecture. From that perspective, changes in artifacts and burial customs suggested a historical process punctuated by successive cultural periods, each characterized by the presence of a distinctive racial group. Indeed, given the abundance of human remains, race assumed particular importance as the driving force of culture change. For example, Nubia's A-Group period was characterized culturally as one of transition between hunting-gathering and food production. Racially A-Group people were described on the basis of cranial features as Egyptian or Caucasoid. Nubia's B-group was characterized both as a period of cultural decline as well as a time of Negroid invasion. In a similar manner each of Nubia's succeeding periods was described in largely cultural-racial terms.

The International Campaign to Save the Monuments of Nubia (1959-69) provided a more comprehensive approach to the study of population relationships. Unlike earlier salvage efforts, the campaign emphasized the systematic excavation of entire village assemblages. What emerged was compelling evidence for cultural continuity ".. *influenced by events and ideas from abroad, but involving the same basic population from beginning to end* ."[9] Analysis of the human remains supported the same conclusion. Greene observed important dental evidence for biological continuity from Mesolithic through modern times.[10] It became equally apparent that populations along the Nile Valley were closely related - forming an overlapping series (cline) from north to south.[11]

Until the excavations at Kulubnarti, opportunities to evaluate clinal patterns between adjacent Nubian populations were limited to comparisons between material from Upper Egypt and Lower Nubia. The purpose of our Kulubnarti investigation was to allow a comparison of craniofacial and dental evidence from Lower Nubia and from the *Batn el Hajar* region.

Data from Lower Nubia were obtained from 44 Meroitic, 94 X-Group, and 36 Christian crania excavated and measured by members of the University of Colorado 1964

[8] e.g. George A. Reisner, *The Archaeological Survey of Nubia, Report for 1907-1908* (Cairo, 1910).

[9] William Y. Adams, "Continuity and Change in Nubian Cultural History", *Sudan Notes and Records*, vol. 48 (1967), p. 17-18.

[10] David L. Greene, "Dentition and Biological Relationships of some Meroitic, X-Group, and Christian Populations from Wadi Halfa, Sudan." *Kush*, vol. 14 (1966), pp. 285-288.

[11] David L. Greene in D. R. Brothwell and B. A. Chiarelli, eds., *Population Biology of the Ancient Egyptians* (London, 1973), pp. 315-324.

TABLE 15
SUMMARY STATISTICS OF THE WADI HALFA CRANIAL REMAINS

Measurement	Meroitic X	Meroitic S	X-Group X	X-Group S	Christian X	Christian S
Cranial Length	178	6.9	179	6.7	179.2	9.2
Cranial Width	131	5.2	132	5.1	129.8	7.4
Basion/Bregma Height	127	6.3	130	6.1	126.9	8.4
Auricular Height	107	6.6	107	6.6	107.1	7.1
Endobasion/Prosthion Length	93.3	5.6	94.9	6.1	92.1	7.8
Bizygomatic Diameter	119	8.6	120	7.3	118.7	10.6
Nasion/Prosth. Ht	61.2	6.6	65.1	5.5	59.2	7.7
Palatal Length	45.5	4.2	49.9	5.2	45.5	4.6
Palatal Width	37.1	4.2	35.5	3.4	36.8	3.8
Mandibular Length	84.3	7.9	84.1	5.8	79.4	8.9
Mandibular Thickness	14.5	1.7	14.9	4.3	14.1	1.9
Bigonial Width	91.9	11.3	88.8	8.6	86.6	10.1

Expedition to the Sudan.[12] All sites were located near Wadi Halfa at the Second Cataract. Of the total Kulubnarti sample, 44 crania from the island cemetery 21-S-46 and 74 from the mainland cemetery 21-R-2 were suitable for analysis. All crania in the Wadi Halfa and Kulubnarti samples were adults and both contained a 1:1 male-female ratio.

data were subjected to a multiple discriminant function analysis in order to determine temporal and spatial relationships within and between the Wadi Halfa and Kulubnarti samples.

Figure 11 illustrates group centroids graphed on the first and second discriminant functions. Error bars indicate one

TABLE 16
SUMMARY STATISTICS FOR THE KULUBNARTI REMAINS

Measurement	21-S-46 X	21-S-46 S	21-R-2 X	21-R-2 S
Cranial Length	181.4	6.2	180.6	7.8
Cranial Width	129.8	5.1	130.1	4.1
Basion Bregma Height	128.5	4.8	128.1	5.2
Auricular Height	108.2	5.5	108.6	5.5
Endobas/Prosthion Lt.	95.3	5.5	95.7	5.6
Bizygomatic Diameter	124.1	5.3	123.1	6.1
Nasion/Prosthion Ht	64.3	4.9	64.2	4.7
Palatal Length	51.3	3.3	50.7	4.1
Palatal Width	38.3	2.5	39.7	3.1
Mandibular Length	73.2	5.7	74.5	5.6
Mandibular Thickness	13.6	1.4	13.5	1.6
Bigonial Width	91.8	6.3	88.3	6.7

Twelve standard craniofacial measurements were chosen for comparison, based on their availability for the Wadi Halfa remains (Tables 15 and 16). For the basic methodology see William Bass, *Human Osteology*.[13] All

standard error for each centroid. It is clear that there is substantial overlap among the Wadi Halfa samples as well as between the Kulubnarti samples. It is also apparent that the samples form two distinct clusters, one corresponding to the Wadi Halfa group and the other representing Kulubnarti. According to analysis of variance (Table 17), the probability of significant difference among the group centroids is greater than 99.9%. The nature of the differences, therefore, warrants further consideration.

[12] See G. J. Armelagos, G. H. Ewing, D. L. Greene, and K. K. Greene in *Kush*, vol. 13 (1965), pp. 28-29.
[13] *Human Osteology: a Laboratory and Field Manual* (Columbia, MO, 1971).

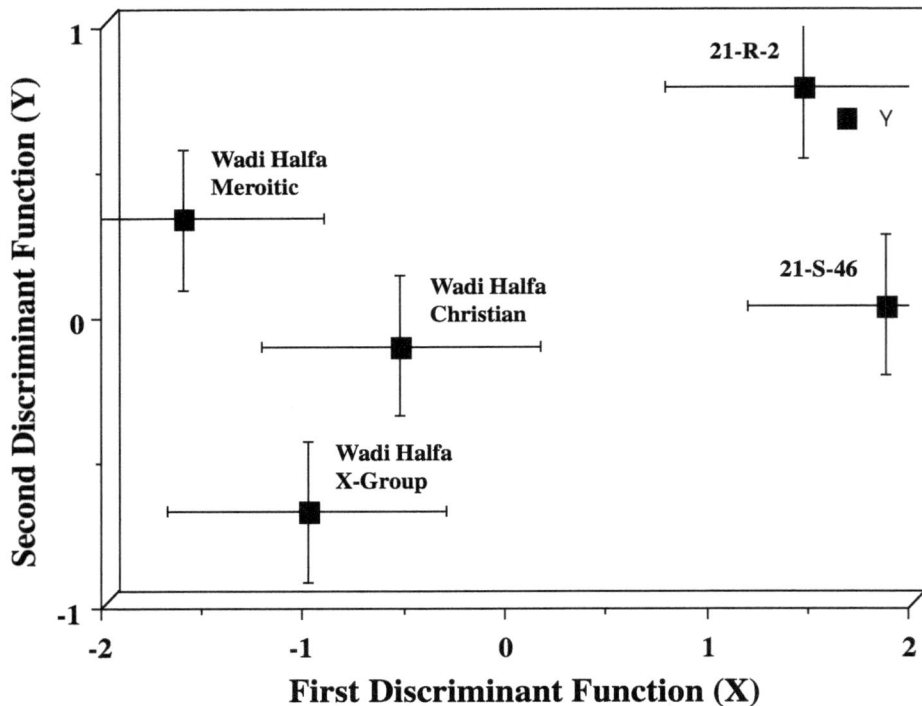

Figure 11. Group centroids for Wadi Halfa and Kulubnarti crania.

In order to accomplish this, it is necessary to consider the numerical values associated with the discriminant analysis.

TABLE 17
F MATRIX FOR THE WADI HALFA AND
KULUBNARTI POPULATIONS

	Wadi Halfa Meroitic	Wadi Halfa X-Group	Wadi Halfa Christian	21-S-46
Wadi Halfa (X-Group)	7.77**			
Wadi Halfa (Christian)	2.99**	6.22**		
21-S-46	23.24**	21.65**	12.42**	
21-R-2	23.93**	27.80**	12.13**	2.12*

*p<0.01   **p<0.001

Computation of eigenvalues and cumulative percentages (Table 18) permits the determination of each discriminant function's contribution to the total discrimination.

The first function accounted for over 77% of the total discrimination while the second contributed only an additional 16%. Associated eigenvalues for these functions were 1.99716 and 0.42112, respectively. Given the dramatic reduction in discrimination between the two functions, only the first was subjected to further analysis.[14]

Inspection of group centroids associated with the first discriminant function (x axis in Figure 11) reveals a pattern of considerable interest. The Wadi Halfa populations all share negative centroid values and cluster closely together relative to the Kulubnarti samples. The Kulubnarti samples form a second and distinct cluster of positive centroids. It is indeed clear that the principal discrimination along the first axis is between Wadi Halfa and Kulubnarti. Analysis of variance of the group centroids (Table 17) confirms this interpretation. The largest F values are consistently associated with group comparisons between Kulubnarti and the various Wadi Halfa series. Conversely, the least significant difference is between the mainland and island Kulubnarti samples.

Inspection of the scaled eigenvectors (Table 18) associated with the first function makes further interpretation of the function possible. The variables contributing primarily to the discrimination are mandibular length (-1.30972) and bizygomatic diameter (+0.39839). Sign contrasts indicate that the discrimination between Wadi Halfa and Kulubnarti is based on an inverse relationship in which the Wadi Halfa

---

[14] In all, four discriminant functions can be calculated for five groups. Functions 3 and 4 together accounted for less than 6% of the total discrimination.

76

TABLE 18
DISCRIMINANT FUNCTIONS FOR KULUBNARTI
AND WADI HALFA CRANIA

Discriminant Function	I	II
eigenvalue	199.7	0.421
cumulative percentage	0.778	0.942
Eigenvectors		
Cranial Length	0.154	-0.006
Cranial Width	-0.109	0.061
Basion/Bregma Height	0.038	0.44
Auricular Height	0.155	-0.128
Endobasion/Prosthion Length	0.179	-0.606
Bizygomatic Diameter	**0.398**	0.035
Nasion/Prosthion Height	0.137	**0.469**
Palatal Length	0.302	**0.967**
Palatal Width	0.357	**0.656**
Mandibular Length	**-1.31**	-0.058
Mandibular Thickness	0.01	0.108
Bigonial Width	0.009	-0.31

Substantially loaded variables in bold

samples have a proportionately longer mandible (lower face) and narrower bizygomatic diameter (mid face). Conversely, the Kulubnarti crania are distinct by virtue of a shorter, wider face.

It is interesting to note that this same function distinguishes the Wadi Halfa populations diachronically. The trend toward a shorter wider facial architecture is broadly consistent with an evolutionary trend in Lower Nubia related to reduced masticatory stress, changed masticatory function, and dental reduction first noted by Greene and Armelagos[15] and later by Van Gerven and co-workers,[16] Carlson,[17] and Carlson and Van Gerven.[18]

The position of the Kulubnarti samples relative to Wadi Halfa is of additional interest. While both Kulubnarti groups lie closer to the Wadi Halfa Christians than they do to either the Meroitic or X-group samples, the mainland Kulubnarti series is the closer of the two. Given the evidence for economic differences between the mainland and island communities, a northern origin for the economically advantaged mainland community may be worthy of further investigation.

Interpretative summary of the cranial evidence

Earlier investigations of human remains from Wadi Halfa

found strong evidence for biological continuity extending from Mesolithic through Christian times.[19] At the same time, comparisons between Upper Egypt and Lower Nubia suggested the likelihood of a biological gradient of genetically and anatomically overlapping human populations extending along the Nile Valley. Our investigation lends strong support to that interpretation.

The cranial remains from Wadi Halfa and Kulubnarti form two distinct but overlapping morphological clusters. Furthermore, while the Kulubnarti samples are predictably most like one another, they show a strong similarity to their northern Christian counterparts. Nevertheless, the pattern of similarity between Wadi Halfa and Kulubnarti is somewhat surprising. The idea of a gradient of human populations extending southward along the Nile Valley has often invoked the image of a corresponding increase in African or Negroid morphological features.[20] Our analysis does not support that view.

Lower facial prognathism (a projecting lower face) typically associated with an African or Negroid cranial morphology is more reduced at Kulubnarti than to the north at Wadi Halfa. Indeed the Kulubnarti Christians are most distinct in having a relatively short, broad face. The implications seem clear. While populations of the Nile Valley may form a gradient of overlapping morphologies, the gradient is not due to a simple Africanization of the southern groups. Indeed, from the perspective of facial morphology, the Kulubnarti populations appear less "African" than their counterparts to the north.

Discrete dental variation

Inasmuch as the original test of biological continuity among the populations of Wadi Halfa was based on Greene's analysis of discrete dental morphological characters,[21] an incorporation of this approach into the Kulubnarti analysis was clearly warranted. The purpose of this phase of our analysis was to apply the Smith-Grewal statistic,[22] not previously applied to Nubian dental traits, to assess biological affinities between Wadi Halfa and Kulubnarti.

In 1967 Berry and Berry first applied the Smith-Grewal statistic to biological distance in human populations using discrete skeletal variants.[23] In 1973 Sjovold further developed its theoretical rationale,[24] and in 1976 Green and Suchey demonstrated that the Freeman-Tukey transformation could be used to stabilize variances in small samples.[25] Consequently in the present study, each discrete

[15] Armelagos et al., op. cit. (n. 12); David L. Greene and George Armelagos, *The Wadi Halfa Mesolithic Population. Research Report No. 11*, Department of Anthropology, University of Massachusetts, Amherst (1972).

[16] Dennis P. Van Gerven, P. Rohr and George Armelagos in *Man*, vol. 12 (1976), pp. 270-277.

[17] D. S. Carlson in *AJPA*, vol. 45 (1976), pp. 467-484.

[18] D. S. Carlson and Dennis P. Van Gerven in *AJPA*, vol. 46 (1977), pp. 495-506.

[19] Greene, op. cit. (n. 10).

[20] cf. Eugen Strouhal in *Anthropological Congress Dedicated to Ales Hdlicka* (Prague, 1971), pp. 541-574.

[21] Greene, op. cit. (n. 10); id., *Dentition of Meroitic, X-Group, and Christian Populations from Wadi Halfa, Sudan. University of Utah Anthropological Papers*, no. 85 (1967).

[22] M. S. Grewal in *Genetics Research*, vol. 3 (1962), pp. 226-237.

[23] A. C. Berry and R. J. Berry in *Journal of Anatomy*, vol. 101 (1967), pp. 361-379.

[24] T. Sjovold in *Homo* vol. 24 (1973), pp. 204-233.

[25] R. F. Green and M. Suchey in *AJPA*, vol. 45 (1976), pp. 61-68.

trait frequency of occurrence was transformed using: $\phi = 1/2\sin^{-1}(1-2k/n+1)+1/2\sin^{-1}(1-2(k+1)/(n+1))$, where k equals the occurrence of a trait and n equals the total number of observations. Mean measures of divergence (or distance) were then found:

$$D = \frac{(\phi_{1i}-\phi_{2i})2 - (1/n_{1i}+1/2) + 1/(n_{2i}+1/2))}{r}$$

where r equals the number of pairs of traits considered, r is the transformed frequency of the *ith* trait in the first population, n_{1i} the total number of observations for the ith trait in the first population, ϕ_{2i} the transformed frequency of the ith trait in the second population, and n_{2i} the total number of observations for the ith trait in the second population. The variance of a mean measure of divergence then equals: $2/r \ (1/(n_{1i}+1/2)+1/(n_{2i}+1/2))^2$ and the standard deviation equals the square root of the variance.

The traits chosen for the present study are as follows:

1. *Carabelli's Trait on the Maxillary First Molar:* cusp, pit, and groove combined as present. Genetic studies indicate that cusps, pits, and grooves may be variable manifestations of the same genotype.[26] This is further supported in Nubian populations by bilateral concordance studies.[27]

2. *Four Cusps on the Maxillary Second Molar:* The 4 and 4- categories used in the earlier Wadi Halfa study are combined.

3. *Three Cusps on the Maxillary Third Molar:* Both 3+ and 3 categories are combined.

4. *Five Cusps on the Mandibular First Molar.*

5. *Four Cusps on the Mandibular Second Molar.*

6. *Four Cusps on the Mandibular Third Molar.*

7. *Shoveling on Central Maxillary Incisors:* Hrdlicka's trace or moderate shoveling categories are combined.

When both right and left teeth were present and observable, observations were made from the left teeth. When only one or the other was present or observable, it was used. All observations were made on permanent teeth and both sexes were combined.

As with the cranial analysis, Meroitic (site 6-B-16), X-Group (site NAX), and Christian (site 6-K-3) samples were chosen for comparison to Kulubnarti. These were the largest Wadi Halfa samples available.

As Sjovold has pointed out,[28] the Smith-Grewel measure of biological divergence D (or distance) is a multivariate statistic comparable to the discriminant function statistic applied to the crania. The statistic D can be positive or negative and becomes significant as it diverges from zero.

[26] See B. S. Kraus in *American Journal of Human Genetics,* vol. 3 (1951), pp. 348-355; and T. Tsuji in *Japanese Journal of Human Genetics,* vol. 3 (1958), p. 21.

[27] Greene, op. cit. (n. 21).

[28] Op. cit. (n. 24).

If the absolute value of a D value exceeds twice its standard deviation, then the difference is statistically significant at 0.05. When the Freeman-Tukey transformation is used to calculate ϕ as in the present analysis, then if the D value exceeds twice its standard deviation the difference is significant somewhere between 0.05 and 0.03.[29]

Table 19 provides the D (standard deviations in italics) values for the Wadi Halfa and Kulubnarti populations. The

TABLE 19
DISTANCES *F* FOR THE WADI HALFA AND KULUBNARTI POPULATIONS

	Wadi Halfa X-Group	Wadi Halfa Christian	21-S-46	21-R-2
Wadi Halfa Meroitic	-0.0028 *0.236*	0.0155 *0.11*	0.0574 *0.047*	-0.0299 *0.031*
Wadi Halfa X-Group		0.0212 *0.031*	0.0108 *0.045*	0.0061 *0.029*
Wadi Halfa Christian			-0.0053 *0.005*	0.0192 *0.039*
21-S-46				-0.0422 *0.059*

clear lack of significant difference among the Wadi Halfa populations reconfirms Greene's earlier argument for biological continuity in that area. The results further demonstrate that this pattern of biological continuity extends from Wadi Halfa to Kulubnarti.

While the Kulubnarti populations do not differ significantly from any of the Wadi Halfa samples, the pattern of difference corresponds closely to the craniometric results. When compared to Wadi Halfa, the island Kulubnarti sample is closest dentally to the Christians and morphologically most unlike the Meroitic series. In this sense, the island population follows the pattern of diachronic change observed for Wadi Halfa. The mainland group, however, behave differently. Indeed, the mainland group are dentally more like the Wadi Halfa X-group (D = 0.0061) and Wadi Halfa Christian (0.0192) and even the Wadi Halfa Meroitics (-0.0299) than they are to their counterparts on Kulubnarti island. This pattern lends further support to the possibility that the mainland Kulubnarti group represent an immigration from the north with genetic roots closer to Wadi Halfa than the *Batn el Hajjar.*

Interpretative summary of discrete dental variation

Anatomical features of the human dentition, particularly the discrete patterns of cusps and fissures of the molar crown, have long been viewed as expressing a strong genetic

[29] Green and Suchey, op. cit. (n. 25).

influence.[30] Dental traits have accordingly been used extensively to assess biological (genetic) relationships among human populations. Our investigation indicates a close correspondence between these dental traits and the anatomical characteristics of the crania.

When they are compared to the samples from Wadi Halfa, the Kulubnarti samples are most like their Wadi Halfa Christian counterparts. Furthermore, the mainland 21-R-2 sample is more similar to the Wadi Halfa Christians than is the 21-S-46 (Island) sample. Taken together, the anatomical and genetic evidence suggests that the Kulubnarti populations may trace their biological (and possibly cultural) roots to Lower Nubia.

Demography

Any attempt to understand the adaptation and biological well-being of an ancient population must proceed from a demographic perspective. Whether represented in the form of simple survivorship curves or the more elaborate form of composite life tables, mortality patterns provide the essential context from which other interpretations can be made. While the use of life tables has been a particular source of debate,[31] the quality of preservation, delineation of cemeteries, and archaeological context, argues strongly in favor of the technique's applicability. The appropriateness of these remains is further enhanced by the preservation of virtually complete skeletons from birth to old age to which, as previously discussed, multiple aging criteria could be applied.

Life tables (Tables 20 and 21) for the island and mainland cemeteries include number of individuals dying per age interval (d'x), the number dying based on a standard population of 1000 (dx), the number of individuals surviving at the beginning of each age interval (lx), the probability of dying at each age interval (qx), the number of individuals at the end of each age interval (Lx), and the mean life expectancy at each interval expressed in intervals (e°*x) and in years e°x). The critical value for the present analysis is mean life expectancy. However, before life expectancy can be interpreted as a legitimate demographic construct, two potential sources of distortion must be considered. The first source arises from truncation of the oldest age group into an open-ended 51+ category and the second arises from the

[30] For full discussion see David L. Greene, *Genetics, Dentition, and Taxonomy. University of Wyoming Publications,* vol. 22, no. 2 (1967).

[31] See J. L. Angel in *AJPA,* vol. 30 (1969), pp. 427-437; A. C. Swedlund and G. J. Armelagos in *Annales: Economie, Sociétés, Civilisation,* vol. 24 (1969), pp. 1287-1298; J. A. Moore, A. C. Swedlund, and G. J. Armelagos in *Population Studies in Archaeology and Biological Anthropology: a Symposium,* pp. 57-70. *Society for American Archaeology Memoir* no. 30 (1975); J. Bocquet-Appel and C. Masset in *Journal of Human Evolution,* vol. 11 (1982), pp. 321-333; Dennis P. Van Gerven and G. J. Armelagos in *Journal of Human Evolution,* vol. 12 (1983), pp. 353-360; J. Bacquet-Appel and C. Masset in *Journal of Human Evolution,* vol. 14 (1985), pp. 107-111; and David L. Greene, Dennis P. Van Gerven, and G. J. Armelagos in *Human Evolution,* vol. 1 (1986), pp. 193-207.

TABLE 20
LIFE TABLE FOR BURIALS IN CEMETERY 21-S-46

Age	d'x	dx	lx	qx	Lx	eo*x	eox
Birth to 1 year	48	224	1000	22.4	888	4.54	10.6
2-3 years	24	112	776	14.4	720	4.71	13.1
4-6 years	45	211	664	31.8	558.5	4.42	14.1
7-9 years	12	56	453	12.4	425	5.24	20.2
10-12 years	18	84	397	21.2	355	4.91	20.5
13-15 years	8	37	313	11.8	294.5	5.1	23.5
16-20 years	5	23	276	8.3	264.5	4.71	23.5
21-25 years	6	28	253	11.1	239	4.1	20.5
26-30 years	3	14	225	6.2	218	3.54	17.7
31-35 years	6	28	211	13.3	197	2.75	13.7
36-40 years	9	42	183	23	162	2.1	10.5
41-45 years	7	33	141	23.4	124.5	1.56	7.8
46-50 years	14	66	108	61.1	75	0.89	4.4
51+ years	9	42	42	100	21	0.5	2.5
Total	**214**	**1000**	**0**				

ever-present risk of infant under-enumeration.

In order to determine the extent of these biases, the Kulubnarti life tables were expanded by Greene and co-workers, using Weiss' graduation technique based on the Gompertz function.[32] This approach was selected because

TABLE 21
LIFE TABLE FOR BURIALS IN CEMETERY 21-R-2

Age	d'x	dx	lx	qx	Lx	eo*x	eox
Birth to 1 year	12	65	1000	6.5	967.5	6.77	18.9
2 to 3	20	109	935	11.7	880.5	6.21	20.1
4 to 6	22	119	826	14.4	766.5	5.96	21.8
7 to 9	9	49	707	6.9	682.5	5.88	23.4
10 to 12	8	43	658	6.5	636.5	5.28	22.4
13 to 15	11	59	615	9.6	585.5	4.61	21
16 to 20	12	65	556	11.7	523.5	4.05	20.2
21 to 25	12	65	491	13.2	458.5	3.52	17.6
26 to 30	7	38	426	8.9	407	2.98	14.9
31 to 35	11	59	388	15.2	358.2	2.22	11.1
36 to 40	25	135	329	41	261.5	1.53	7.6
41 to 45	17	92	194	47.4	148	1.25	6.2
46 to 50	11	59	102	57.8	72.5	0.92	4.6
51+	8	43	43	100	21.5	0.5	2.5
Total	**185**	**1000**	**0**				

it is sensitive to many of the problems of smoothing and estimation intrinsic to demographic analysis of small, living anthropological populations. In constructing idealized or model life tables for groups such as the !Kung San, Weiss had to deal with incomplete data sets, small sample sizes,

[32] Greene, Van Gerven, and Armelagos, op. cit. (n. 31).

and age estimation difficulties similar to that encountered for archaeological populations.[33] In essence, Greene began with the age group known to have the lowest mortality in living populations (age 14) and used a mathematical function (the Gompertz function developed by Weiss) to systematically project expected mortality patterns in the direction of the older and younger age categories. These expected frequencies could then be compared to the observed life table frequencies calculated for the Kulubnarti data. At no point were the observed frequencies significantly different from those predicted using Weiss' technique. There were, however, some differences worth noting.

Projections based on this model life table approach suggest that 8.8% of the island and 7.3% of the mainland Christian samples are likely to have lived beyond their fifties. However, because adequate age estimations could not be

patterns makes it likely that the Kulubnarti life tables offer a legitimate view of mortality in these ancient Nubian communities.

A comparison of the two cemeteries (Figure 12) from the perspective of mean life expectancy reveals a pattern of considerable interest. It appears that while differences in mortality after childhood are minimal between the two communities, patterns of infant and childhood mortality are strikingly different. Indeed from birth through age 8 infant mortality on the island is consistently higher. Most notably mean life expectancy at birth on the island is only 10.6 years compared to 18.9 years on the mainland. The average reduction among newborns to 8 year olds on the island is 6.5 years.

If infant and childhood mortality is viewed as a more sensitive barometer of a population's well-being than that

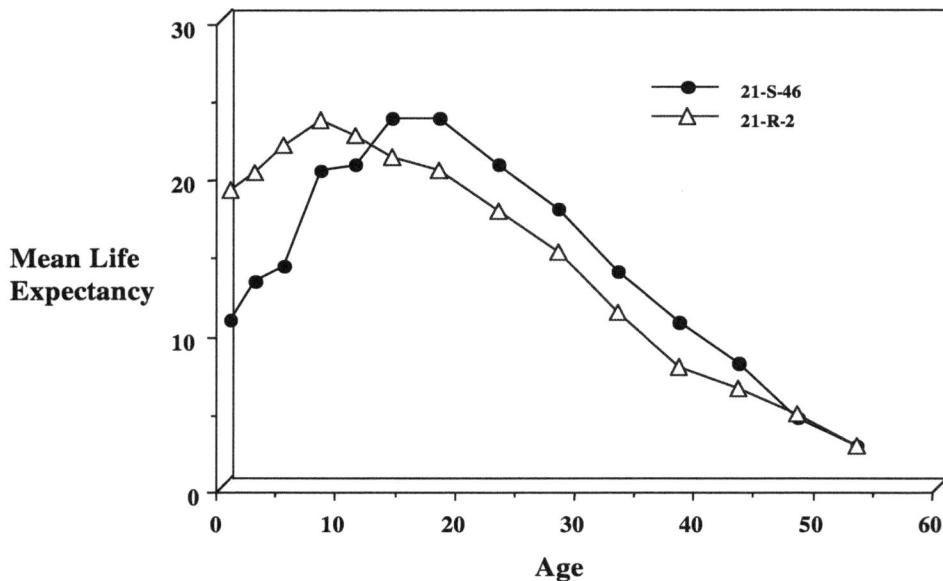

Figure 12. Mean life expectancy for individuals buried in the Kulubnarti cemeteries.

made beyond the 51+ category, this fraction of the population could not be analyzed for distinct age changes in survivorship. Fortunately, this small percentage is unlikely to have an important impact on the interpretability of the data. The proportion of infants and children observed in the samples is also consistent with the frequencies predicted using Weiss' tables. Indeed the island population is virtually identical to Weiss' expected values while observed infant frequencies for the mainland group are about 8% lower that would be expected. Inasmuch as the island cemetery was completely excavated while the mainland cemetery was sampled, the lower than expected frequency of infants on the mainland may reflect sampling bias. Even so, the close approximation between observed and predicted mortality

evidenced in the mortality of adolescents and adults, these differences in childhood mortality can be used to frame a pair of testable hypotheses. For example, if these differences in childhood mortality are due to differences in stress, these data predict a corresponding elevation in the skeletal manifestations of stress among the island children. On the other hand, if no such correspondence between mortality and stress can be demonstrated, an alternative explanation presents itself. What appears as lower mortality on the mainland may reflect a lowering of fecundity. This second interpretation, if confirmed, would suggest a lower degree of health and adaptation on the mainland.

Nutritional stress

The first measure of stress and morbidity investigated at Kulubnarti was the skeletal lesion of children known as

[33] K. M. Weiss, *Demographic Models for Anthropology. American Antiquity,* vol. 38, part 2 (1973).

cribra orbitalia. This lesion of the superior surface of the eye orbit is a response of the growing, or sub-adult skeleton to anemia.[34] The anemia may result from a combination of causes including dietary iron insufficiency, parasitic infection, and weaning diarrhea. The iron deficiency hypothesis has been of particular importance given the nature of the Nubian diet.

Like their modern counterparts, the people of Kulubnarti subsisted as sedentary agriculturists practicing small scale farming. Their diet consisted primarily of cereal grains supplemented by small amounts of animal protein.[35] Clinical research has demonstrated a strong relationship between this type of diet and iron deficiency. Specifically, iron deficiency frequently results from the low bioavailability of iron in many cultigens, particularly cereal grains high in phytate.[36] The impact of low levels of dietary iron is often intensified by parasitic infections typically accompanied by gastrointestinal bleeding.

The age distribution of the lesion at Kulubnarti (Table 22) is also consistent with the clinical pattern of iron deficiency anemia. Just as with living children, osteological signs of iron deficiency are rare among the youngest Kulubnarti infants. This is because iron stores accumulated *in utero* provide for the neonate. However, by the end of the fifth or sixth month, these stores are exhausted,[37] and iron deficiency becomes increasingly prevalent among infants and children.

Clinically, the frequency of iron deficiency shows a further increase with weaning as children are introduced to adult foods and are increasingly exposed to gastrointestinal pathogens.[38] The resulting weanling diarrhea leads to further deterioration of nutritional status due to decreased appetite and increased metabolic loss of essential nutrients, including iron.[39]

Absence of the lesion in the youngest infants at Kulubnarti is followed by a dramatic increase beginning in the second year of life (Table 22). This trend peaks with 78% of those between 4 and 6 years exhibiting the lesion. This pattern appears to reflect the increasing impact of iron deficiency accompanying weaning and weanling diarrhea.

This association is further clarified by the distinction between those with and without active (unhealed or unhealing) lesions (Table 22). All of the Kulubnarti infants and children with *cribra orbitalia* show active lesion development at the time of death. With age, however, an increasing number of individuals show signs of healing, with all affected children showing some signs of healing by age

---

TABLE 22

CRIBRA ORBITALIA IN THE COMBINED SAMPLE FROM THE TWO KULUBNARTI CEMETERIES

Age	Total n.	Percent with *Cribra Orbitalia*	Percent with Active Lesions
0 to 1 year	41	17.1	100
2 to 3	34	50	58.8
4 to 6	54	77.8	38.1
7 to 9	19	73.7	28.6
10 to 12	24	75	16.7
13 to 15	16	50	0
16 to 20	16	37.5	0
21 to 30	25	28	0
31 to 40	46	37	0
41 to 50	42	23.8	0
51+	17	17.7	0
Total	**334**		

12. Such a pattern lends strong support to Stuart-Macadam's hypothesis that *cribra orbitalia* is a childhood condition even though the underlying anemia may continue throughout life.[40]

A comparison between the cemeteries 21-S-46 and 21-R-2 further supports the hypothesis of increased stress among the island community. As illustrated in Table 23, lesion frequencies are higher in the sample from 21-S-46. The lesion also appears a full year earlier and is maintained at a high frequency longer. Indeed from birth through age 12, significantly more island children express active lesions (p<0.05). The lesion also had a more pronounced impact on childhood mortality in the island community. From birth through age 15, island children with the lesion have substantially lower mean life expectancies than those on the mainland. While this difference in survival is no doubt due to a multiplicity of factors, it appears that one major contributor was a more frequent and longer lasting childhood anemia.

Growth and development

Studies of long bone growth in archaeological populations are relatively rare in the literature. A major reason for this is that large samples of sub-adults are seldom available. Such studies are also based on children that failed to survive and thus comparisons to longitudinal data from living children are tenuous. As Johnston pointed out in his study of long bone growth for children from Indian Knoll, "... some degree of error is introduced by the very fact that the sample is skeletal. It does not represent the normal, healthy, population from which it was drawn."[41]

However, when growth data from archaeological remains are used comparatively and in the context of other stress

---

[34] P. Stuart-Macadam in *AJPA*, vol. 66 (1985), pp. 391-398.

[35] See William Y. Adams, *Nubia, Corridor to Africa* (London, 1977), pp. 50-54.

[36] See E. R. Morris in W. Mertz, ed., *Trace Elements in Human and Animal Nutrition* (San Diego, 1987), pp. 79-142.

[37] See I. Bernat, *Iron Metabolism* (New York, 1983), p. 131.

[38] J. E. Gordon, I. D. Chitkara, and J. B. Wyon in *American Journal of Medical Science*, vol. 245 (1963), pp. 345-377.

[39] Ibid.

[40] Stuart-Macadam, op. cit. (n. 34).

[41] F. E. Johnston in *AJPA*, vol. 20 (1962), pp. 249-254.

TABLE 23

CRIBRA ORBITALIA RATES FROM CEMETERIES 21-S-46 AND 21-R-2 COMPARED

| | | 21-S-46 | | | 21-R-2 | |
Age	Total n.	Percent with *Cribra Orbitalia*	Percent with Active Lesions	Total n.	Percent with *Cribra Orbitalia*	Percent with Active Lesions
0 to 1	31	22.6	100	10	0	0
2 to 3	20	65	61.5	14	50	28.6
4 to 6	35	74.3	50	19	84.2	18.8
7 to 9	10	80	12.5	9	66.7	50
10 to 12	16	88	21.4	8	50	0
13 to 15	8	63	0	8	37.5	0
16 to 20	4	25	0	12	41.7	0
21 to 30	8	37.5	0	17	23.5	0
31 to 40	13	38.5	0	33	36.4	0
41 to 50	16	25	0	26	23.1	0
51+	9	22.2	0	8	12.5	0
Total	**170**			**164**		

indicators, a fuller understanding of growth and morbidity among historic and prehistoric peoples can be facilitated. Such information may provide important insights into the adaptation of earlier human societies. This is particularly true when sub-adult remains are well preserved and the cultural context is well documented, as at Kulubnarti.

As a first step in our analysis of growth and development, length of the femoral diaphyses was measured for 124 island and 56 mainland sub-adults ranging in age from newborns to 16 years. Distance curves for the cemeteries (Figure 13) reveal that growth patterns are quite similar until the 9th year, when the 21-S-46 children fall behind and never fully catch up. Here again, the data suggest that stress was more severe in the island community. This view is further confirmed when skeletal development is examined.

It has been well documented that development of the human skeleton responds more readily to environmental stress than does the genetically timed eruption of the teeth.[42] More specifically, the rate of skeletal maturation slows considerably in individuals and populations experiencing nutritional stress.[43] Since skeletal age and dental age both develop in accordance with chronological age, they should, under normal conditions approximate one another. Consequently, instances in which dental age advances ahead of skeletal age may be interpreted as evidence for retarded skeletal development. Such a finding at Kulubnarti, in combination with the other evidence available, has enhanced our ability to assess the merits of our hypothesis of greater

stress in the island 21-S-46 community.

Independent estimates of skeletal and dental age were made for 21 island and 23 mainland sub-adults ranging in age from 12 to 23 years. The sample represents all individuals for which adequate dental and skeletal age comparisons could be made. Individuals were placed in dental age categories by comparison to standard dental eruption charts.[44] These categories were then further refined according to estimates of dental attrition based on the method described by Miles.[45]

Estimates of skeletal age were based upon standard criteria for epiphyseal union,[46] and thus individuals under age 12 lacking such union could not be included in this phase of the analysis. Nine separate sites of union were scored. These included the proximal and distal humerus, femoral head, distal femur, iliac crest, primary elements of the innominate, ischial tuberosity, distal radius, and medial clavicle. A final skeletal age estimate was determined using modification of the Tanner-Whitehouse method for the evaluation of skeletal maturity.[47]

A comparison between dental and skeletal age is presented in Table 24. For the combined samples, 70.5% of the individuals examined had a dental age exceeding their skeletal age, while only 13.6% had a skeletal age greater than their dental age. Seven individuals (15.6%) produced no difference between the two age estimates. This bias in the direction of skeletal retardation is statistically significant at the 99.9% confidence level.

A comparison of individuals by cemetery indicates that

[42] S. J. Garn and C. G. Rommen in *The Pediatric Clinics of North America*, vol. 13 (1969), pp. 353-379; G. W. Lasker in *Science*, vol. 166 (1969), pp. 1480-1486; and D. F. Roberts in *British Museum Bulletin*, vol. 37 (1981), pp. 239-246.

[43] W. A. Stini in E. S. Watts, F. E. Johnston, and G. S. Lasker, eds., *Biosocial Interrelations in Population Adaptation* (The Hague, 1975), pp. 19-41; J. M. Tanner, *Fetus into Man* (Cambridge, 1978), pp. 78.

[44] D. H. Ubelaker, *Human Skeletal Remains* (Chicago, 1978), pp. 47.

[45] A. E. W. Miles in D. R. Brothwell, ed., *Dental Anthropology* (London, 1963), pp, 191-209.

[46] Ubelaker, op. cit. (n. 44), pp. 53.

[47] Tanner, op. cit. (n. 43), pp. 120-129.

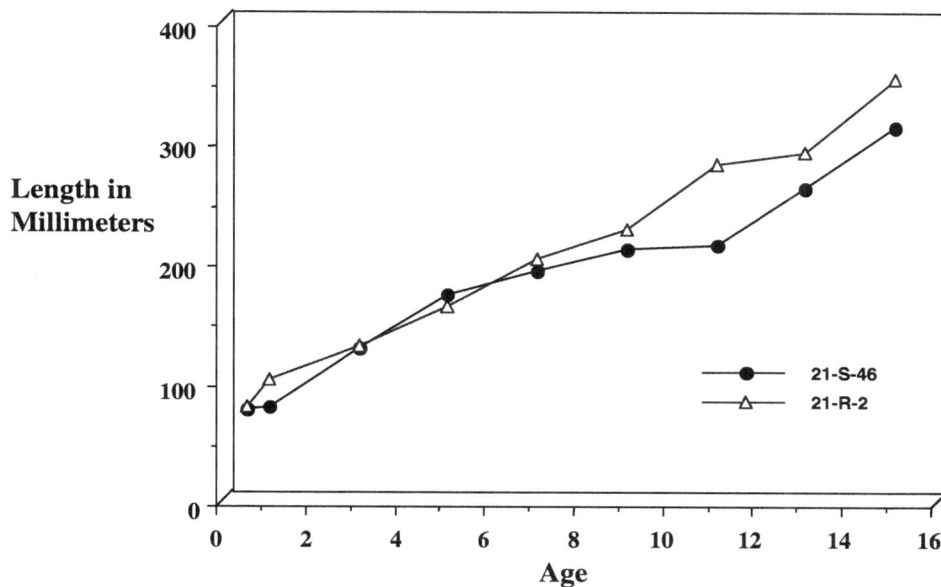

Figure 13. Length of the femoral diathesis among individuals in the Kulubnarti cemeteries.

sub-adults in the island population experienced a greater disparity between skeletal and dental ages with skeletal age averaging 86.5% of dental age. In the mainland population, skeletal age averaged 89% of dental age.

Because sexual differences in the skeleton do not appear until near the end of the growth period, analysis of maturational patterns by sex for skeletal remains is rarely undertaken. In the case of Kulubnarti, however, 23 of the 44 individuals in the combined sample were sufficiently mummified to allow positive sexing. On average, female skeletal age is 102% of dental age. This disparity is not statistically significant. Males on the other hand show a significant retardation of skeletal age, with a mean value of 85.3% relative to dental age.

This pattern is of particular interest in light of male-female differences observed among living children experiencing nutritional stress. Such research has demonstrated that females are frequently less affected than are males.[48]

Dental and skeletal growth asymmetry

Asymmetries in the development of bilateral features of the dentition have long been used as indicators of stress.[49] Earlier studies of cusp pattern stability based upon dental field theory suggest that while mandibular and maxillary crown patterns should show a high degree of bilateral concordance, that might not be the case for the Carabelli Trait. The Carabelli trait is typically an extra enamel cusp

located on the inside forward corner of the first and second molars.[50] Yeagley scored the cusp patterns observed on the second deciduous molar and the permanent molars in 93 individuals from the island 21-S-46 cemetery and 59 from the mainland 21-R-2 cemetery.[51] Those individuals were then evaluated for concordance or disconcordance for the expression of morphological cusp traits between left and right teeth of their mandible and maxilla. Finally, Chi-square tests of homogeneity were used to compare the frequency of concordance and disconcordance between the two cemeteries for each left and right dental pair. Mandibular cusp pattern and maxillary cusp pattern concordance were not significantly different. However, the island cemetery was significantly (p<0.001) more disconcordant than the mainland cemetery for the bilateral expression of the Carabelli trait.

Albert conducted a detailed examination of the timing and patterning of epiphyseal union in up to 66 sites of skeletal union in 36 individuals from the island cemetery and 54 individuals from the mainland, all between 11 and 31 years old at death.[52] She found that both cemetery samples showed disruptions in the epiphyseal union process when compared to standards derived from modern, healthy samples from the United States. In addition, the island cemetery exhibited even more delays in timing and patterning than was observed for the mainland sample.

Yeagley's and Albert's studies strongly indicate, as have all other studies, that developing individuals in the island

[48] Stini, op. cit. (n. 43); Roberts, op. cit. (n. 42).

[49] R. G. Scott and C. G. Turner in *Annual Review of Anthropology,* vol. 17 (1988), pp. 99-126.

[50] Greene, op. cit. (n. 10).

[51] Yeagley, op. cit. (n. 4).

[52] Albert, op. cit. (n.5).

community were stressed more severely than were their mainland counterparts.

Enamel hypoplasias

An additional approach to the analysis of childhood stress at Kulubnarti has involved the analysis of enamel hypoplasias. These are dental defects that appear as bands or pits on the enamel surface. Resulting from the disruption of ameloblast (enamel-forming cell) activity and corresponding deficiency in enamel thickness,[53] hypoplasias typically appear as zones of depressed enamel. These defects have been clearly associated with periods of physiological stress and interrupted growth. Their sequential appearance in combination with the known sequence of enamel formation has also made it possible to reconstruct age relationships and thereby add a demographic dimension to the interpretation of their occurrence. While a number of factors including poor nutrition may underlie their appearance, there is little doubt that, in contrast to *cribra*

developed for assessing the timing of hypoplastic events on all teeth,[55] the relationship between location of the enamel (distance from the cemento-enamel junction) and age varies substantially. The canine was chosen because it is stress sensitive and, relative to other teeth, its formation is slow and constant. Consequently, the location of a hypoplasia could easily be converted to an age of occurrence from birth, when crown formation begins, to age 6.5 when formation is completed.

The frequency of hypoplasias in both Nubian populations (Figure 14) is extremely high with 100% of the subjects expressing at least one hypoplastic event. This is more than twice the frequency (40%) reported for the more prosperous populations of Lower Nubia.

The 21-S-46 sample has a modal frequency of three hypoplasias, while the 21-R-2 sample is bimodal at 3 and 5 years of age. The most striking differences, however, occur at the distributional extremes. The island population has 8% fewer individuals with only one hypoplasia and 5% more

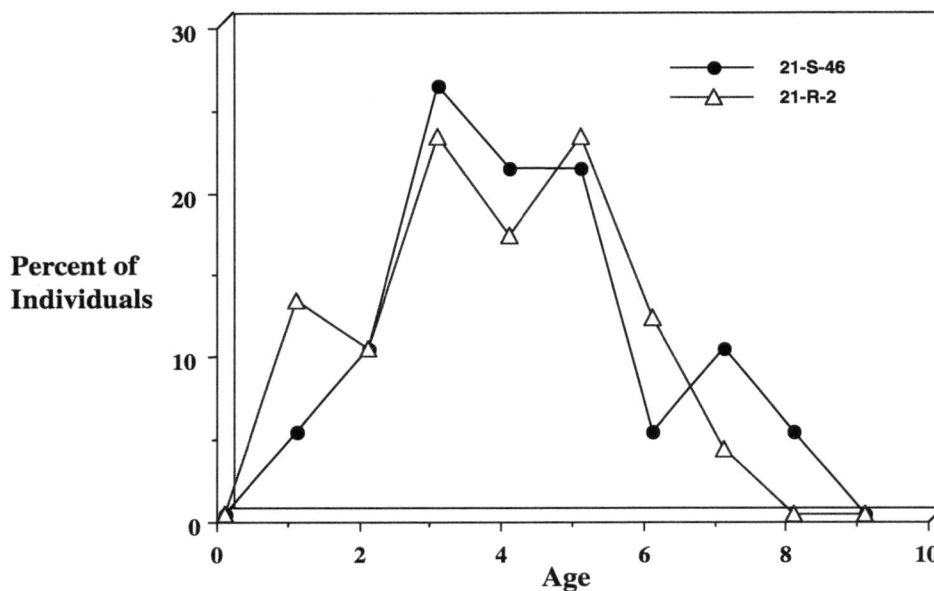

Figure 14. Frequency of enamel hypoplasias among individuals buried in the Kulubnarti cemeteries.

orbitalia, bouts of infectious disease play a major role in their formation.

The hypoplasia investigation was conducted on a sample of 31 island and 56 mainland individuals.[54] The inclusion of each was based on the presence of at least 1 mandibular canine sufficiently unworn to permit data collection.

Selection of the canine for study was based largely on developmental considerations. While standards have been

with seven or eight defects. This contrast at the extremes is once again suggestive of increased stress among the island children.

Examination of hypoplasias by age of formation also supports this suggestion. Both the 21-S-46 and 21-R-2 samples (Figure 15) show a rapid increase in the incidence of hypoplasias between birth and age 4. After that, however, the populations diverge. While the 21-R-2 incidence drops rapidly, the 21-S-46 children show no decline for an additional 1.5 years. This prolonged period of hypoplastic activity among the island children corresponds well to their mortality. Probabilities of dying are not only higher for the island children, mortality remains high longer.

Additional support for the stress hypothesis comes from

[53] A. H. Goodman, G. J. Armelagos, and J. C. Rose in *Human Biology*, vol. 52 (1980), pp. 515-528.

[54] Van Gerven, Beck, and Hummert, op. cit. (n. 6).

[55] See Goodman, Armelagos, and Rose, op. cit. (n. 53).

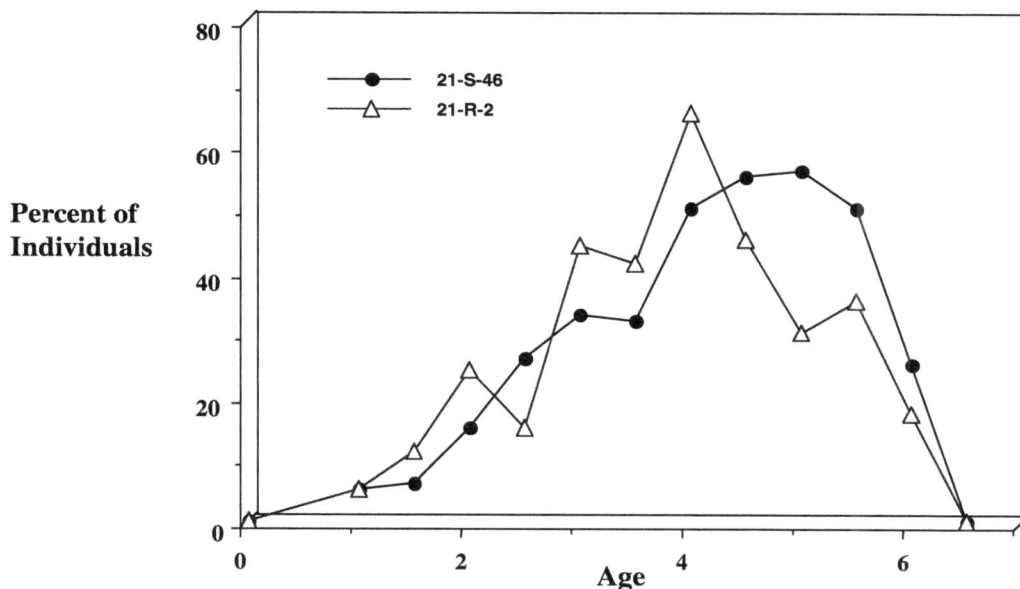

Figure 15. Age of formation for enamel hypoplasias found at Kulubnarti.

an examination of recovery patterns observed as areas of normal enamel between hypoplastic events. Among the earlier children, a majority (74%) of adjacent hypoplasias appear in successive age categories suggesting a continuous succession of stress events. Among the later children, on the other hand, a majority (61%) of adjacent bands are separated by 1 year. It appears from these data that the mainland population was not only less stressed but more likely to recover when conditions permitted.

Adult bone maintenance

Following childhood and adolescence, differences in mortality between the island and mainland populations diminish. The lesions of *cribra orbitalia* become healed, and the growth process is completed. Were the adults in the two communities equally capable of withstanding the stresses and strains of life in the *Batn el Hajjar*, or did the differences experienced by the sub-adults continue into adult life? Patterns of adult bone maintenance can provide an answer. Our data suggests that rates of cortical bone loss through the adult years reflect the continuing stresses of infancy and childhood.

Age related bone loss *(osteopenia)* among adults aged 20 through 51+ is consistent with that observed in other ancient and modern populations - including those from Lower Nubia.[56] Percent cortical areas (the percentage of bone tissue within the total cross-section of femurs cut at midshaft) measured from midshaft sections of 16 island and 34 mainland males (Figure 16) indicate substantial

maintenance of bone cortex from young adulthood through old age. This pattern is typical of males in other ancient and modern populations.

Females, on the other hand, reveal (Figure 17) a pattern of dramatic bone loss beginning in the youngest age group. This pattern of rapid pre-menopausal bone loss followed by a continuation after menopause was first reported for Nubia by Dewey and coworkers, who investigated the condition in Meroitic, X-Group, and Christian remains from Wadi Halfa.[57] Similar patterns of bone loss were subsequently observed over a wide range of ancient human populations. Dewey interpreted this pattern to reflect an interaction between nutritional stress and aging. In essence, young women lost bone due to the demands of pregnancy and lactation while older women lost bone due to the hormonal changes of menopause.

This hypothesis received strong support by Martin and co-workers.[58] Microscopic examination of the femora examined macroscopically by Dewey revealed distinct differences between bone loss in young and old Nubian women. Young females turned over 3.8mm^2 of bone per year compared to 2.8mm^2 turned over by older (post menopausal) females. According to Martin *et al.*, the younger females were not just aging, they were mining (through bone turnover) their skeletons for essential minerals needed by the developing foetus and neonate.

[56] J. R. Dewey, G. J. Armelagos, and M. H. Bartley in *Human Biology*, vol. 41 (1969), pp. 13-28.

[57] Ibid.

[58] D. L. Martin and G. J. Armelagos in *AJPA*, vol. 51 (1979), pp. 571-577; D. L. Martin, A. H. Goodman, and G. J. Armelagos in B. Gilbert and J. Mielke, eds, *The Analysis of Prehistoric Diets* (Orlando, 1985), pp. 227-279.

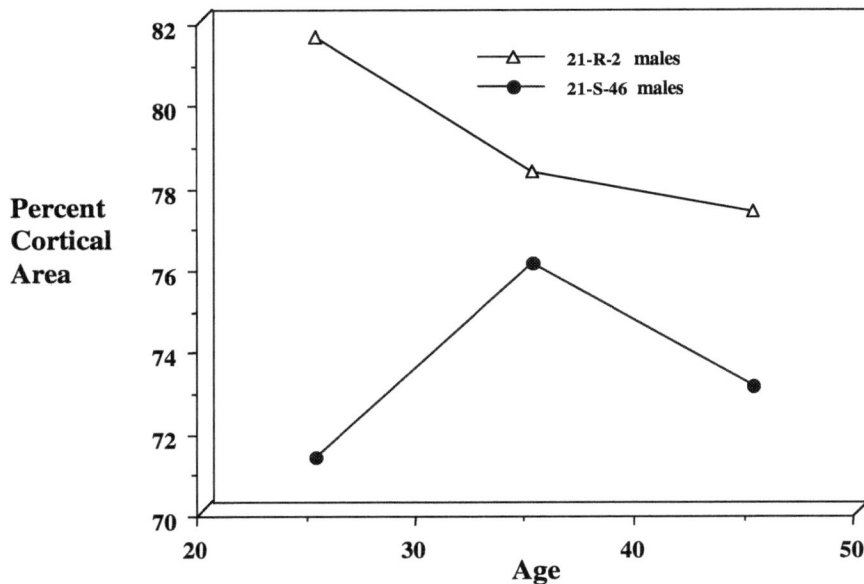

Figure 16. Percent of femoral cortical bone preserved among the Kulubnarti male burials.

While the pattern of bone loss by sex at Kulubnarti is typical of those observed at Wadi Halfa and elsewhere, a comparison by cemetery reveals important differences. For both males and females, percent cortical areas are reduced across all age groups at the island site. The apparent gain followed by loss among the males is a likely result of growth retardation and delayed maturation. Failing, however, to catch up by their mid-thirties, the island males, like their mainland counterparts, begin the gradual process of age-related bone loss.

Because females experienced less growth retardation (as evidenced in the comparison between skeletal and dental ages) it is not surprising that the island females begin their adult years with amounts of bone tissue nearer to their mainland counterparts. Having reached adulthood with only slightly less bone, the island females then lose progressively more bone throughout their reproductive years. A difference of 1% in the twenties advances to a difference of 8.5% by the mid-forties and then vanishes by the last age category. This pattern of divergence in the premenopausal years

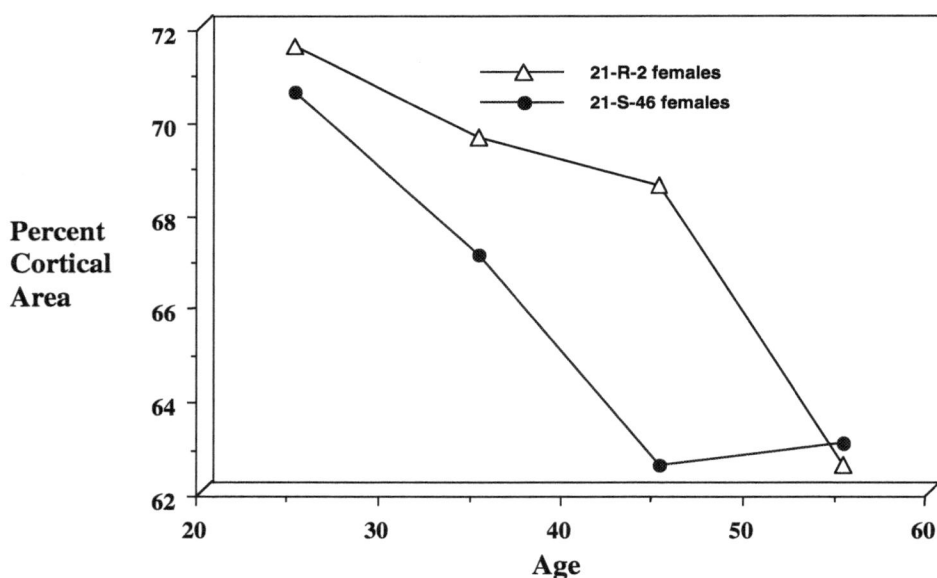

Figure 17. Percent of femoral cortical bone preserved among the Kulubnarti female burials.

86

TABLE 24
COMPARISON OF DENTAL AGE AND SKELETAL AGE FOR BURIALS IN THE TWO KULUBNARTI
CEMETERIES

CEMETERY 21-S-46					CEMETERY 21-R-2				
DA	SA	DA-SA	SA/DA	SEX	DA	SA	DA-SA	SA/DA	SEX
12	12	0	100	-	14	12	-2	86	M
13	12	-1	92	-	14	12	-2	86	-
13	12	-1	92	-	14	14	0	100	F
15	13	-2	87	-	14	12	-2	86	-
15	12	-3	80	-	15	14	-1	93	-
15	12	-3	80	-	15	16	+1	107	F
16	12	-4	75	-	16	12	-4	75	-
16	12	-4	75	-	16	12	-4	75	-
18	18	0	100	M	16	12	-4	75	-
18	13	+5	72	-	17	15	+2	88	-
18	12	-6	67	M	17	12	-5	71	-
18	12	-6	67	-	18	18	0	100	M
19	17	-2	89	-	18	16	-2	89	F
19	24	+5	126	F	18	14	-4	78	-
20	12	-8	60	-	18	15	-3	83	M
20	17	-3	85	M	19	20	+1	105	F
21	19	-2	90	M	19	20	+1	105	F
21	21	0	100	M	19	18	-1	95	F
22	24	+2	109	F	19	19	0	100	F
23	16	-7	70	M	20	16	-4	80	M
23	23	0	100	F	21	23	+2	109	F
					22	18	-4	82	F
					22	17	-5	77	M

N=21   XSA/DA = 86.5%   N=23   XSA/DA = 89.0%
         XDA-SA = -2.4   XDA-SA = -1.9
DA = DENTAL AGE   SA = SKELETAL AGE

followed by convergence in the oldest age group is informative. Premenopausal differences are most likely to reflect environmental stress and predictably the island women are most greatly affected.

Thus, while less apparent in death rates and overt manifestations of disease, the adults of Kulubnarti carry forward through the life cycle patterns of stress begun in infancy. The island males began the descent into old age having never attained the cortical development of their mainland counterparts. For the females, the demands for childbearing in a difficult environment were also greatest in the island community.

Conclusions

Over some 20 years of research, the human remains at Kulubnarti have provided important insights into both the identity as well as the lives of these ancient people. Because our evidence is inherently circumstantial it has been important, wherever possible, for us to pursue independent lines of investigation. The results are most compelling when these independent lines of inquiry lead to the same or similar conclusions. We have been fortunate in this regard.

Analysis of cranial anatomy based on adult remains from the island 21-S-46 and mainland 21-R-2 cemeteries revealed a high degree of anatomical similarity between the two communities. This is not surprising given their close spatial and temporal proximity combined with the virtual identity of their mortuary practices. There also appear to be strong biological ties between the Kulubnarti folk and the populations of Lower Nubia. Our comparisons between Kulubnarti and Meroitic, X-Group, and Christian populations from Wadi Halfa revealed two overlapping but clearly delineated clusters of similarity - one Lower Nubian and one at Kulubnarti. The point of greatest similarity between these regional clusters was between the Wadi Halfa and Kulubnarti Christian samples.

This pattern of similarity, while satisfying from a historical perspective, also provides us with intriguing questions worthy of future inquiry. A trend toward facial shortening observed at Wadi Halfa from Meroitic through Christian times, is most pronounced at Kulubnarti and this is particularly true for the mainland 21-R-2 population. In this sense, the Kulubnarti folk are less "African" then their counterparts to the north. These results challenge the notion of a north-south gradient of increasingly Africanized populations and suggests one of two possibilities. Either the populations of Kulubnarti evolved *in situ* more rapidly than did populations to the north, or one or both of the Kulubnarti populations came to the *Batn el Hajjar* as northern immigrants.

Our independent investigation of dental morphology leads to the same conclusion. Here again, the Kulubnarti remains form a distinct genetic cluster when compared to Wadi Halfa, and here again the Kulubnarti Christians, particularly the mainland Christians, are most like their Christian counterparts to the north. The dental evidence may, however, provide additional clarity. While cranial changes such as facial reduction are relatively simple, and may evolve in parallel among local *in situ* populations, multiple independent dental features are far less likely to do so. The patterns of dental similarity observed between the Kulubnarti and Wadi Halfa Christians strongly support the hypothesis that the mainland Kulubnarti group had strong genetic roots in the north. The island community exhibits a more complex combination of local and northern influences. Unfortunately, the issue cannot be resolved further without the excavation of additional remains to the south of Kulubnarti.

Our analyses of adaptation at Kulubnarti have also resulted in a consistent interpretation across multiple lines of investigation. All of our studies of adaptation to date have led to the same conclusion; the people of the island 21-S-46 community experienced higher mortality and were more adaptively stressed than their mainland counterparts. These differences in survivorship and health may well have had an important impact on the long-term success of mainland and island communities.

Estimates of sub-adult mortality for the island 21-S-46 cemetery imply one of two possibilities. Barring continuous immigration, the population either maintained a birth rate beyond the known modern human maximum or the population experienced a steady decline in its numbers - a trend leading either to extinction or abandonment of the area. In contrast, the mainland community experienced lower infant mortality, and could have maintained its numbers with normal levels of fertility. This striking difference in mortality is corroborated by our independent investigations of childhood and adult health.

Patterns of *cribra orbitalia,* indicative of childhood iron deficiency anemia, correspond closely to the patterns of mortality estimated for the island and mainland communities. While frequencies of the lesion were high at both sites, the lesion appears a full year earlier among the island children and occurs more frequently in that group throughout the childhood years. The island children likewise grow more slowly and experience greater growth retardation than their mainland counterparts. The island children also express higher frequencies of enamel hypoplasias indicative of illness and interrupted growth as well as a greater degree of asymmetric growth, also indicative of nutritional and

disease stress. These signs of increased stress within the island 21-S-46 community are not limited to the sub-adult segment of the population. Among adult males and females alike, progressive age-related bone loss, osteopenia, is most pronounced in the 21-S-46 remains.

Taken together, all of our research to date based on paleodemographic reconstructions, paleopathology, as well as studies of dental and skeletal growth, development, and degenerative changes lead to a single conclusion. These neighboring Christian communities with powerful genetic ties, did not experience comparable levels of survival and biological wellbeing. While we may never fully understand the underlying causes or consequences of this difference, it is intriguing to note that the mainland cemetery has remained in continuous use to the present time, while no remains appear in the island cemetery beyond the early Christian period. While this difference may or may not reflect the ultimate fate of the two communities, the causes of their striking differences in health and survival continue to elude us.

Speaking to this question, Adams makes the following observations:

The combination of cultural and biological evidence from Kulubnarti suggests a wholly unexpected possibility: that this region in Early Christian times was home to two racially and culturally identical, but socially distinct, communities, one of which was considerably better off than the other.

For the moment there is no obvious explanation for this anomaly... we are left to imagine a single culturally homogeneous but socially stratified Nubian population; yet there is neither textual evidence nor archaeological evidence from other sites to support such an interpretation.

At this time we join Adams in his call for further investigation.

بأجزاء منها. أيضاً تم العثور على رفات امرأة شابة و هي ترتدي سترة من القطن جيدة الصنع و يبدو كما لو أنها لم تستخدم إلا لذلك الغرض. بعض الأجساد تم تكفينها بأكفان مستوردة و على الرغم من الترقيع و الرتق الذي نالها إلا أنها احتفظت بألوانها الزاهية. أما بقية الأكفان فقد عملها تم بخياطة قطعتين أو أكثر من القماش دائماً ما تكون مختلفة عن بعضها البعض. و بالإضافة إلى استخدام القماش، تم العثور على سبعة أجساد مكفنة بالجلد و على ثلاثة من الأحداث تمت تغطيتهم بجلود الأغنام.

و بالرغم من التباين الذي أبرزته المواد التي استخدمت في صنع الأكفان إلا أنها في مجموعها تنتمي إلى الفترة المسيحية القديمة و هي تختلف بدرجة كبيرة عن منسوجات الفترات المتأخرة. و قد سجلت المنسوجات الصوفية حضوراً أعلى من القطن و الكتان حيث لم يعثر عليهما إلا في مناسبات قليلة، كما و أنه لا توجد أمثلة لاستخدام الحرير. و من المؤكد أن الكتان و الذي تم استخدامه خصيصاً لأغراض الدفن كان مستورداً من مصر، أضف إلى ذلك المنسوجات الصوفية الملونة و المصبوغة. غير أن الجزء الأعظم من المنسوجات الصوفية و القطنية تم إنتاجه بمنطقة النوبة.

كان من الموجودات غير المألوفة استخدام الشعر الآدمي في عمل الأكفان في كلا المقبرتين ، ففي مواضع عدة عثر عليه في شكل حبال و أشرطة هذا بالإضافة إلى ثلاثة بُسُط تم نسجها بالكامل من الشعر الآدمي. ويعد هذا الإكتشاف الأول من نوعه في كل المواقع النوبية الأخرى التي تم التنقيب فيها.

و كما جرت العادة فإن المدافن المسيحية لم تشتمل على الكثير من اللقى الأثرية بلستثناء المواد المنسوجة. إلا أن الشاهد في هذه المدافن يشير إلى العثور على إحدى عشرة صليباً صغيراً من الحديد وجدت حول عنق الميت متدلية بخيط. أيضاً عشر على ثلاث قلادات من الخرز و أخرى من الحديد هذا بالإضافة إلى قرط من البرونز، كل هذه اللقى أو معظمها تم العثور عليها بمدافن الأحداث. و من أميز ما عثر عليه قبر كبير الحجم لإنسان راشد و هو مسجاة على عنقريب –سرير خشبي- و قد تم تغطية الجثة بدثار و عليه ألوان زاهية. من محتويات القبر الأخرى جرة و مصباح من الفخار وضعتا بجانب رأس الميت. و من الواضح أن هذا القبر يرجع تاريخه إلى الفترة المسيحية المتأخرة.

المدافن المسيحية القديمة بكلبنارتي

في سنة ١٩٦٩، قامت بعثة جامعة كنتكي بإجراء حفريات إختبارية بمقبرتين مسيحيتين بالنوبة السفلى، تمت الأولى بجزيرة كلبنارتي و كانت الثانية على مقربة منها بالضفة الغربية لنهر النيل. و قد كان من نتائج ذلك الكشف العثور على معظم الجثث و هي محنطة طبيعياً و احتفظت العظام ببقايا اللحم و الجلد و الشعر عليها.

و تعد هذه الحالة من الفرص النادرة لدراسة الأحوال الصحية و التغذية و معدل الوفيات في أوساط المجموعات السكانية بالنوبة المسيحية بصورة أكثر اتساعاً عما إذا اقتصر الدليل الآثاري على مخلفات العظام بمفردها.

و للقيام بمثل هذه الدراسة، تم إرسال بعثة ثانية إلى كلبنارتي في ١٩٧٩، و كان ذلك تحت رعاية جامعتي كنتكي و كلورادو. و في ذلك الوقت أسفرت عمليات التنقيب عن الكشف عن ٢٠٠ قبراً تقريباً في كلا المقبرتين. و تم إرسال المخلفات الإنسانية إلى جامعة كلورادو بينما احتفظت جامعة كنتكي باللقى الأثرية و معظمها أكفان من النسيج.

المدافن

أسفرت أعمال التنقيب عن حقائق مميزة. و أظهرت نتائج البحث أن كلا المقبرتين تعودان إلى فترة زمنية واحدة و يمكن أن يؤرخ لهما بالفترة ما بين ٦٠٠.-٨٥٠ م. و تشير جميع المدافن إلى وحدة نموذجية في ما يتعلق بالطقوس و الشعائر الجنائزية، فكل المدافن مستطيلة الشكل و موجهة من الشرق إلى الغرب و تم تغطية أكثرها بحجارة مسطحة الشكل رصفت عند عند مستوى سطح الأرض . أمثلة قليلة من تلك المدافن تم رصف أسطحها بالآجر المحروق. غير أن البحث لم يستطع أن يبرهن على وجود مصطبة الآجر و التي اشتهرت بها مدافن الفترة المسيحية في النوبة السفلى. معظم ممرات المدافن احتوت على قاعدة مستوية، باستثناء ما يقرب من الـ ١٠٪ منها و التي احتوت على قواعد أكثر إتساعاً كما تم حفر حجرة جانبية صغيرة بالجانب الشمالي في أغلب الأحوال. تم العثور على معظم الجثث مستلقية على ظهورها، إلا أن ما يقدر بحوالي ٢٧٪ من الجثث بمدافن الجزيرة و ٤٣٪ بمدافن الضفة الغربية تم العثور عليها مستلقية على جانبها الأيسر مستقبلة اتجاه الشمال. تم تغطية وجه الميت بالآجر أو بكسر من الفخار كبيرة الحجم، و القليل من هذه الجثث تم تغطيتها بالكامل بالآجر أو الحجارة. و باستثناء النسبة العالية للجثث الموضوعة على جانبها الأيسر فإن كل ما ذكر آنفاً من طقوس يتناغم و ما هو متعارف عليه فيما يختص بالعلاقات و الممارسات الجنائزية الخاصة بالمدافن النوبية المسيحية.

مخلفات المدافن

يبدو جلياً أن كل الجثث قد تم تكفينها ولف أشرطة و خيوط حولها ساعة الدفن. كما تم استخدام مواد مختلفة لتغطية الجثث، فأقلية منها قد تم تكفينها بأكفان بيضاء صنعت خصيصاً لهذا الغرض. و تم تكفين البقية بأكفان كانت مستخدمة من قبل. بعض الموتى و معظمهم من الأحداث تم دفنهم بكامل ثيابهم أو

A. *General view.*

B. *General view.*

C. *X-Group tumulus 12.*

D. *X-Group tumulus 12.*

E. *Stone outline superstructure. Grave 69.*

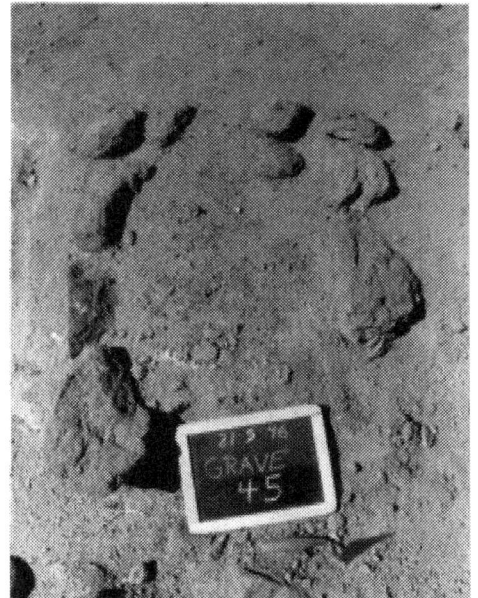
F. *Stone outline superstructure, Grave 45.*

Plate 1. Cemetery 21-S-46: general views and superstructure types

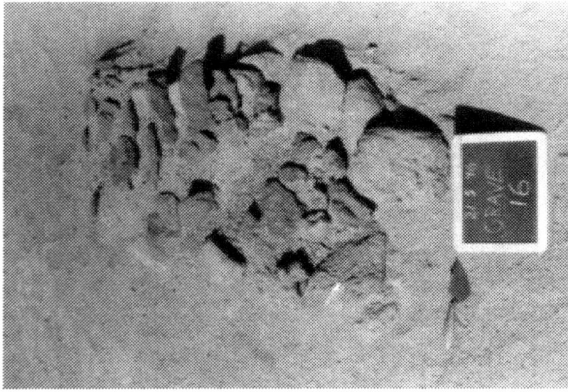

A. Stone pavement superstructure, Grave 16.

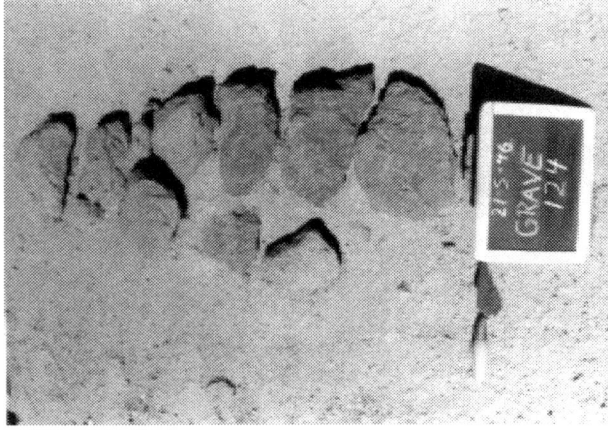

B. Stone pavement superstructure, Grave 124.

C. Stone pavement superstructure, Grave 17.

D. Stone pavement superstructure, Grave 35.

E. Flat brick superstructure, Graves 186 and 185.

F. Rollag brick superstructure, Grave 188.

Plate 2. Cemetery 21-S-46: superstructure types.

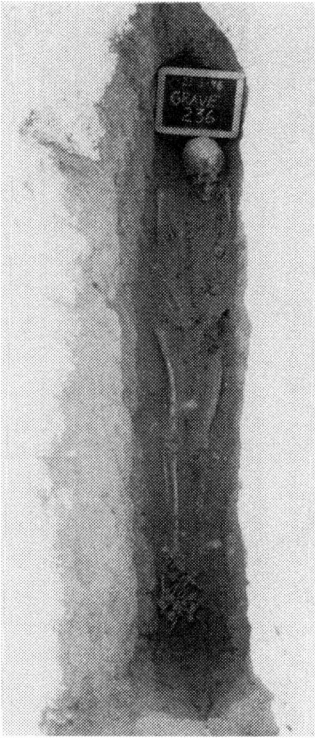

A. Slot Grave 236.

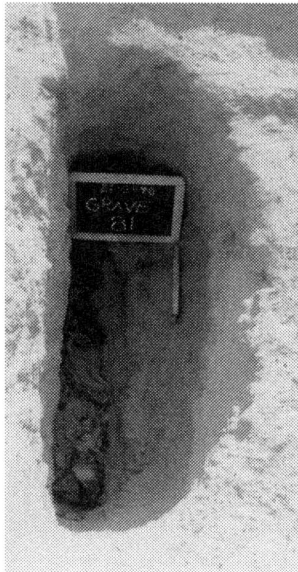

B. Side niche Grave 81.

C. Stone body covering, niche Grave 30.

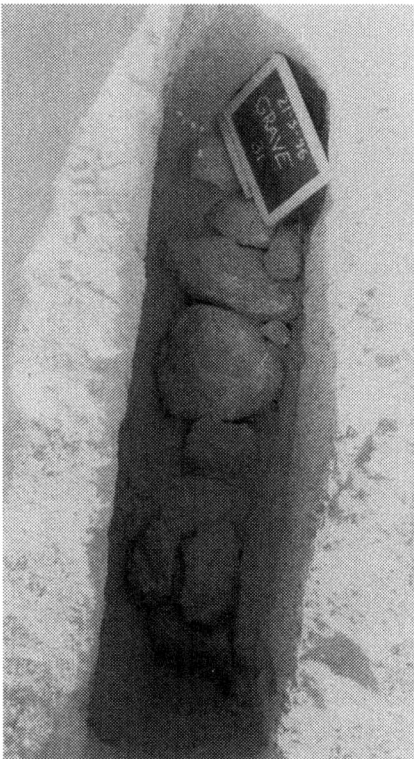

D. Stone body covering, niche Grave 31.

E. Stone body covering, slot Grave 41.

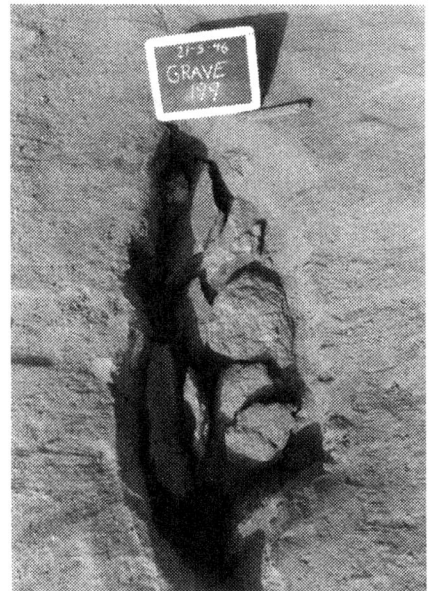

F. Stone body covering, slot Grave 199.

Plate 3. Site 21-S-46: grave shafts and body coverings.

A. Dorsal burial with head to left, Grave 5.

B. Burial on left side, Grave 162.

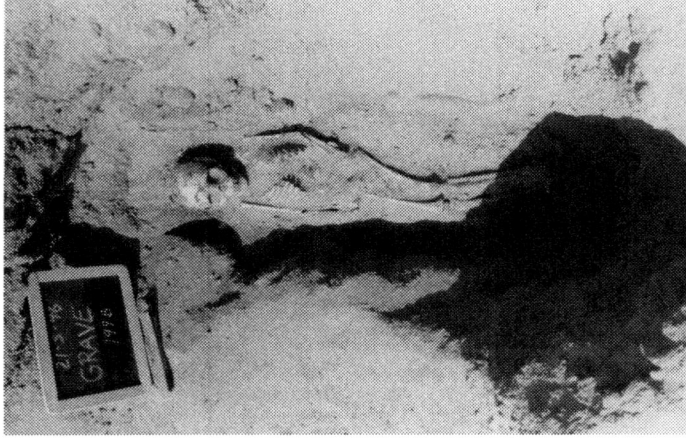

C. Dorsal burial with head facing up, Grave 199B.

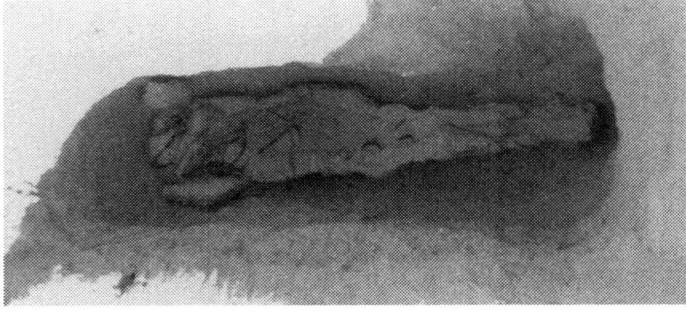

D. Fully shrouded burial, Grave 178.

E. Foetal burial in amphora, Grave 71.

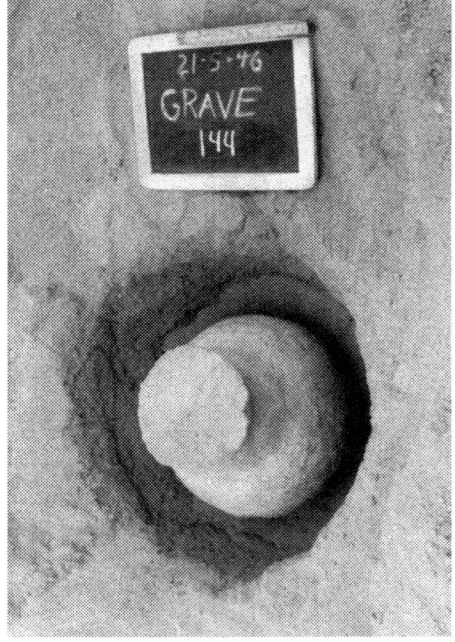

F. Foetal burial in pot, Grave 144.

Plate 4. Site 21-S-46: treatment of the bodies.

A. General view over the cemetery area, looking east.

B. General view of the cemetery area, looking southeast. Church 21-R-1 is at the extreme left.

C. View of the cemetery surface, looking west. Church 21-R-1 is in the center.

D. Excavations in progress in the cemetery.

Plate 5. Site 21-R-2: general views.

A. Stone pavement superstructure, Grave C4.

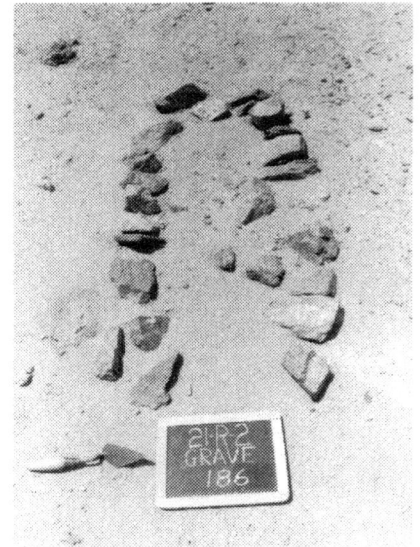

B. Stone outline superstructure, Grave 186.

C. Stone and brick superstructure, Grave A1.

D. Rollag brick pavement superstructure, Grave C2.

E. Large rollag brick pavement superstructure, Grave B4.

Plate 6. Site 21-R-2: superstructure types.

F. Unusual brick pavement superstructure, Grave 188.

A. *Stone slab covering of Grave 185.*

B. *Unopened brick vault, Grave B7.*

C. *Overlying brick corbel, Grave B3.*

D. *Bed burial in brick vault, Grave B3, accompanied by* qulla *and lamp.*

E. *Burial on left side in Grave C1, with stones covering head.*

Plate 7. Site 21-R-2: unusual tombs; body coverings.

F. *Dorsal burial in Grave A4, with bricks covering head.*

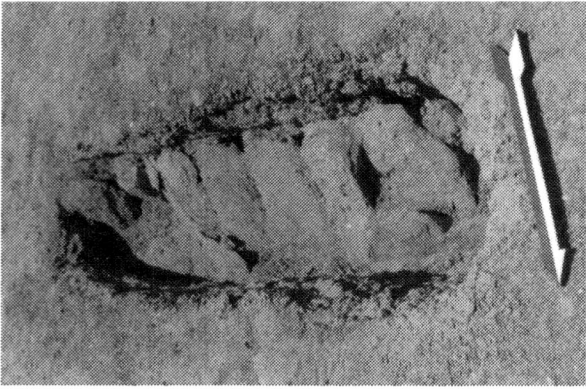

A. Stone slab body covering, niche Grave B8.

B. Stone body covering, slot Grave 136.

C. Body on left side, niche Grave C5.

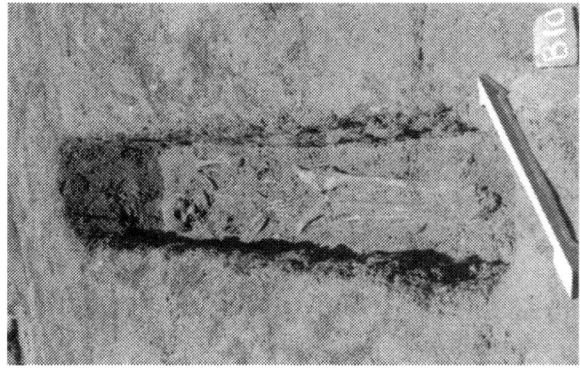

D. Dorsal burial in slot Grave B10.

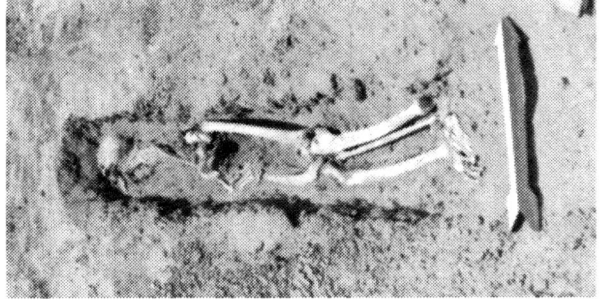

E. Body on right side, slot Grave A5.

F. Fully shrouded burial in slot Grave 20.

Plate 8. Site 21-R-2: body coverings and body positions.

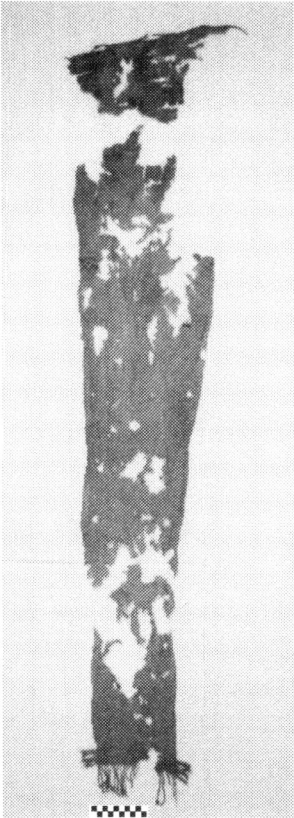

A. Portion of loincloth:
21-S-46, Grave 16,
Cloth 14A.

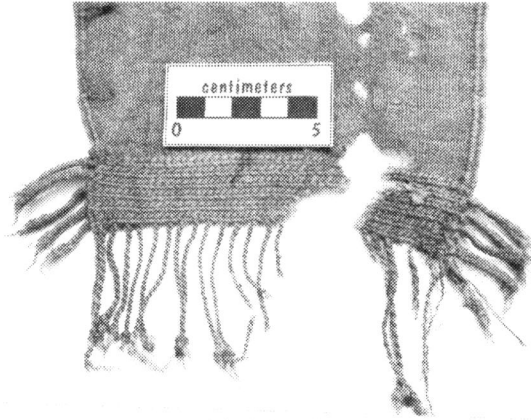

B. Twining and fringe at loincloth end 21-S-46,
Grave 16, Cloth 14A.

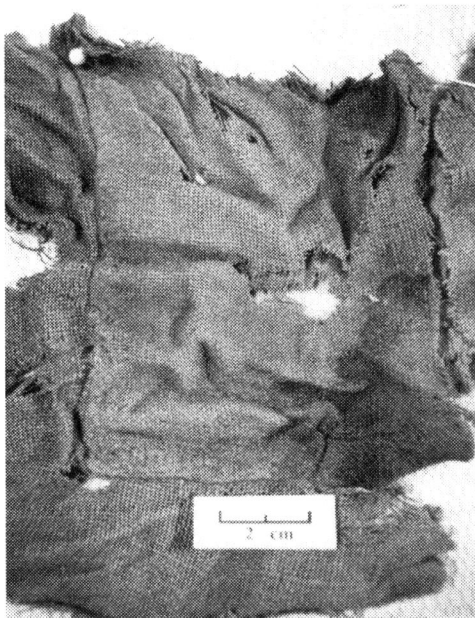

C. Underarm gusset of tunic: 21-R-2,
Grave 162, Cloth 128A.

D. Portion of tunic: 21-R-2,
Grave 162, Cloth 128A.

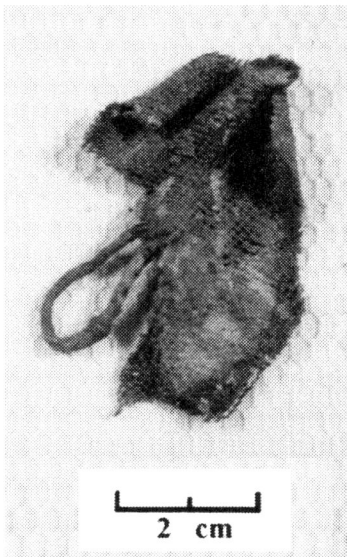

E. Button loop of tunic: 21-R-2,
Grave 162, Cloth 128A.

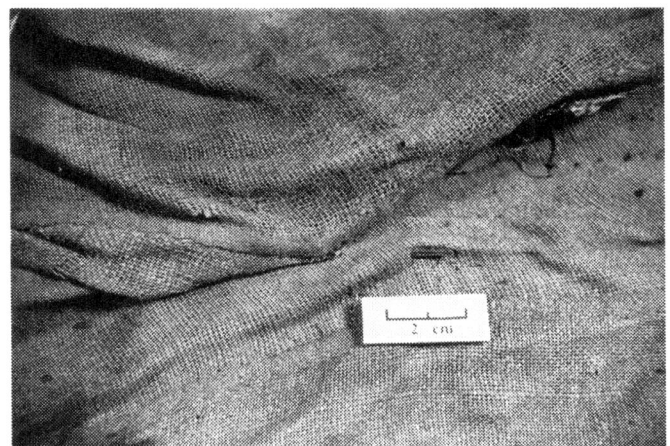

F. Well-made seams of tunic and wooden splinter pin, 21-
R-2, Grave 162, Cloth 128A.

Plate 9. Garments.

A. Threads: left: 21-R-2, Grave 108, Cloth 127; right: 21-R-2, Grave 151, Cloth 136.

B. String: 21-S-46, Grave 29, Cloth 17.

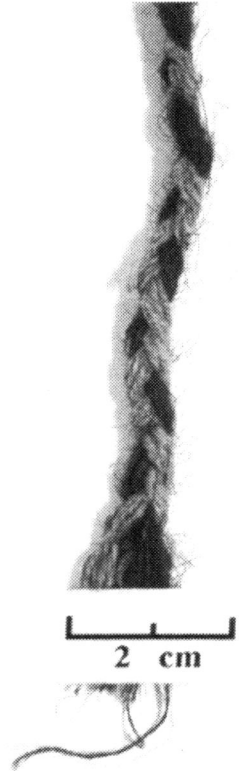

C. Braid: 21-R-2, Grave 14, Cloth 118C.

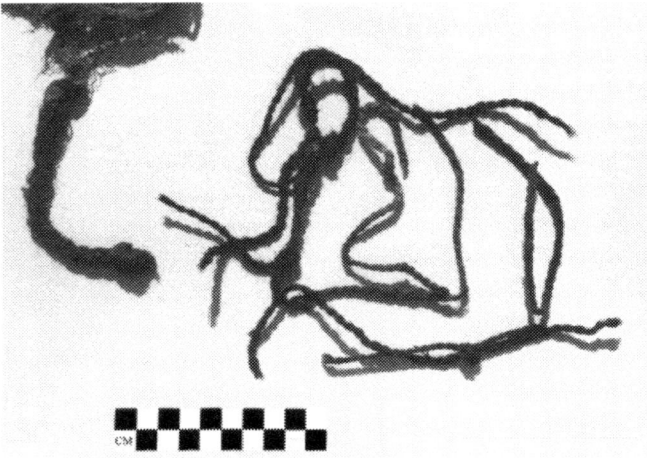

D. Cord: 21-S-46, Grave 33, Cloth 19.

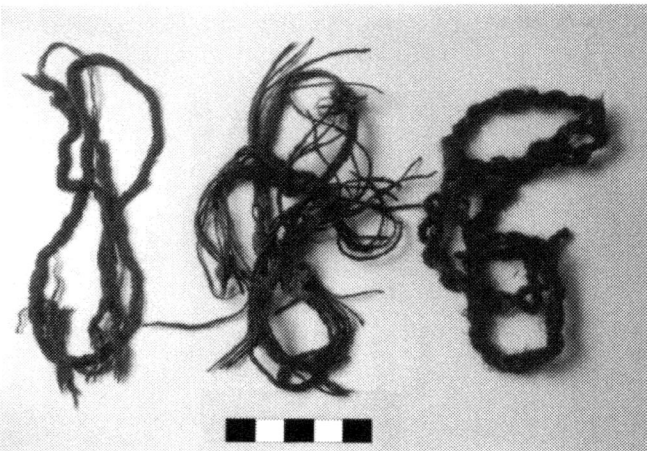

E. Bindings made of human hair: left: cord, 21-R-2, Grave 68, Cloth 135B; center: string, 21-R-2, Grave 2, Cloth 228; right: braid, 21-R-2, Grave 6, Cloth 237B.

Plate 10. Burial Bindings.

F. Tape: 21-R-2, Grave 197, Cloth 211B.

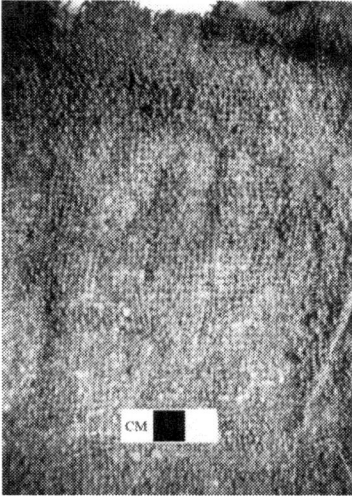

A. Type A-coarse: 21-R-2, Grave 19, Cloth 184A.

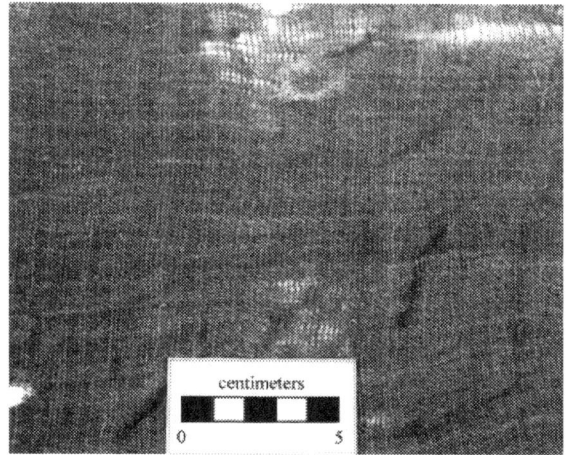

B. Type A-fine: 21-S-46, Grave 26, Cloth 8.

C. Type B with reinforced selvedge and end cord: 21-S-46, Grave 217, Cloth 88A.

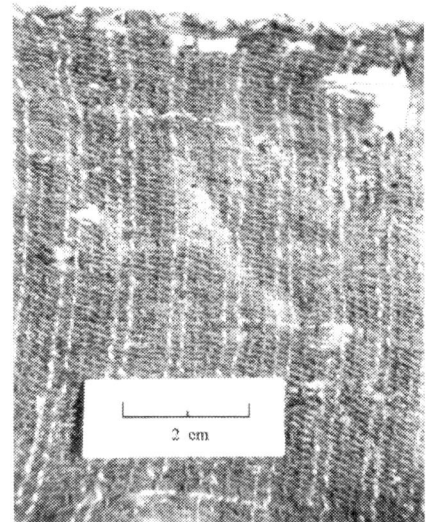

D. Type C variant with starting border: 21-R-2, Grave 34, Cloth 236A.

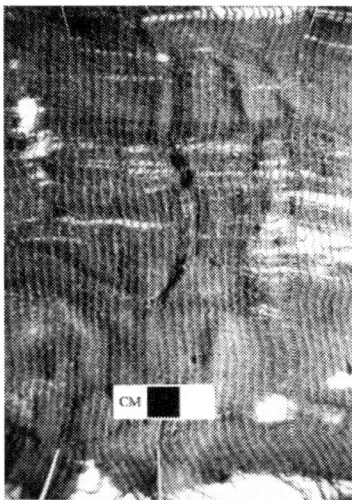

E. Type C variant: 21-R-2, Grave 118, Cloth 221A.

Plate 11. Fabric Types A-C.

F. Type C variant with reinforced selvedge: 21-R-2, Grave 34, Cloth 236A.

A. Type D: 21-R-2, Grave 32, Cloth 235A.

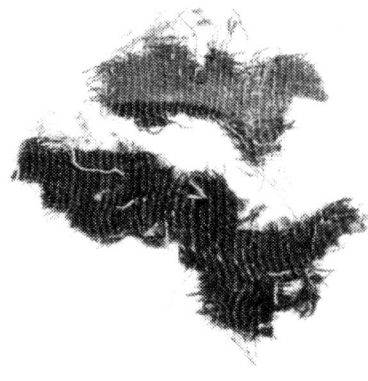

centimeters

0   5

B. Type E variant: 21-R-2, Grave 167, Cloth 133A.

C. Type E variant with end cord and hemmed edge: 21-R-2, Grave 83, Cloth 193.

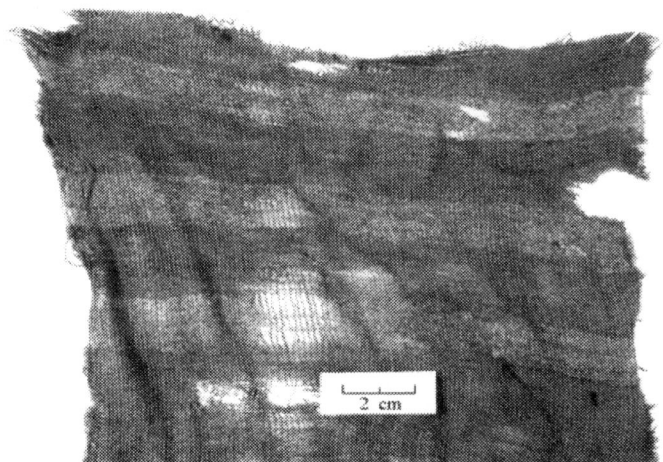

2 cm

D. Type F variant with blue and brown bands: 21-S-46, Grave 73, Cloth 113B.

centimeters

0   5

E. Type F variant with blue and "natural" bands: 21-S-46, Grave 217, Cloth 88C.

Plate 12. Fabric Types D-F.

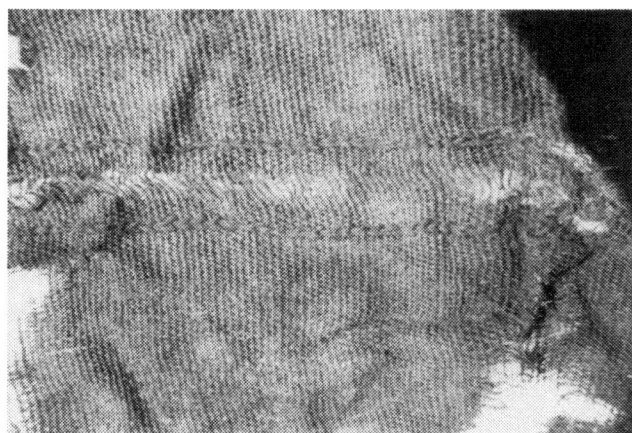

F. Type F variant blue with red band and countered twining: 21-S-46, Grave 195, Cloth 26A.

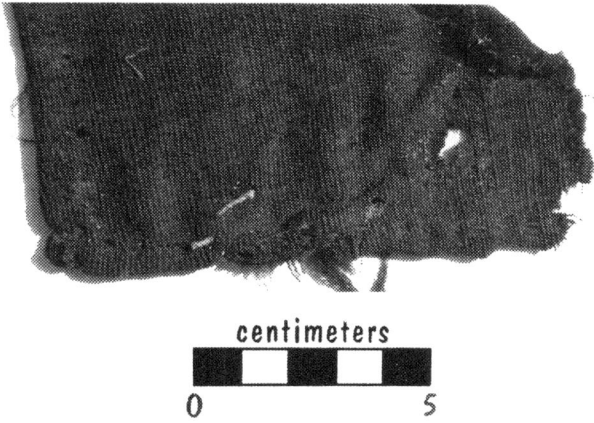

A. Type G: blue with weft-faced weave: 21-R-2, Grave 6, Cloth 237C.

B. Type H: red with balanced open weave: 21-S-46, Grave 14, Cloth 29A.

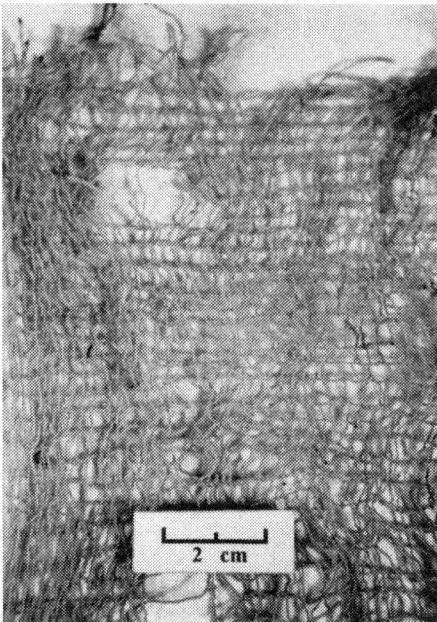

C. Type I: 21-S-46, Grave 17, Cloth 18.

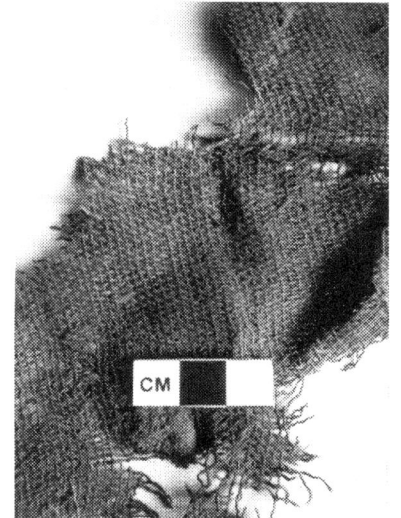

D. Type J: 21-R-2, Grave 95, Cloth 215B.

E. Type K: 21-R-2, Grave 68, Cloth 135A.

Plate 13. Fabric Types G-L.

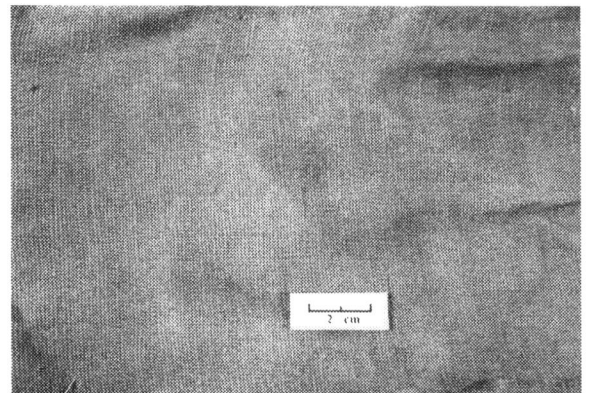

F. Type L with balanced close weave: 21-R-2, Grave 162, Cloth 128A.

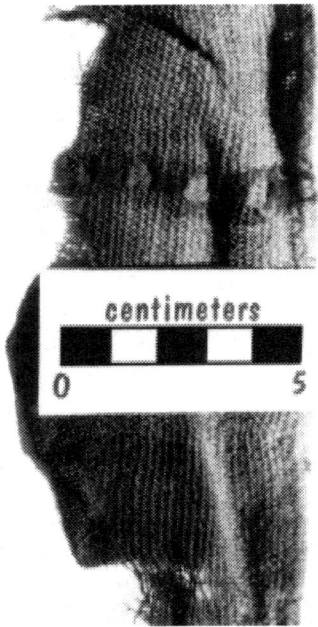

A. Selvedge pattern, woven in: 21-S-46, Grave 222, Cloth 163.

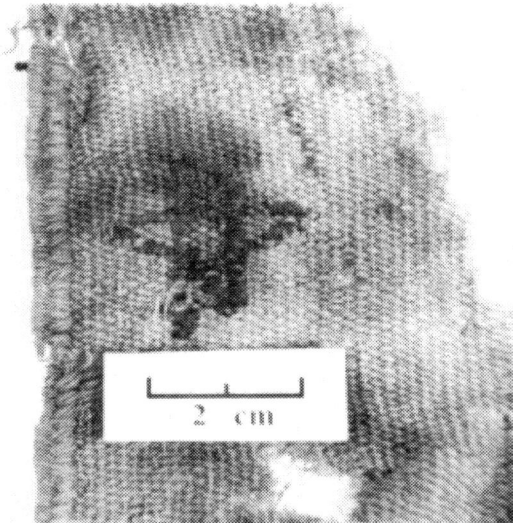

B. Selvedge pattern, embroidered: 21-R-2, Grave 197, Cloth 211A.

C. Example of half-basket weave: 21-R-2, Grave 167, Cloth 133A.

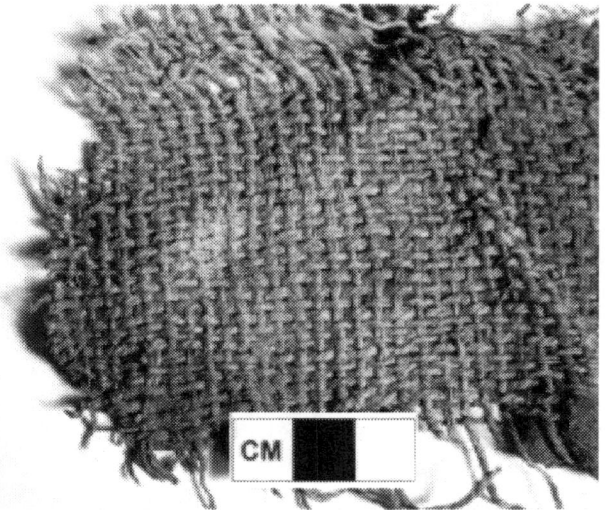

D. Untyped fabric with archaic spinning style: 21-R-2, Grave 80, Cloth 188A.

E. Several fabrics stitched together: 21-S-46, Grave 217, Cloth 88A-C.

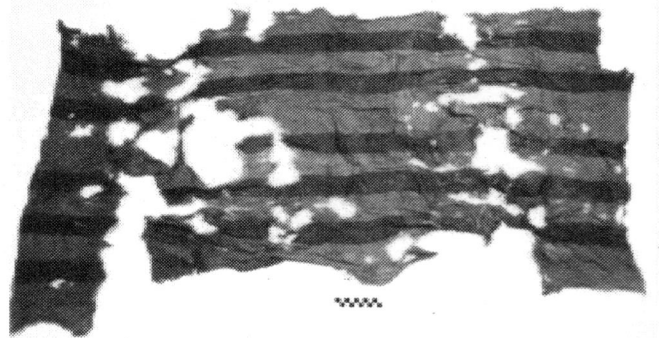

F. Mantle, Type F fabric: 21-R-2, Grave 38, Cloth 114A.

Plate 14. Miscellaneous Textiles.

A. Incomplete mat: 21-R-2, Grave 168, Cloth 190.

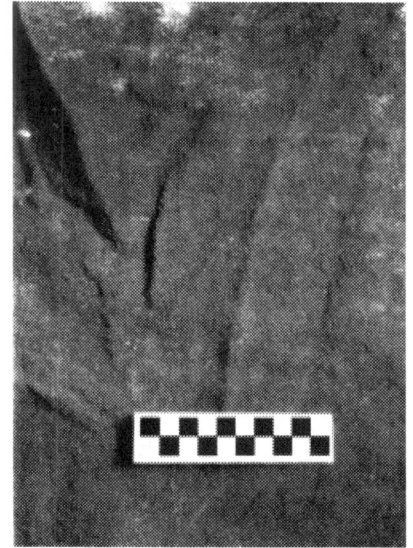

B. Subtle shades of brown in bands: 21-R-2, Grave 168, Cloth 190.

C. Complete mat: 21-R-2, Grave 70, Cloth 225C.

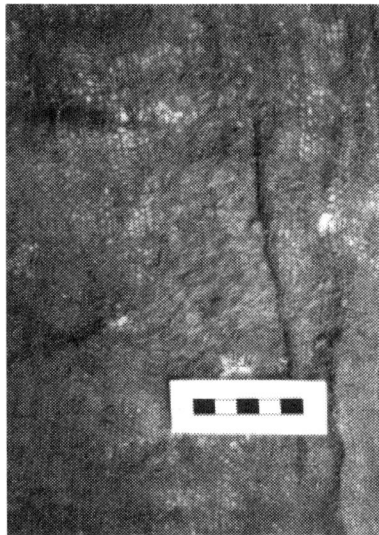

D. Darned area: 21-R-2, Grave 70, Cloth 225C.

E. Complete mat: 21-S-46, Grave 172, Cloth 1.

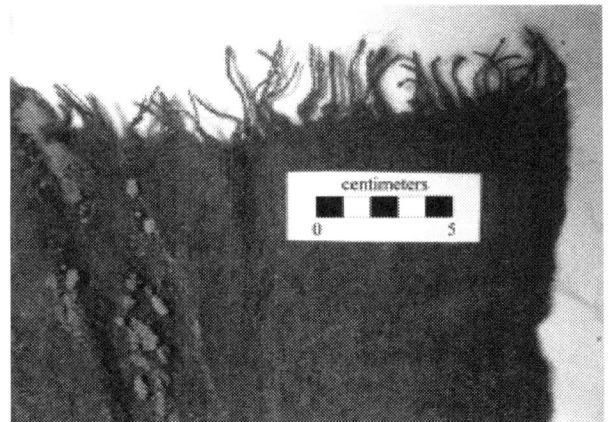

F. Looped, fringed edge: 21-S-46, Grave 172, Cloth 1.

Plate 15. Mats Made of Human Hair.

A. X-Group bottle: 21-S-46/27.

B. X-Group cup: 21-S-46/26.

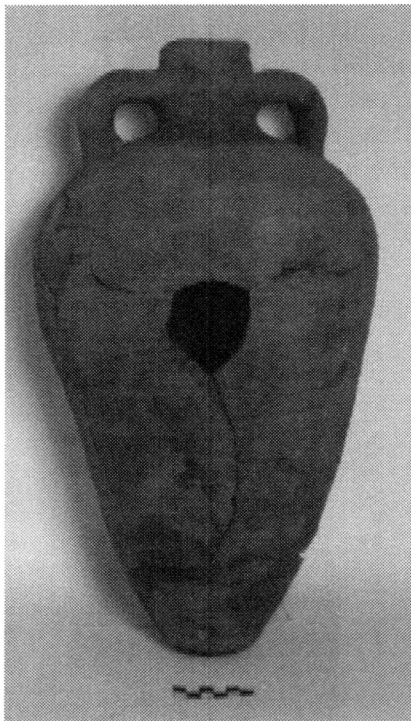

C. Amphora:
21-S-46/7.

D. Amphora: 21-S-46/6.

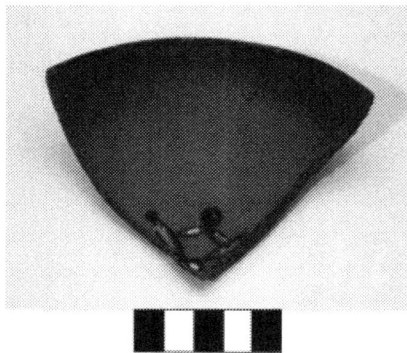

Plate 16. Pottery.   E. Saucer: 21-R-2/1.   F. Saucer: 21-R-2/19.

A. Iron cross: 21-S-46/19.

B. Miscellaneous beads: 21-S-46/24.

C. Framed cross: 21-R-2/16.

D. Bead bracelet: 21-S-46/22.

E. Small cross: 21-S-46/18.

F. Bead bracelet: 21-R-2/15.

Plate 17. Crosses and Beads.

A. Higab: 21-R-2/4.

B. Bangle: 21-R-2/10.

C. Bead pendant: 21-R-2/7.

D. Pendant: 21-S-46/21.

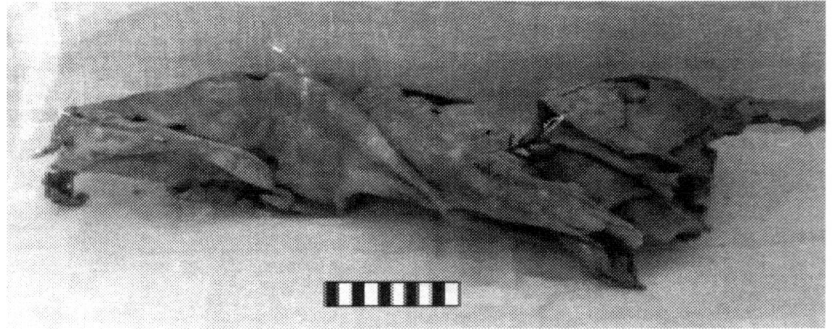

E. Leather wrapping: 21-S-46/28.

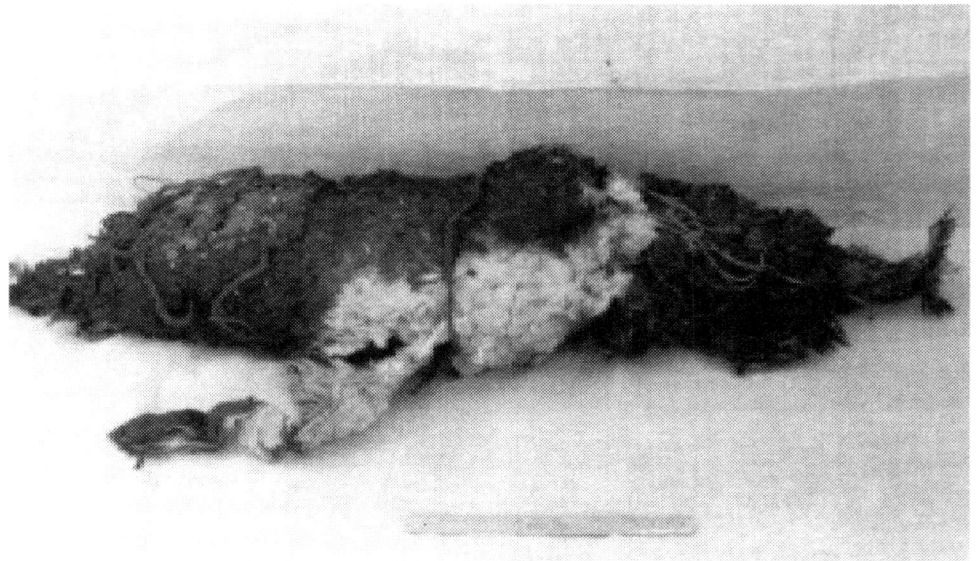

F. Sheepskin wrapping: 21-S-46/29.

Plate 18. Miscellaneous Objects.

www.ingramcontent.com/pod-product-compliance
Lightning Source LLC
Chambersburg PA
CBHW061005030426
42334CB00033B/3365